THE LIFE & PUBLIC SERVICES

OF

SIMON STERNE

Respectfully
Simon Sterne

THE

LIFE & PUBLIC SERVICES

OF

SIMON STERNE

BY

JOHN FOORD

London
MACMILLAN AND CO., LIMITED
NEW YORK : THE MACMILLAN COMPANY
1903

TO MY

NOBLE BROTHER,

WHO DEVOTED HIS LIFE TO
THE PUBLIC GOOD.

L. Sterne.

London, 1903.

PREFACE

THE following pages are designed to perpetuate the memory of a man whose life was devoted to the service of humanity. Simon Sterne never held executive office, but he did much to raise the standard of responsibility attached to the administration of a public trust; he never sat in the State or National Legislature, but no man of his generation exercised so much influence in elevating the character of legislative methods; he never occupied a place on the Bench, but the interpretation of the law affecting railroads and corporations owes more to him than any one of his contemporaries. His life was full of activity, and from his twenty-second year to his death there was no year in it which was not rich in effort that redounded to the benefit of his fellowmen. The author of this volume disclaims other credit for its contents than that which belongs to the judicious compiler and conscientious interpreter. All of the book that is his is the arrangement of its contents, and the thread of narrative and explanation on which the subject-matter is strung.

CONTENTS

CHAPTER VII

CHAPTER VIII

CHAPTER IX

CHAPTER X

CHAPTER I

BIOGRAPHICAL

Simon Sterne was born in Philadelphia on July 23, 1839. His parents were Henry and Regina Sterne. After leaving public school he was sent to Europe, and had the advantage of a short course of study at the University of Heidelberg, whence he returned to enter the law department of the University of Pennsylvania. At this stage of his career his health was far from robust, but he had early learned the lesson of self-denial, and in after years he reaped the full advantage of the temperance, industry, and indomitable tenacity of purpose which became impressed upon his character early in life. He was graduated from the Law School on June 6, 1859, having also pursued his legal studies in the office of Mr. John H. Markland and in that of Judge Sharswood. He was admitted to the Philadelphia bar in the year of his graduation.

The achievement was a remarkable one, considering that young Sterne had barely reached manhood, and had been handicapped in his years of preparatory study not only by poor health, but also by the necessity of earning enough to pay for his tuition. There is ample evidence, however, that his preparation for the work of his profession was more than usually thorough, and that outside of his legal studies he had found time to be a diligent worker in the field of politico-economical research. His mastery of the principles of what he found by no means a "dismal science" must be regarded as extraordinary in one so young, and the conclusions he reached were not by any means those which found general acceptance in Pennsylvania. Whether from a lack of sympathy with his environment, or the desire to secure a larger field for the exercise of his talents, or partly for both reasons, young Sterne moved to New York in 1860, and immediately secured admission to the Bar in that city. But he had not yet definitely cast in his lot with the profession of law, the exposition and study of the practical side of political economy apparently presenting a career more attractive. It was in obedience to this dominant impulse that, on the "solicitation and request" of Mr. Peter Cooper and others, he agreed to prepare a course of lectures on "The Science of Government and Political Economy," to be delivered in the spring of 1863 at the Cooper Institute. The spirit in which he undertook this work of free public instruction is indicated in the following letter to his friend Judge Sharswood of Philadelphia :—

NEW YORK, *March* 9, 1863.

Honourable GEORGE SHARSWOOD.

Dear Sir—A few weeks ago I took the liberty to send to you an invitation for a course of lectures on "Political Economy."

Since that time the lectures were delivered in the large hall of the Cooper Institute, and were the most successful discourses—the number of persons present at every lecture ranging from 2500 to 3000—upon a scientific subject in this city, since O. K. Mitchell delivered his celebrated lectures upon Astronomy.

As the sciences of Political Economy and Sociology are so wofully neglected, not only by the public at large, but also by our present race of legislators, I have been induced, at the request of some of the leading citizens of New York who were familiar with my predilection, for the science and conception of its importance to write the course of lectures referred to.

The success which attended them proved to me that the present time is most auspicious to awaken public attention to the study of that science, which, by reason of the rapid strides it has made of late years, may justly be termed the science of liberty. In consequence of the vicious empiricism of the politicians of the present day, we are likely to experience the same difficulties and evils in reference to the matter of a depreciated currency and taxation as were entailed upon the old nations of Europe until experience had taught them the natural laws governing these subjects. But we, unmindful of the past, and seemingly regardless of the future, rushed madly on, seeing our dearest rights and privileges sacrificed in consequence of the incapacity of our present race of politicians to deal with the most trivial subjects of government in accordance with the laws of political economy.

The Society for the Advancement of Political and Social Science of this city, of which I have the honour to be the corresponding secretary, have requested me to continue a career so auspiciously begun, and believing that I can render thereby more valuable services to my fellow-citizens than conducting a lawsuit between John Doe and Richard Roe, I will continue my efforts if they are at all seconded by the public interest and approval.

. . . . . .

SIMON STERNE.

It was while in this mood that he became one of the leader writers of the New York *Commercial Advertiser*, which had become the property of one of his clients, and engaged in the work of journalism in 1863 and 1864. In 1864, with David Dudley Field and Alfred Pell, he founded the American Free Trade League, and in 1866 the Personal Representation Society, of which he became the first secretary. Meanwhile he continued the practice of law, but his tireless literary energy found vent in the editorship of the newly established *New York Social Science Review*, which began a brief but useful career in 1865. In the same year he visited England, and formed friendships which lasted throughout their lives with John Bright, John Stuart Mill, Herbert Spencer, Professor Fawcett, Walter Morrison, Thomas Hare, and other leaders of the political thought of the time. His acquaintance with Mr. Bright had a somewhat unpromising beginning. It was at a dinner at the house of Mr. Morrison, M.P. for Plymouth, between whom and Mr. Sterne there existed from the first a strong sentiment of mutual regard. It happened that, in the course of this visit to London, Mr. Sterne had been asked to speak at St. James's Hall, as an American, on the extension of the franchise, which was then the absorbing topic of political discussion in England. Instead of putting in a plea for lowering the qualifications of voters, Mr. Sterne had made a careful presentation of what he conceived to be the dangers of universal suffrage. This fact had not passed unnoticed by Mr. Morrison's guests, who comprised all the distinguished men above mentioned, except Mr. Hare, with the addition of Captain White, M.P. for Brighton, and Leonard Courtney. At the mention of Mr. Sterne's name, Mr. Bright said loud enough to be heard, "Is that the crack-brained philosopher who, having been in England only a few days, undertakes to tell us how to conduct our politics?" To this Mr. Sterne, in his characteristically incisive way, made reply: "It may be hardly modest to discuss English politics on so short an acquaintance, but it is not so bad as to speak confidently about American politics without having been in the country at all." Mr. Bright apparently took the rejoinder good-naturedly, since he conceived a lasting respect for the earnestness and aggressiveness of the younger man, and was always ready to extend to him a helping hand in the investigation of subjects in which both were interested.

With Thomas Hare, Mr. Sterne kept up a constant correspondence, and maintained a close personal intimacy. To Hare's influence he owed the formation of what may be called his strongest political conviction, that in minority, or proportional representation, was to be found the cure for most of the evils of our system of Government.

Hare was never tired of recognising the value of the younger man's advocacy of his principles, and when Mr. Sterne undertook to adapt Hare's work on proportional representation to American readers, its author gave him the fullest authority to use the knife at his discretion. Hare's system scored some of its earliest triumphs in the United States, and thanks mainly to the fervour of the convictions of his American disciple, The agitation for its general adoption had a longer life and better sustained activity there than in the country of its origin. How thoroughly Mr. Hare appreciated the value of Mr. Sterne's services to the cause may be inferred from the following letter, written after the news of the assassination of President Garfield had been received in England :—

LONDON, *July* 23, 1881.

My dear Mr. Sterne—I have been several days thinking of writing to you on the present circumstances as they affect our agitation for what should be as nearly as possible a really "pure" democracy. I have been reading over again your last excellent and exhaustive letter of February last. You were then not without hope that, being no longer in active participation with the local party organisation, you might be able to devote more thought and time to the greater object of obtaining a real political representation. I can, however, well understand that the multiplicity of other labours at the Bar and elsewhere may have stood in your way. But I cannot help thinking that the late horrible attempt on the life of the President, which has given so great a shock to all thinking persons in the States and in the civilised world, and which has evidently awakened a profound feeling of sympathy throughout the Union, might justify and give countenance and encouragement to a revival of our efforts to give a new and healthy and pure tone to public and political life. Whether the would-be assassin was sane or mad, the act is equally an outcome of the system which, founding political action on the part of large numbers of persons on the mere hope of personal profit, creates the bitterness and rage of disappointment when they fail in their object. I trust that the great and powerful nation which has grown up around the nucleus planted by the emigrants of the *Mayflower* may not sink into a parallel either with the despotism or the nihilism of Russia. I want to see your institutions great and glorious, the envy and admiration of the Old World. You have all the materials for making them so, if we can but eliminate the prolific germs of evil that now taint and corrupt public life. . . .—Ever yours sincerely,

THOMAS HARE.

The early fervour displayed by Mr. Sterne in pleading the cause of free voting and free trade did not interfere with his attainment of a recognised position at the Bar. The fact that he was known as an ardent Democrat doubtless had something to do with his selection as one of the counsel retained for the defence of Jefferson Davis, but the choice necessarily involved a recognition of his professional standing as well. That his own estimate of this was very modest is as evident from the following letter as that his sense of professional propriety was exceedingly keen :—

October 18, 1866.

Gentlemen—You were kind enough at some time in the year 1865 to retain me as one of the counsel of the Hon. Jefferson Davis. Actuated by the hope that I should procure for Mr. Davis a speedy trial, I accepted the high trust of counsel in his behalf.

At that time, Mr. Davis was not allowed to communicate with any one outside his prison walls, and the only way for him to obtain counsel was either by voluntary offer on the part of members of the Bar to act as such, or to have them retained by means of the earnest endeavours and kindness of his friends.

Mr. Davis is now in position to communicate with whomever he desires. He has already signified his willingness to be represented by Charles O'Conor and William B. Reed, Esqrs., and under the circumstances I earnestly ask your permission to retire from the cause.

So far as I am concerned, the cause stands as though I were a physician who had been called to attend Mr. Davis, in consequence of his having suddenly fallen sick with congestion of the brain. So long as Mr. Davis is in an unconscious state, of course his friends are in duty bound to obtain for him such medical aid as they have confidence in, but just as soon as the patient is in condition to have his own wishes in that respect complied with, the physician called in at the emergency should retire, unless especially requested by the patient himself to continue his attendance.

Trusting that you will agree with me as to the propriety of this step, I am, respectfully yours,

SIMON STERNE.

J. W. LEWELLEN, ESQ., AND OTHERS.

Mr. Sterne was always very jealous of the honour of his profession, and he was profoundly impressed with the idea, years before the Association of the Bar of the State of New York was thought of, that the representative lawyers of the city owed it alike to themselves and their profession to do something to elevate its standards, and render it impossible for grossly ignorant and unfit men to be elevated to the Bench. It was in pursuit of an effort to enlist the aid of some of his fellow lawyers in an organised movement for the reform of the Bar (which found expression in an article on "Law and Lawyers in the United States" in the *New York Social Science Review* of July 1865), that he elicited the following characteristic letter from Charles O'Conor :—

NEW YORK, *September* 5, 1865.

Dear Sir—Your favour of the 22nd ult. is received. I shall be happy to see you at any time and to converse with you on the interesting subject referred to. Truth sanctions this statement; and independently of any emotion that might justly be excited by the complimentary tone of your letter, common courtesy requires its utterance.

To the end, however, that your valuable time may not be wasted in the attempt to enlist a co-operation not likely to be available, I am bound in fairness to apprise you of a very deeply-seated disinclination to participate in efforts at reform, such as the one advised in the article on Law and Lawyers. I do not disapprove them, but am conscious of an almost total inability to aid in them. Therefore, as qualification for really useful labour in these directions is not given to me but to others, theirs should be the task of performing them, and theirs the honours and rewards that are justly due to valuable public service.

I would not plead guilty to the imputation of being extremely indolent, or impeach myself for want of benevolence or public spirit. All I mean to say is, that my power of being useful, if any I may claim, is best adapted to employment in other and different spheres of action.—I am, dear sir, with great respect, yours truly,

CH. O'CONOR.

MR. STERNE.

No man of Mr. Sterne's type could have been a close student of public affairs in New York in the later '60's without being moved to indignant protest against the political corruption which was then rampant, and which, though most flagrantly in evidence in the City Government, had visibly affected the conduct of public affairs both in the State and Nation. Speaking, in February 1869, in a public lecture in the Cooper Union, Mr. Sterne made the following allusion to this subject which indicated with sufficient clearness his attitude toward it :—" If you tell me that New York city is not a fair criterion by which to judge our political system, I ask you, is the whole of New York State a fair gauge ? The senatorial dignity of the Empire State was but lately the subject of a most disgraceful bargain and sale. Go to Washington and witness the activity of that swarm of vermin called the Lobby, and ask yourselves whether they could exist except upon corruption of the worst character. If you tell me that in our sparsely settled districts a purer atmosphere prevails, I answer that if sparseness of population is the only safeguard for the purity of the ballot box and the independence of electors, then, from year to year, as we increase in population, we must be content to bear with a greater and greater load of political demoralisation and iniquity."

One of the men who at that time were most deeply in sympathy with such views, was Friedrich Kapp, to whom New York owed its Emigration Commission, and the correction of a long-standing system of immigrant swindling and oppression.

Speaking at a memorial service, held after the death of his friend, in 1884, Mr. Sterne recalled the impulses by which he was led to take a prominent part in the movement against the Tweed Ring in the following terms :—

> From 1860 to 1870 it was my privilege to be on very intimate terms with Mr. Kapp, and my personal and social relations with him were to me a constant source of pleasure and intellectual profit. No man more sincerely than Mr. Kapp regretted and deplored the then existing political conditions in the city of New York just prior to 1870, when the old Tweed Ring had almost complete control of the judicial and legislative organisation, not only of the city, but of the state of New York, and doubtless his resolution to return to his native land under the then improving political condition of his own country was quickened by the lamentable condition of the Judiciary in the city of New York. From no man more than from Mr. Kapp did I receive words of encouragement in my own determination to do all in my power to assist in the destruction of ring rule in the city of New York. He frequently told me at that period of time, that he could not take part (as he intended to return to Europe) in the struggle which he saw was inevitable between honest men and the thieves in the city of New York; but he expressed the hope that a constant endeavour to crystallise the opposition to ring rule and to get rid of the corrupt judges, venal legislators, and complacent lawyers would be persisted in by the few bold spirits who were then buckling on armour for that memorable struggle.

On June 8, 1870, Mr. Sterne married Mathilde Elsberg, sister of Doctor Louis Elsberg, the celebrated laryngologist. His married life was of the happiest, and all the natural geniality of his character was revealed in the intercourse of home.

Absorbed in public affairs and the promotion of movements of public utility as he was all through his life, his love for home remained one of his dominant characteristics. From first to last his private life was above reproach; anything that savoured of social impurity was as distasteful to him as anything that partook of falsehood or dishonesty. One who came to know him intimately, shortly after this time, Mr. Joseph H. Choate, now the Ambassador of the United States to Great Britain, pays the following sympathetic and discriminating testimony to the strong points of Mr. Sterne's character:—"His keen and subtle intellect, well nourished and enriched by an excellent education, and his playful humour and unvarying good-nature which nothing could ruffle, made conversation with him always attractive and delightful, and I am indebted to him for many pleasant hours. We rode often in the Park together, and his bright sallies and quick responses constantly cheered the way. Whatever subject came up, he was always exceedingly suggestive, and his active mind and ready sympathy of thought made everything easy to him. His enthusiasm—I might call it his intellectual enthusiasm—was a most marked trait, and made his life always fresh and interesting. It always seemed to me that he lived on a higher plane than most lawyers. Although his profession absorbed very much of his attention, it never absorbed his whole energy, which was very great. He loved it, and laboured and succeeded in it, but he loved other things better. He was always very watchful of social movements, in the higher sense of the word, being a very careful and constant student of those things in which the welfare of the community was involved. He had a keen appreciation of the pleasures of sense, but it always seemed to me that his chief delight was in intellectual sport and labour, and to him this kind of labour was sometimes in the nature of sport, as I think his published writings occasionally show. He was full of resource and invention even to the verge of speculation. He did not care so much what other men thought, but was always sure of his own ideas, however much they differed from established standards, and he had a great contempt for mere convention and social prescription."

To this may be added the brief personal tribute of another lifelong friend: "Simon Sterne was a rare spirit, and but few men were his equals intellectually. As a lawyer he was unexcelled, and in all economic questions bearing on the welfare of society, he was a recognised authority, always taking a broad, unselfish, patriotic view. In his home life he was a most charming host, brilliant in conversation and repartee, and yet so kindly in his nature that he never wounded the feelings of those with whom he came in contact. A very kindly, generous friend was he—a very gentle gentleman."

The story of Mr. Sterne's activity in connection with the Committee of Seventy and its work of correction and reform is told in another chapter. But perhaps no better indication could be given of the dominance of Mr. Sterne's ideas in the constructive and legislative work of the Committee than is afforded by the brief allusion to them in the following letter from Mr. William C. Whitney, then a young lawyer who was coming into political prominence as a Reform Democrat :—

New York, *February* 21, 1872.

Dear Sterne—I have to make you my acknowledgments and thanks for remembering me in connection with your meeting of last evening, but singularly enough, I neither saw my name in the newspapers nor anywhere else, and your note which I received at about five o'clock yesterday on my return from the hall was the first notification I had had upon the subject. It came after I had made two engagements for the evening, one of which it was impossible for me to postpone, besides the fact that I am not so thoroughly up on the questions involved in the present charter as to be competent to speak upon it at a moment's notice. My views would be somewhat at variance with yours I doubt not on the whole subject—and yet at this time I see no other result likely to be attained—but this charter or none, or a partisan Republican charter, and I think you will find a great many men coming to your support who will view it in precisely that light.

I particularly admire in this whole matter the ability that has been able to push radical principles of reform legislation into the foreground, and keep them ahead of every rival project—so that it is your charter or *nothing*—or at least nothing *desirable*.—Hastily yours,

W. C. Whitney.

From the date of his assumption of the duties of Secretary of the Committee of Seventy down to his last illness—a period of thirty years—Mr. Sterne was continuously engaged in some work prompted by the desire to be of service to his fellow-men. It may be said, without qualification, that in all of this varied and protracted labour for the public he willingly accepted the task that was most exacting, and in some of it he left but little for his associates to do. It is the design of the following chapters to give some connected account of the chief public movements in which Mr. Sterne was a leading figure in the course of his busy life. It has been deemed most conducive to clearness and compactness of statement to group his chief public activities under separate heads, rather than to deal in detail with the successive periods of his career in their chronological order. Broadly speaking, the promotion of the following great reforms engrossed most of the time which was not devoted to the practice of his profession :—Reform in the relations between labour and capital ; reform in the methods and political standards of the Democratic Party ; reform in the representative system by the introduction of some plan of cumulative voting ; reform in the methods of legislation by the elimination of haste and confusion from the introduction and consideration of bills ; reform in municipal administration by increasing the influence and enlarging the opportunities of the best men in the community, and reform in the relations between the great transportation companies and the public by greater explicitness in their published accounts, by the substitution of stability for uncertainty of rates, and of equal treatment to all for discrimination and favouritism to the profit of a few. His work in all these directions was of an eminently practical kind. He kept in actual contact with the activities of commerce and with the men who had the conduct of public affairs, and to legislator and business man alike he could talk with all the authority derived from an intimate knowledge of the sphere occupied by both. He never accepted any salaried public office, but he never shirked the full measure of responsibility for his performance of public work. A career so absolutely disinterested it would be difficult to find among the men of his generation. He literally spent himself in the service of the community, and he had no other reward save the approval of his associates and fellow-workers, and the consciousness of having done what he believed to be his duty.

The brief duration of the influence of the Committee of Seventy probably deepened Mr. Sterne's conviction that the successful prosecution of the work of political reform was incompatible with the acceptance of office by those engaged in it. He at least acted uniformly on the rule that the reformer should hold himself as free to criticise those placed in power by his own efforts as those whom they had displaced. When, pursuant to a concurrent resolution of the Legislature of 1875, Governor Tilden appointed a Commission to devise a permanent and uniform plan for the government of the cities of the State, Mr. Sterne was naturally marked out for one of its members. His associates on this Commission were :—Messrs. William M. Evarts, Samuel Hand, E. L. Godkin, Edward Cooper, John A. Lott, James C. Carter, Oswald Otendorfer, William Allen Butler, J. M. van Cott, and Henry F.

Dimock—probably as thoroughly capable a body of men as ever undertook the performance of such a public service. The two years gratuitous work of this Commission, though denied immediate acceptance, furnished much of the material for subsequent legislation. The proposal which doomed the Commission's scheme to defeat was that of entrusting the control of the financial affairs of great cities to a Board, elected by the votes of property owners and rent-payers only. As the report of the Commission put the case, its members had been led, in view of the manifold disorders of our municipal governments, and of the notorious failure of popular elections to supply the needed correctives, to entertain doubts whether the general application of the method of universal suffrage in the election of the local guarders and trustees of the financial interests of these public corporations was in accordance with sound principles, or consistent with our present condition, and their conclusion was that the choice of these trustees of the financial concerns of cities should be lodged with those who for two years should have paid an annual tax on not less than 500 dollars of property, or a yearly rent of not less than 250 dollars. Mr. Sterne proposed, as a substitute for this scheme, that, in view of the popular prejudice against property qualifications, a remedy might be found, and the object of giving to the property-holding constituency a voice in municipal government might still be attained, by the adoption of some plan of minority representation in the election of members of Boards of Aldermen. It was only when he found that he could not induce his associates to accept his views, that he adopted what he felt was the only alternative—the creation of an entirely new organisation to exercise a veto power over expenditures, leaving to universal suffrage the choice of mayor, aldermen, and all other elective officers, and enlarging, instead of diminishing, their functions. Nevertheless, all through his public career, there were newspaper critics who insisted on accusing Mr. Sterne of a desire to restrict the suffrage, and who persisted in confounding the principles of minority representation with the property qualification scheme of the State Commission of 1875-76. Replying to these, on many occasions, Mr. Sterne declared the object of minority representation to be not the restriction of the suffrage, but its extension, so as to have in our legislative halls a body thoroughly representative of the whole community, and not merely of about one-half, thus excluding the minority from any representation at all. He pointed out that legislative bodies thus representing about one-half of the people, and only requiring for the passage of any laws the votes of a majority, are, in fact, in the expression of their will, merely representative of about one-fourth of the people. As it requires only a majority vote of the legislative body to pass a law, this majority vote represents about one-half of the whole legislative body, which itself represents about one-half of the people. It was explained that the system proposed by Mr. Sterne and many well-known publicists was intended to give representation to the whole community, so that the legislative bodies should be, as it were, a reduced photograph of that community, and any action taken by such legislative bodies should thus represent the voice of the great majority of the people.

Even before his work on the Tilden Commission had begun, Mr. Sterne was called upon to take the lead in a movement of far-reaching importance, whose purpose it was to effect a satisfactory readjustment of the relations between the great transportation companies and the public. As counsel for Mayor Havemeyer on the questions arising out of the law requiring the city to pay half the cost of abating the dangerous nuisance of the railroad occupation of Fourth Avenue, Mr. Sterne had become profoundly impressed with the extent of the political power wielded by the railroad corporations, and his intercourse with the leading business men of New York brought to his attention the hindrances to the commercial development of the city interposed by the arbitrary character of the prevailing railroad methods. He was one of the founders of the New York Cheap Transportation Association, and it was on his motion that the name of this body was changed in 1877 to that of the New York Board of Trade and Transportation. In his frequent visits to Europe, Mr. Sterne had devoted close study to the question of the relation of railroad corporations to the Government in other countries. As early as 1874 Mr. Sterne, as chairman of a committee of the original Board of Trade, drafted a State Railroad Commission Bill, and a Bill providing for minority representation in Boards of Direction of all corporations. From 1874 to 1878, with the exception of one year, the Commission Bill was presented to the Legislature, and argument made upon it by its author. By this time the burdens laid by the railroads on the city of New York had become too grievous to be borne, and merchants and business men of all degrees found it necessary to demand an investigation of existing abuses as the basis of remedial legislation. Mr. Sterne was invited to address a mass meeting called for April 19, 1878, to give expression to what were virtually the sentiments of the entire commercial community. The invitation was couched in terms highly appreciative of the services which Mr. Sterne had already rendered in his disinterested advocacy of the Railroad Commission Bill. In calling the meeting to order, Mr. Charles Stewart Smith said that probably no man in the city had given more conscientious study to this overshadowing question than Mr. Sterne. Mayor Ely, who occupied the chair, congratulated an unusually representative audience on the fact that they were to have the privilege of listening to some suggestions on the subject from one who had made it, both theoretically and practically, an especial study. Out of this meeting came the appointment of the Legislative Committee of 1879, known as the Hepburn Committee, for the purpose of taking testimony in regard to the abuses in the railway system of the State. On the appointment of this committee, Mr. Sterne acceded to the request of the Chamber of Commerce and the

Board of Trade to conduct the investigation. The Committee began its sessions in Albany on March 26, 1879. The two commercial bodies made elaborate and specific charges against the management of the New York railways. This was followed by a similar series of charges on behalf of the State Grange and Millers of Rochester and various other interests in the State. The Presidents of the New York Central and Erie railways replied by a "joint letter," in which they denied *seriatim* the justice of the complaints, and insisted that investigation would show them to be wholly groundless. The Committee thereupon met in the city of New York to take testimony, and both the complaining commercial bodies by their counsel adduced evidence in support of their charges. The railways were also represented by counsel, and testimony was taken with the same care and under the same rules of evidence as are established in courts of justice. The Committee sat, at short intervals, for about nine months, and submitted at the conclusion of its labours an elaborate report, signed by all the members save one, substantially finding that the charges of the commercial bodies and agricultural interests of the State had been fully proved. At the sessions of this committee, the leading experts and railway managers were examined. The salient points of the testimony were spread before the community from day to day, and the report of the Committee, together with the recommendations which accompanied it for legislation, was received as the first serious and well-directed attempt to deal with the great transportation companies in a statesmanlike manner. The Legislature of 1881 approved of the report of the Hepburn Committee, and the Railroad Commission Bill was finally passed almost precisely as it had been drafted by Mr. Sterne in 1874.

It is difficult to realise the impression which the work of the Hepburn Committee made on students of the railroad problem in every part of the United States and throughout the world. For twenty years after its completion, Mr. Sterne's correspondence abounds with requests for copies of the report and testimony, information as to the character of the evidence on one or other of the special subjects of investigation, and with acknowledgments of the obligations of the inquirers to the immense amount of information in regard to the practical workings of the railroad system which was then elicited. Ten years after the report was published, Mr. Henry D. Lloyd makes the following reference to it in a letter addressed to Mr. Sterne :—" I have during the past week occupied myself by going all through the report and the testimony of the Hepburn Committee. You must allow me to express to you the great admiration with which the study of your work has filled me, both for your patriotic spirit and the immense—I use the word advisedly—the immense intellectual power it discloses. The ten years which have passed make its value only the more apparent. It would be impossible to name any public official who has rendered the State of New York as great service as your labours in this matter have been." In a subsequent letter Mr. Lloyd characterises the work before the Hepburn Committee as "a monument of genius and industry which fills me with renewed admiration of you whenever I look at it." From the office of the British Railway Commissioners, in the House of Lords, came a request for the printed proceedings of the Hepburn Committee, and an acknowledgment from Mr. J. H. Balfour Browne of the interest and pleasure with which he had read Mr. Sterne's admirable "opening," and with which he had followed him throughout the testimony. From New Zealand came expressions of interest in the Hepburn testimony and subsequent correspondence with Mr. Sterne in regard to the suggestions which it contained for the guidance of railway reformers at the Antipodes. From many of the States of this Union came testimonies of the powerful interest which had been excited by the New York methods of dealing with the grievances against the railroad companies, and from senators and members of Congress of the United States came repeated calls for the drafting of some scheme by which national control could be exercised over the railroads engaged in interstate commerce.

As Governor of the State of New York, Mr. Cleveland had been thoroughly familiar with Mr. Sterne's work in regard to the relations between the railroads and the State, and shortly after his accession to the Presidency in 1885, he commissioned Mr. Sterne to report on the relation of the railways of Western Europe to their Governments. This was a subject to which Mr. Sterne had already devoted a good deal of study, but the special report thus called for enabled him to give a unity and comprehensiveness to his treatment of the entire question, which had a special value in shaping the legislation which was already being prepared for the creation of an Interstate Commerce Commission. Mr. Sterne was consulted by Senator Cullom and his associates at every stage of their preliminary work of investigation into the conduct of the railroad business of the country, and as a witness before their committee he made the most valuable contribution of the whole voluminous body of testimony. The report of the Cullom committee was based on his work, and essential provisions of the Interstate Commerce Act were drafted by him. After the Interstate Commerce Commission was formed, he was retained as counsel in some of the most important suits between that body and the railroads, and during the first ten years of the operation of the Act no man was more closely identified with the details of its judicial interpretation.

The last important public appointment conferred on Mr. Sterne was that of one of the five Commissioners to report to the State Legislature a plan for improving the methods of legislation. This was a subject which had occupied Mr. Sterne's attention for many years, and in regard to which he read an elaborate paper before the American Bar Association at Saratoga in 1884. This paper was an elaboration of the views which had found expression several years before that time in various magazine articles and addresses by Mr. Sterne. About the same time he had reported on the subject as chairman of a committee of the Bar Association of New York, and several years later, as chairman of a committee of the New York Board of Trade and Transportation, he had submitted suggestions for amendments to the constitution designed to methodise legislation. When Governor Morton, therefore, in the summer of 1895 appointed him one of the commissioners provided for by an Act of the Legislature of that year, Mr. Sterne threw himself into the work with even more than his usual ardour. One of the first steps he took was to get the consent of his associates to allow him to make a systematic study of the legislative methods and procedure of the countries of Europe. This he followed up by a request to Mr. Richard Olney, then Secretary of State, to make a direct inquiry to the various persons in the diplomatic service of the United States in the countries of Europe as to the methods, rules, and requirements of legislation adopted in the countries in which they exercise their official functions. In response to an inquiry to the Department of State as to the precise purpose of this investigation, Mr. Sterne said: "In this country we suffer exceptionally from slipshod and corrupt legislation. I assume, indeed I know, that the paramount cause for this is absence of method, responsibility, and proper rules for originating and giving notice of proposed legislation if it is to affect personal or local interests; also in defective formulation of the Acts and the absence of proper machinery for ascertaining the effect of proposed changes in the law, and in investigating pending progress of legislation through the Chambers. As to public legislation, there is an entire absence of coupling the due measure of responsibility for legislation with the party in power. Other countries which have legislative bodies have advanced beyond ourselves in the scientific treatment of legislative matters. This is due to improved methods, and these methods do not rest in unwritten tradition, but in formulated rules and prescribed forms which are accessible to a friendly governmental inquiry." He therefore submitted a series of inquiries to be addressed to foreign Governments in regard to the prevailing rules of their legislative procedure. The Department of State lent itself very cordially to the prosecution of this inquiry, and within a few months after it was instituted elaborate replies were received from the Ministers, Chargés d'Affaires, or Secretaries of Legation at London, Paris, Berlin, Rome, Stockholm, Copenhagen, Brussels, the Hague, Vienna, Madrid, Lisbon, Athens, Tokyo, Mexico City, and Berne, as well as from the consular officers of the Government in Australia and Canada. In the same spirit of thorough and minute study of the subject in hand, which was so characteristic of Mr. Sterne, inquiries were addressed to the governors of most of the States in the Union for copies of the legislative manuals and other rules or constitutional requirements bearing on the question of methods of legislation.

In studying the mode of procedure adopted by Mr. Sterne in this and other departments of his public activity, one cannot fail to be impressed at once with his supreme conscientiousness and his amazing capacity for work. The labour incident to a large and successful legal practice, dealing mainly with matters of great complexity and importance, would have been to most men a sufficient draft on their intellectual energy. But Mr. Sterne's appetite for work was so insatiable that he found time to duplicate in unrequited public effort quite as much energy as was required for the discharge of his professional obligations. He "stumped" the Eastern States for Tilden in the Presidential campaign of 1876, and was one of the most active and earnest defenders of the legality and finality of the election of the Democratic ticket in that year. He threw himself with equal energy into the campaign for Hancock in 1880, and the cause of Democracy, as represented by Cleveland in 1884 and 1888, had no more convincing or untiring advocate than he. In the campaign of 1896 he gave renewed evidence of how deeply interested he was in keeping alive the traditions of pure Democracy by devoting himself, without stint of time or energy, to the support of the ticket headed by John M. Palmer.

The campaign of 1896 was no sooner over than we find Mr. Sterne engaged in the preparation of resolutions relating to the draft of the Greater New York Charter, and in protracted conferences bearing on the same subject, while also serving on and doing as usual most of the work of a committee appointed to consider the question of high buildings in the city of New York. It is difficult to convey a satisfactory idea of the exacting character of the public duties accepted by Mr. Sterne to those who have had little or no experience of what the work of committees, the drafting of resolutions, the addressing of public meetings, and the active participation in the never-ending labour of social, political, legislative, or administrative reform really mean. Mr. Sterne's private correspondence contains almost from day to day some call to serve on a committee, to speak at a public dinner, to act as trustee of a club, to do a piece of work for a colleague, to contribute funds for a movement, or to perform his part in one or other branch of the multifarious activities for which his fellow-citizens appear to have regarded him as specially fitted. Considering the ardour which Mr. Sterne displayed in the doing of anything to which he set his hand, the drain both on his mental and physical resources which all this extra labour involved could not fail to prove exhausting.

Without going into tedious details it is impossible to do more than superficially indicate the number and variety of the services which Mr. Sterne performed for the community in which he lived. In addition to those which are considered at some length in the succeeding pages, his share in the work of preserving the Adirondack forests will be gratefully remembered, as also the yeoman's service he did in exposing the Ramapo water job, and in resisting the Amsterdam Avenue grab. The calls made upon him for public service were at no time more numerous than in the years when his system had begun to yield to the approaches of disease, and when perhaps a timely regard to the warnings of nature might have lengthened his life. Probably no man ever opposed to the advance of physical infirmity a more imperious will or a more masterful resolution to refuse to be conquered by bodily weakness. But after surmounting one protracted and painful malady, the finely tempered and resolute spirit had to yield at last, and on September 22, 1901, Simon Sterne passed peacefully away, still fresh in mind, hopeful and genial in disposition, young in vigour, and not old in years. He left to mourn his loss a widow who in thirty-one years of married life had been the unfailing sympathiser in all his aspirations, and a daughter who inherited a notable share of his ability. The feeling which the loss of such a man inspires in the community for whose interests he laboured so faithfully and so long is necessarily confined to those who were his co-workers in the various causes with which he was identified, and among these the death of Mr. Simon Sterne left a feeling of sorrow all the more profound from the conviction that, in sober literalness, he left a place which no other man could adequately fill.

The best known products of Mr. Sterne's literary activity are the two volumes to which reference has already been made :—

On Representative Government and Personal Representation, 1871. J. B. Lippincott and Co., Philadelphia.

Constitutional History and Political Development of the United States, 1882. 1st edition. Cassell, Petter, and Galpin, London. 1888. 4th edition. G. P. Putnam's Sons, New York.

But in addition to these, Mr. Sterne was the author of a large number of pamphlets, magazine and newspaper articles, contributions to cyclopedias, and introductions to other men's work relating, more or less intimately, to the subjects which, from time to time, engaged his study and enlisted his efforts. A complete list of these would be a highly formidable one, and the one appended gives a decidedly impressive indication of the broad range of the multifarious avocations of Mr. Sterne's busy life. The list is given in its chronological order, omitting fugitive contributions to newspapers, and magazine articles which were not separately published :—

The Tariff: its evils and their remedy. 1861.

Law and Lawyers in the United States. *New York Social Science Review.* July 1865.

Report to the Constitutional Convention (New York) on Personal Representation. 1867.

Representative Government: its evils and their remedy. Lecture at Cooper Union. 1869.

Legal Responsibility and Accountability. A paper read before the Medico-Legal Society of New York. November 26, 1873.

Arguments for New York Cheap Transportation Association on Bill to provide for Railway Commissioners and for Minority Representation in Boards of Directors of R. R. Co.'s. March 1874.

Arguments for New York Cheap Transportation Association on Bill to provide for Railway Commissioners. March 28, 1876.

Report of Commission to devise plan for the Government of the Cities of the State of New York. March 6, 1877.

Argument before New York Assembly Committee

on Railways on Bill to create Board of Railway Commissioners. March 28, 1877.

Speech before Assembly Committee on Railways on Bill to organise Board of Railway Commissioners. July 18, 1877.

The Administration of American Cities. *International Review*, September 1877.

Speeches at Taxpayers' Meeting at Steinway Hall in favour of Constitutional Amendments relating to the Government of Cities. October 23, 1877.

Suffrage in Cities. A Lecture delivered at Cooper Institute, December 15, 1877. *Economic Monograph*, VII. G. P. Putnam's Sons. 1878.

Opinion on Constitutionality of separate submission of 6th section of Constitutional Amendment relating to the Government of Cities. January 31, 1878.

Argument before Assembly Committee on Railways on Bill entitled "An Act relating to Horse Railroads in the Cities of New York and Brooklyn." March 5, 1878.

Argument before Committee on Railroads on Bill to create a Board of Railroad Commissioners. March 7, 1878.

The Railway in its Relation to Public and Private Interests. Address before Merchants and Business Men of New York at Steinway Hall, April 19, 1878.

Hindrances to Prosperity, or Causes which retard Financial and Political Reforms in the United States. Address before New York Free Trade Club, November 21, 1878. *Economic Monograph*, XIII. G. P. Putnam's Sons. 1879.

Our Methods of Legislation and their Defects. Paper read before the New York Municipal Society. January 6, 1879.

The English Methods of Legislation compared with the American. Address before the Philadelphia Social Science Association, March 13, 1879. *Penn. Monthly*, May 1879.

The Railway Problem in the State of New York.

Opening Statement before Assembly Special Committee on Railroads on behalf of Chamber of Commerce and Board of Trade and Transportation of New York. June 12, 1879.

Railroad Pooling and Discriminations. Information in answer to questions propounded by the Chief of the Bureau of Statistics, Treasury Department of the United States. June 27, 1879.

Closing Argument on behalf of Chamber of Commerce and Board of Trade and Transportation of New York before Special Assembly Committee on Railroads. December 2 and 3, 1879.

Address on Interstate Railroad Traffic, before the National Board of Trade. December 11, 1879.

The Corporation: its Benefits, its Evils: as Benefactor, as Monopolist. Lecture delivered before the General Society of Mechanics and Tradesmen. January 8, 1880.

The Railway Problem. *National Quarterly Review.* April 1880.

Administration of American Cities. From Lalor's *Cyclopedia of Political Science, Political Economy, and United States History.* 1881.

Remarks at Special Meeting of Board of Directors of New York Board of Trade and Transportation on Death of Peter Cooper. April 5, 1883.

Representation. From Lalor's *Cyclopedia of Political Science, Political Economy, and United States History.* 1883.

Legislation. From Lalor's *Cyclopedia of Political Science, Political Economy, and United States History.* 1883.

Monopolies. From Lalor's *Cyclopedia of Political Science, Political Economy, and United States History.* 1883.

Introduction to Wealth-Creation, by A. Mongredian. Cassell, Petter, Galpin and Co. 1883.

Crude Methods of Legislation. Article in the *North American Review.* August 1883.

Railways. From Lalor's *Cyclopedia of Political Science, Political Economy, and United States History.* 1884.

Remarks at 14th Annual Meeting of the National Board of Trade at Washington. January 25, 1884.

Arguments before Committee on Commerce in relation to Bills referred to the Committee proposing Congressional Regulation of Interstate Commerce. January 29, 1884.

The Prevention of Defective and Slipshod Legislation. Paper read before American Bar Association at Saratoga, New York. August 24, 1884. G. P. Putnam and Sons, 1885.

Memorial Resolutions and Remarks on Death of Friedrich Kapp, at meeting of Medico-Legal Society. November 19, 1884.

Report of Committee of Bar Association of City of New York on Plan for Improving Methods of Legislation of this State. March 10, 1885.

Address before Joint-Committee on Cities of Senate and Assembly on the New York Park Bill. March 25, 1885.

The Railway Question: Statement to the United States Senate Select Committee on Interest to Commerce at Fifth Avenue Hotel, New York City. May 21, 1885.

Report to President Cleveland on the Relations of the Governments of the Nations of Western Europe to the Railways. January 18, 1887.

Address before German American Citizens' Association on the proposed Constitutional Convention and the work before it. February 4, 1887.

Some Curious Phases of the Railway Question in Europe. Paper read at the meeting of the American Economic Association at Boston. May 24, 1887. *Quarterly Journal of Economics*, July 1887.

Protection—A Delusion and a Snare. Address before Harlem Democratic Club. May 8, 1888.

Nicaragua Canal, Argument in opposition to the

Signature by the President of the United States of Bill to incorporate the Maritime Canal Company of Nicaragua. February 14, 1889.

Oppressive Telephone Charges. Speech before New York Assembly Committee on General Laws. January 30, 1889.

Railway Reorganisation. *The Forum.* September 1890.

The Greathead Tunnel Electric Railway. *The Forum.* August 1891.

The Salaries of the United States Supreme Court Justices. *The Counsellor*, of the New York Law School. January 1892.

Recent Railroad Failures and their Lessons. *The Forum.* March 1894.

Suggestions for Constitutional Provisions to Methodise Legislation. Report of the Special Committee of the New York Board of Trade and Transportation, adopted May 9, 1894.

Representative Reform in its Relation to the Civil Service. *Proportional Representation Review.* December 1894.

The Relation of the Railroads to the State. Paper read before the Wharton School, University of Pennsylvania. November 27, 1895.

The Telephone Bill. Argument before New York Assembly Committees. February 5 and 19, 1895.

Proportional Representation. *Proportional Representation Review.* September 1895.

Report of the Commission to Recommend Changes in Methods of Legislation. November 30, 1895.

The Reconquest of New York by Tammany. From *The Forum.* January 1898.

CHAPTER II

CONTRIBUTIONS TO THE SOLUTION OF THE LABOUR PROBLEM

THE dominant impulse of Mr. Sterne's earliest activity in the field of public usefulness was a desire to diffuse among the common people some intelligent conception of the truths of political economy. The Cooper Institute was in the early sixties, as it is to-day, a centre of diverse agencies of popular education, but at least one of these must strike the present generation as being characteristic either of different habits of mind or different racial elements from those which enter into the composition of the wage-earning community of New York to-day. That successive courses of lectures on social and political science should have been attended by audiences consisting of from 1000 to 2000 working people, suggests the existence of a higher degree of intellectual curiosity than now prevails among the same class, if not also a higher level of mental capacity. Doubtless much of the popularity of these lectures was due to the personality of the lecturer—to the impressive earnestness, the convincing force, and the contagious enthusiasm which he brought to the exposition of what is commonly deemed one of the least attractive departments of human knowledge. But there must have been, a generation ago, a greater openness of mind than exists to-day among the working population of New York in regard to what has come to be known as the labour question, to make it possible for them to fill the benches, week after week, at Mr. Sterne's lectures. His treatment of this question was deficient neither in frankness nor in fairness, and it dealt very unceremoniously with some of the cherished illusions of organised labour. As a contribution to the better understanding of a question which is every year becoming more acute in the United States, the following synopsis of some of these lectures may not be without value. As a revelation of the extraordinary maturity of thought and judgment attained by a young man, still in his twenty-fifth year when the last of this course was delivered, their subject-matter is of more than ordinary interest.

The first course, which consisted of six lectures, was delivered in the spring of 1863, at the invitation of the Board of Trustees of the Cooper Institute of the city of New York. The second course was delivered in 1864, at the invitation of the Association for the Advancement of Social and Political Science, and consisted of four lectures. The third course was delivered in the spring of 1865, and was published in full in the *Trades Advocate*, the official organ of the working-men's union, a journal devoted to the interests of the working classes, published in the city of New York. This latter course, bearing more particularly on the problems of our own time, is selected for analysis. To appreciate the value of the instruction therein conveyed, the fact must be borne in mind that it was addressed to an audience of working people, ignorant, for the most part, of the rudiments of political economy, and presumably under the influence of false impressions in regard to the share due to labour in the division of the profits of industrial enterprise. After an introductory sketch of the natural growth of the subdivision of labour and the accumulation of capital, Mr. Sterne pointed out that it was part of the harmony of the social organisation that man is not remunerated in proportion to the amount of effort or labour he has expended on a commodity, but according to the estimate formed by society of the value of his services. All labour, to be productive, must be free. Every artificial enactment which interferes with that right on the specious pretext of better regulating the partition or remuneration of labourers, is radically false and injurious. There is not a commercial privilege nor industrial monopoly which is not a source of suffering and misery to some one. The interest of man should be the sole arbiter of his conduct. Let that be rightly understood, and he will always be a useful member of society.

The labourer has no right to any greater or higher remuneration than such as results either from the exercise of his muscular force, his manual dexterity, the application of his intelligence, the loan of his capital, or the advancement of his credit. The results obtained through natural agents or the collective power of society, in their nature gratuitous, should and do inure to the benefit of mankind at large. In proportion as the intellect of man is developed, he calls to his aid natural forces which were wholly unproductive before he made them subservient to his will. For instance, he has utilised the waterfall by compelling it to turn a mill. He makes use of the evaporation of water to drive his engines, and he has discovered an invisible agent to carry his messages with incalculable speed, making him more powerful than the ancient Greeks deemed their gods. If it were not for the aid of natural forces which, from time to time, have been subjected by the intelligence of man, the greater part of his wants would have to remain unsatisfied. All these natural forces become in a short time gratuitous. All can to-day employ and make use of steam or electricity without having to pay for their use. We are compelled to pay for the steam-engine and the Morse instrument, but the price simply represents the labour expended upon the manufacture of an implement which facilitates the employment of a natural force. We simply pay for the shackles which hold the slave in subjection.

Only second to the employment of natural forces is the immense aid to production arising from the division of employment. This increase of productive power is largely due to the increased dexterity of each particular workman, and it necessarily tends to lessen the price of the product ;

besides enabling the consumer to obtain a commodity at a less expenditure of effort than would otherwise be necessary, the division of employment raises the wages of labour and adds to the productiveness of capital. Wherever a single person is found acting at the same time as mason, farmer, weaver, and shoemaker, the condition of society to which he belongs is necessarily barbarous. In other words, the division of labour is the associate of civilisation, and both cause and effect of progress. If commerce were entirely free, it was Mr. Sterne's conviction that a division of employments would take place between nations similar to that which exists between individuals, and the mutual dependence of the civilised countries of the world would be such that wars between them would be as rare an occurrence as violent differences between bakers and shoemakers. Labour is an article of merchandise with which the labourer comes into market and disposes of to the highest bidder. The value of it, like its results, depends principally upon the cost of production, and the skill, ingenuity, and industry of the labourer. The price of it is fixed like that of any other commodity purchased and sold according to the law of supply and demand. The larger the number of persons who seek a particular kind of employment, the greater the competition between the labourers, and the lower the salary in that branch of human activity.

When a commodity is to be produced, two things are necessary for its production—capital and labour. In the present organisation of society, these two elements are generally supplied by different classes. The capitalist advances the necessary raw material—the tools and buildings required for the manufacture of the commodity. The labourer provides his labour, more or less skilled, and which is more or less remunerative in proportion to his skill. The union of these forces produces a commodity, an article of merchandise, which is the joint property of the labourer and the capitalist. Wages being simply the payment by the capitalist to the labourer of his presumed share in the products, the justice of the share thus apportioned obviously involves much matter of controversy. That this sum can never amount to the full value of this share is both natural and just, otherwise there would be no compensation to the capitalist for the considerable element of risk which his advantages entail. For example, a vessel has to be built or a house to be erected. The capitalist supplies the necessary implements and machinery as well as the material to work upon. The mechanic whose only fortune consists in his skill and industry, supplies the labour. The capitalist must be careful not to expend his all in the enterprise, and must have sufficient to live upon until at least part of the work is finished, and to preserve him from poverty if the enterprise should result in a loss. But the labourer cannot wait six months or a year before he receives a dollar as his compensation, nor can he run the risk of being deprived of all remuneration in the event of no profit being forthcoming. He, therefore, says to the capitalist: "I will renounce all extraordinary profits on condition that you assume all the risk, and will take a smaller sum as my share in consideration of the security I enjoy of being able to supply myself and family with necessary food, clothing, and shelter, by reason of your paying me a fixed rate for my co-operation in the work of production." Both the capitalist and the labourer have been benefited by this interchange of services. The capitalist has the sole direction of affairs and the hope of larger profit. The labourer gains the certainty of making a livelihood instead of running the risk of an entire loss of his efforts, should the enterprise prove a failure.

The cost of production regulates the price of all things. The oscillation around this central point regulates what we call profit or loss. The cost of production regulates the price of labour, or in other words, the value of the productive services of the human faculties, precisely as it regulates the price of a steam-engine. In searching, therefore, for the necessary elements entering into this price of production, we must pay attention not only to the cost of maintenance but also to the cost of reproduction. In the case of a railroad enterprise, it is not only necessary to calculate the cost of surveying and laying out the road, the cost of putting down sleepers and laying the rails, in building rolling stock and machine shops, but also the wear and tear on all these things, and the budget of the road must provide for their renewal. Thus the working-man must have sufficient not only to maintain himself, but he must also be enabled to support his family. If he does not earn sufficient to enable him to do this, he cannot be deemed prosperous, as a new generation does not supply the wear and tear of the old one. The lowest ebb to which the remuneration of unskilled labour can permanently sink is the cost of maintaining life ; and between that level and the highest point of remuneration we meet with all grades of pay depending upon the value to mankind of the services of the labourer.

Here Mr. Sterne touched what he recognised as a source of discontent and heartburnings to many a mechanic, and he went on to show that this difference of remuneration was in strict conformity with the principles of justice and equity. He asked, what would any journeyman say if his employer put an apprentice on a par with himself with reference to wages? He would think it clearly unjust. Why is it unjust? Simply because the apprentice has not yet earned this extra salary by the development of his intellect, the devotion of his time, or the service he renders. In the industrial world it is conceded to be necessary that wages should correspond with services. Such a world in which there should be an equality of wages and remuneration would be a sort of fool's paradise in which the indolent, the stupid, and the improvident would fare as well as the enterprising, the intelligent, and the provident. But how is it with the remuneration of persons who do not belong to the industrial class? Are they entitled to so disproportioned a share of this world's goods as they appear to enjoy, and, if so, why and how can this be reconciled with the principles of justice? The answer is that consideration must be taken of the amount of time necessary for the education of the professional man, the long years of toil, and unremitting and unrequited endeavour of one who devotes himself to a liberal profession. Then there is the uncertainty of success and the increased responsibility of his position; the greater strain upon the intellectual faculties, and the greater waste of the system than in any manual employment. These strains and waste necessitate periods of rest and leisure to restore the needful mental vigour, no less than the use of a greater variety and more expensive character of food than would be sufficient for a day labourer. If a law were passed compelling society to pay the same remuneration to every class of labourers, no one would devote himself to employments requiring long and costly preparation, because by less study and effort he could obtain the same reward. Society would, therefore, quickly relapse into barbarism.

The rate of wages being determined by natural laws, it follows that for their unimpeded action the most complete freedom is essential. As the rate of wages can be justly and equitably fixed by a bargain between employer and employed, no arbitrary authority can so well regulate it for them. It has frequently been said that the capitalist is better able to enforce harsh terms upon the labourer than the labourer is to resist them. This is an assumption not warranted by the facts. When the competition between capitalists for profitable investments is taken into account, it will be perceived that a manufacturer who, by reason of paying a lower rate of wages than the market justifies, earns thereby an exorbitant profit, must attract capital into the same line which will create an additional demand for labour, thus giving the workmen a greater choice of employers as well as increased wages. The working-classes have thus the clearest possible interest in the increase of capital, since the greater the amount of capital employed in any particular industry, and the more extended the credit, the higher will be the rate of wages. In a district where there is but a single factory, the labourer is to some extent at the mercy of the employer. But erect in the same place ten, instead of one, industrial establishments, and the workman becomes independent; he can choose his employer, and competition between masters will increase to its highest natural price the wages of labour. Mr. Sterne therefore asked his auditors: "Who can have a greater interest than yourselves, to watch carefully and jealously the action of your legislators, that they, by short-sighted legislation, do not hinder the growth of capital, or wantonly interfere artificially to regulate the mutually beneficial dependencies and relations of capital and labour?"

Mr. Sterne enumerated the stages of development through which the labourers of the world have passed, and from which they have been gradually emancipated by increased intelligence and machinery as: (1) slavery; (2) serfdom; (3) as workers for hire. That this third stage of development would develop into something higher and better he had no doubt; but whether the workingmen of the world were already ripe for this higher and better development, was a question which he did not undertake to solve. The prevalence of strikes, the constantly recurring arguments on their own part against capital and machinery, seemed to argue against their present fitness for something higher. But the success which had attended the establishment of labour associations and co-operative societies, organised upon strictly scientific principles in Germany, by Herman Schulze-Delitzsch, had been so marked and beneficial, that he regarded it as folly to suppose that a like attempt would not meet with the same degree of success here. Four of these five lectures was intended to lead up to an explanation of how such associations could be organised, and were designed to disabuse the minds of working-men of erroneous conceptions which they had formed in regard to the relations of capital and labour, and on the subject of strikes, population, and what not. Two or three years before the delivery of these lectures, Mr. Sterne had personal experience of the crude and erroneous ideas which the working-men of New York were liable to entertain in regard to their own interests. In the year 1862 there was a strike of some 2000 grain shovellers, measurers, etc., against the use on the part of their employers of the steam grain elevators which were gradually coming into vogue in this part of the country. Having seen the grain elevators operated on a large scale in the West, Mr. Sterne was moved to attend a meeting of the striking grain shovellers of New York to give them some words of practical counsel. Permission to speak was readily given to him, and he pointed out that in striking for an increase of their already high wages, they were drawing attention to the large amount of money paid to men for hand labour which could be done so much cheaper by machinery. He counselled them that instead of striking they should at once go to work and agree to put half their wages aside into a common fund, so that they would shortly have money enough to purchase two elevators and become the owners of them and have an income from that source for all time. Meanwhile, they could continue hand labour until grain shovellers were no longer wanted, and keep making enough money to order more elevators, so as to be first in the field and control the grain-handling business of the port. These suggestions were rejected by the men assembled, and they declined to listen to further arguments from Mr. Sterne on that evening.

In one of the lectures delivered in 1865, Mr. Sterne reverts to this strike to illustrate the folly of all strikes against the use of machinery. He recalled the fact that in 1862 there were about 2000 men employed in the trans-shipment of grain, together with six grain elevators. The steam grain elevator worked by nine men performed the labour in two days that would require five days under the manual system with twelve men and one horse. The lessened price of trans-shipment by the use of steam was twelve cents per hundred bushels. The 2000 men then employed in the business earned, at the time of the strike, an average of $3.50 per day. The immediate inducement to strike was the fear of losing this high remuneration by the gradual and general introduction of the steam elevators. If they had not struck, the introduction of the elevator into general use, like that of every improvement, would have been gradual, and sufficiently slow to have permitted all of them to find some other employment. But as soon as they had struck, they immensely quickened the march of events which they had intended to obstruct. Within a short time twenty elevators were placed upon the stocks, and the President of the Company said that he would have paid the workmen to do precisely what they did. These 2000 men were out of employment by their own voluntary action for the period of five weeks, and lost during that time in wages the sum of $240,000. Had they placed that sum in a common fund, they could have purchased all the elevators then in use in the city of New York for the sum of $20,000 each, making an aggregate of $120,000. They could then have worked them for their collective benefit, and had $120,000 to spare for other purposes. But in consequence of the strike the grain elevators came into general use, so that the number of hands employed in the business was decreased by one-half. Assuming that the grain shippers had assented to the demands of the strikers, the grain elevators would have gone to some other port where vessels would have been loaded more quickly and cheaply, and New York would have lost an important element of its commerce.

That all strikes against the use of machinery should be predestined failures Mr. Sterne declared especially fortunate, since otherwise a particular class could for ever debar mankind from the use of an improvement, beneficial to the vast majority of their interests. When a number of men fraternise for the purpose of using violence of any character, they soon cut loose from the principles which until then had governed their conduct, and their violence, when once begun, takes a wide range, and brings with it an unexpected train of evil consequences. Granting that strikes occasionally take place without being accompanied by violence, the step is none the less an error on the part of the workman. He acts upon the supposition that wages can be arbitrarily regulated by the wishes of employers and employed, instead of depending upon the law of supply and demand and the cost of production. When wages sink in any particular employment, it is by reason of a surplus of hands in proportion to the capital invested or the demand for the product. If not arbitrarily interfered with, the equilibrium will soon be established by the natural course of events. Some workmen will withdraw from employment offering low to one offering higher wages, until gradually the general average is attained. But from the moment the labourer strikes he adds twofold to his difficulty. In the first place, he reduces the capital employed in his industry, thus lessening the fund upon which he must depend. Secondly, he increases the number of persons who in future will compete with him for labour, as the employer will engage new hands during the strike, and thereafter prefer to employ those newly acquired hands as a punishment to the strikers. Thus labourers, by reason of a strike, have frequently for a long time thrown themselves out of employment.

That wages should sink when the trade or vocation is overcrowded with hands is a harmonic natural law, beneficial in its operation. By appealing to the immediate interests of the labourer it advises him to change his vocation or economise in his expenditures. But if, heedless of this advice, he attempts by violent means to increase his wages, penury and misery must necessarily result from his shortsighted proceeding. Should the employer accede to the demands of the employed, the injury may be greater than in case of a refusal, if the state of the market or the limited supply of labour does not justify the increase. In a short time the capital of the employer is exhausted, as others in the same trade can undersell him. And the increase of wages will attract new hands to an already overstocked labour supply, thus increasing the competition between labourers, causing ruin to those hitherto employed, as well as to the others who are attracted to the trade by the temporary increase of wages.

At the time these lectures were delivered, the organisation of labour had by no means reached the point of development which it has since attained, and the tyranny of the trades-union was not felt to any such degree as it is at the present time. But Mr. Sterne clearly perceived the dangers inherent in the system, and proclaimed them with an amount of frankness and courage which cannot be too highly commended, and which has very seldom been imitated by public teachers having the ear of working-men. He defined trades-unions as being associations to protect working-men in any certain employment from the supposed despotism of capitalists. These associations are formed by working-men, and a code of regulations is drawn up, to which not only working-men are expected to conform, but this code is also intended as a guide to the proper management of the affairs of the capitalist himself. All working-men in any particular vocation in which such a union is organised, and who have sufficient independence of spirit and manliness to refuse to be guided by any such self-constituted judges as to the proper wages they should receive, or the hours of their labour, are subject to being coerced into joining the organisation by having every impediment thrown in their way to the obtaining of employment, and by having their intercourse with their fellow-workmen made uncomfortable by manifestations of contempt and dislike.

Trades-unions are the offspring of the system of guilds which governed the industrial world a few centuries ago. These guilds were associations of working-men and employers for the protection of their particular trade against the oppression of government on the one hand, and the encroachments of similar occupations on the other. That these guilds were necessary and useful at one period of their existence no one who believes in the progress of civilisation can doubt. The guilds were the bulwarks which defended in its infancy the growth of the industrial enterprise of the world, just as the Hanseatic League was the first great commercial organisation which tended to develop and foster the commercial intercourse of nations. The wealth acquired by these guilds, the strength of their membership and their cohesion, made them respected by the rulers and robber barons who then governed the civilised world, and who dared not infringe upon the rights of the guilds for fear of the rebellious spirit which might thereby be awakened.

Mr. Sterne quoted from Dunoyer the account of a litigation, which lasted 150 years in the city of Paris, to illustrate some of the absurd disputes which grew out of the guild system, and which foreshadowed some of the petty restrictions of the trades-unions. This litigation was begun by the Guild of Shoemakers against the Cobblers' Guild, to settle the question of how much mending or patching of shoes should be allowed, and where patching ceases and new shoes are in point of fact made. After grave deliberation, the Courts of Law came to the conclusion that putting new soles and heels on old uppers was patching, and putting new uppers on old soles and heels was also patching; but putting new uppers on new soles and heels was not patching, but the making of new shoes, and therefore an interference with the rights of the time-honoured and highly respectable Guild of Shoemakers.

It was maintained by Mr. Sterne that there was this essential difference between the guilds and trades-unions, that while the former had an excuse for their existence, the latter, in their existing form at least, had none. His chief objections to the trades-unions were, that they were based on two radically false and mischievous ideas —that capital and labour are antagonistic, and that the rate of wages can be arbitrarily fixed by the will of some few working-men, instead of being regulated by the law of supply and demand. He admitted, however, that no system, even if its object be objectionable, which tends to bring working-men together, which leads to an exchange of views, which tends to make labourers acquainted with their common wants and necessities, can fail to be of ultimate benefit. Therefore, while their immediate object may be a mistaken one, they are calculated to become the germ of future good in facilitating gradual enlightenment upon the question, the practical solution of which should form the true object of the association. Schulze-Delitzsch found these trades-unions scattered in great abundance throughout Germany, and he converted them all into co-operative societies. The existence of the unions facilitated his labours, because it was not necessary to bring together the working-men engaged in any particular employment; they were already assembled. All that he had to do was to dissipate error and establish truth in the minds of the members of the German guilds, and his cause was won. It was admitted that improvements, such as those introduced by Schulze-Delitzsch were easier to accomplish in Germany than they could be here. The people of Germany, not being possessed of political power, had not been led and misled by demagogues; had not been made vain by flattery; did not suppose themselves intelligent and wise, but were willing to learn from a man who had made the subjects of political economy and labour a life-long study, and they hailed him as their benefactor and guide. With a blunt straightforwardness which excites our admiration, Mr. Sterne told his auditors that while the flatterers and sycophants of Germany plied their miserable arts at the courts of that nation, they did not corrupt the heads of the lower classes, whereas here, the demagogue and pothouse politician can ride to power only on the shoulders of labouring men. He therefore cringes to those who require instruction and not flattery, and to whom a few earnest words of advice and remonstrance is much more wholesome than pandering to their lowest passions and playing on their basest feelings.

Mr. Sterne was an enthusiastic advocate of the application of the co-operative principle to production as well as to distribution, and believed that in this was to be found the true solution of the labour question. The concluding lecture of the series, the first four lectures of which have been already summarised, was devoted to a review of the practical operation of the co-operative societies of England and Germany. Answering the objections which have been urged against co-operative plans of production, Mr. Sterne admitted that there was some justice in the argument that men who co-operate are not as likely to find some disinterested individual who, like the capitalist, will always buy in the cheapest market and sell in the dearest. He admitted that a capitalist directly interested in the results of his labours, whose whole profit was dependent upon his activity or enterprise, was enabled, by reason of the additional spur to action which the hope of gain calls forth, to underbuy and oversell, all other things being equal, any co-operative store or manufactory. But he maintained that all other things were not equal. The capitalist is subject to counteracting influences from which co-operative working-men are free. In the first place, he is in constant practical antagonism toward his working-men, who will give him as little labour as they can for as much wages as they are able to secure; who, uninstructed in the relations between capital and labour, will constantly try to hinder and prevent as much as possible the profits of the capitalist. What with strikes and trades-union regulations, arbitrary laws in reference to the hours of labour, and laziness on the part of working-men, the capitalist is constantly impeded and hindered in the maintenance of regularity in the supply of the commodity which he furnishes. Co-operation changes all this. The working-man is both capitalist and labourer, and he at once perceives, that if he is faithless in his duty as labourer, he injures his interests as capitalist. He begins to understand practically the relations of capital and labour, and with the great mass of mankind practical demonstration is the only teacher. The great curse of the wage-earning class is the bitterness engendered by the idea that labour and capital cannot work harmoniously together. Co-operation removes all this. The little sum originally saved will be carefully watched, and every effort will be made to increase it. Strikes cannot occur, and there will be an immediate perception of the fact that wages depend upon profit, and not upon the arbitrary will of employer and employed. Under the co-operative system the workman would be in every way improved, intellectually and morally. All the inchoate socialism and communism in his nature would be driven out of him by experience.

It was Mr. Sterne's conviction that almost all working-men, not possessed of capital, are socialists and communists without ever having read a line of Proudhon or Fourier. He discerned the probability of another change in the fact that after a year's experience of co-operation, working-men could no longer be led to the polls like sheep to the shambles, well knowing that the votes they cast tend to put some thief in office, but consoling themselves with the delusion that the capitalist pays for it and they do not. Once a capitalist himself, to however limited an extent, the artisan voter would say to the demagogue who tries to cajole him out of his vote: "No, you don't; I tried this sort of business last year, and my taxes have largely increased in consequence. I have learned something by this time." It is true that, property or no property, capital or no capital, the working-man pays the taxes, but he does not know—he does not feel it. It is done indirectly; he never sees the tax-gatherer *in propria persona.* By the co-operative system, he learns to feel the consequences of his wrong, and he will try to avoid its perpetuation.

Another objection to co-operation is that it is a

species of communism, and as such it should be condemned. Mr. Sterne met this objection by a simple denial. It is not communistic at all, but quite the contrary. It is a specific cure against communism. Communism is essentially a system by means of which everybody is to receive an equal share in this world's goods. No matter what his intelligence or stupidity, no matter what his industry or laziness, he is to enjoy the same amount of comfort and luxury as everybody else. Co-operation rightly understood and rightly practised, embodies nothing of all this. It is simply a development of a system of wages; it embodies all that is good and excludes all that is bad in that system. In co-operation, the working-man receives interest on the amount of capital he has himself invested, profit in proportion to his risk and wages in proportion to production, so that the system is the farthest possible remove from communism.

The unanswerable argument in favour of co-operation is that it educates working-men to a higher scale of being than that which they have so far enjoyed. Working-men become masters. They are compelled to watch the changing events of the market. They begin to understand the interlacing and solidarity of human interests. They begin to comprehend the influence of peace and war upon prices, and of plenty or dearth upon profits. They are naturally led to discuss and adjust between each other their various profits and losses. Competition will make them desirous to educate themselves so as to be on a par with other employers. Reading-rooms and mechanics' institutes will spring up everywhere as one of the beneficent results of such a system. Instead of, as now, opposing the introduction of the improvements in machinery, they will seek at the earliest possible moment to avail themselves of these improvements.

The introduction of machinery, while beneficial to all the interests of society, had one deleterious effect, which was, that it tended to keep working-men fixed in their positions. That is to say, the introduction of machinery has so increased the amount of capital requisite to the building and equipping of a successful manufacturing establishment, that it became almost a hopeless task for the working-man to emancipate himself from his position as a journeyman and to swing himself to that of an employer. Mr. Sterne cited, for illustration, a mechanic employed in one of the great iron-mills reflecting on his position and being driven to the conclusion that 100 years of most rigidly enforced economy would not suffice to enable him to possess himself of the huge machines necessary to compete successfully with existing manufacturers. He looks at one of these great machines, and when he calculates that such an instrument of labour alone costs $25,000 his heart sinks within him, and he feels himself as much debarred from the position of master workman as though a law defined his position and enacted that he should for ever remain in it. This absorption of the vast amount of capital by machinery and the influence it has had on the working-man, aside from the fact that it has advanced his wages and lessened the drudgery of his employment, was to Mr. Sterne a sad thing to contemplate. That the vast majority of mankind should be doomed to a perpetual routine of work without the hope of social advancement, would argue that if a remedy cannot be found against so crying a social evil, there is something wrong in our social organisation.

Almost everywhere throughout the world, Mr. Sterne found indications that working-men were entering upon a new phase of social existence, differing as much from the one in which they are at present as working for wages differs from serfdom. He saw that it might take many years before this revolution would be completely effected. For hundreds of years serfdom existed by the side of freedom, and thus, for a century or more, the greater part of labouring men may be compelled to depend upon salary or wages for their sole means of existence. But the question of co-operation is no longer an experiment, and it depends upon the working-men alone as to how soon they will avail themselves of the advantages of the system. Mr. Sterne perceived but one thing in the way of the successful introduction of the Schulze-Delitzsch banks in the United States, and that is the usury law. Fifty years before he spoke, Jeremy Bentham, in his unanswerable plea for usury, had given usury laws their mortal wound, but as if unconscious of the propriety of dying, these laws most unscientifically and unpardonably continue their existence. Since they impeded and delayed the introduction of a great social reform, it was high time, in Mr. Sterne's judgment, that an agitation be commenced for the repeal of these remnants of narrow views and middle age prejudices. Error is really long lived, particularly in governmental institutions; it won't be argued down nor laughed down, but positively insists on being kicked down before it consents to abdicate.

The supreme triumph of the Schulze-Delitzsch Association, Mr. Sterne found to be that, for the first time in the history of labour, the question had been solved of the credit which it could command. The remark had been frequently made that labour is capital, but hitherto it had been a capital upon which little if any credit was given. But it had been demonstrated that it was capital in the sense that it could be hypothecated and pledged for advances made to it. The point which in all this progress was most gratifying was that the improvements in the social condition of working-men had been effected by themselves. The initiative had not come from Governments and did not depend upon Governments for support. There was, therefore, substantial reason for believing it to be real, not factitious, to be enduring, not transient. Nay, more, there appeared to be good reason to believe that the benefits which would arise from these simple co-operative societies might vie in importance with the results which flowed from that meeting of the seven citizens of Manchester, who began the agitation of the question of free trade.

It is instructive to note the vitality of the ideas

formulated by Mr. Sterne for the instruction of his artisan hearers of a generation ago in the latest discussions of the labour problem. At a meeting of the American Academy of Political and Social Science, held in Philadelphia on July 1902, we find Mr. W. H. Pfahler, of the National Association of Iron Founders, making the following generalisations:—"Labour, whether skilled or unskilled, engaged in the reduction of the raw material to the finished product, is also dependent upon the law of supply and demand to fix its value or wage; and any effort to change this value brings the wage-earner in direct conflict with the consumer, through his representative, the employer, whose duty it is to know, and who usually does know, what proportion of the entire cost of any article can be distributed in wage, so as to retain the value of the article at a price not in excess of the ability of the consumer to purchase, and yet within limits which will prevent a more favoured nation or district from furnishing the same article in competition, and thereby causing idleness for the wage-earner and loss to the employer. Capital represents plant, machinery, transportation, interest, and all the factors known as unproductive, and yet absolutely essential for the combination of material and labour. Capital is usually, though not always, the owner of material and the direct employer of labour, and therefore must stand for the silent partner in the combination. What is so frequently called a war between capital and labour is simply an effort on the part of the wage-earner and wage-payer to determine what part of the product of labour, as distinct from material, is represented in the price to the public, and after deducting the proper charge for plant, etc., how the balance, which is profit, shall be divided between the employer and employee—or wage-payer and wage-earner."

From these and similar principles Mr. Pfahler makes deductions which run on all fours with those made in 1865 by Mr. Sterne. He insists that the employee must not forget that the effort to establish a minimum rate of wage, if based upon the lowest standard of efficiency, destroys the earning power of the more competent workman, and lowers the standard of all. That the effort to limit production is false in principle, and can only succeed, if at all, when the demand is in excess of the supply, and when it succeeds it causes the creation of methods and machines which supplant the skill of the mechanic, and bring into competition a lower grade of labour at a lower wage. That the laws, rules, and methods of Labour Unions must be changed to conform to present conditions if the Union hopes to be recognised as a factor in the adjustment of the labour problem. That the right to strike, or refuse to work, under certain conditions, does not involve the right to prevent others from working, if the conditions are satisfactory to them, and involves responsibility for all the damage that may arise. That the standard of wage cannot be measured by the standard of time employed, or energy expended, but by the results attained.

Still more striking is the correspondence between Mr. Sterne's ideas and those of Mr. Alexander Purves, Treasurer of the Hampton Institute, Virginia, which were submitted at the same meeting, in regard to the advantages of industrial co-operation. Mr. Purves enunciates the following principles as sufficiently well established to be used as a basis for working out plans for the reform of prevailing relations of labour and capital :—" (*a*) That whenever there is sufficient confidence on the part of the employees, a direct or an indirect dividend to labour is a good investment for capital. (*b*) That, with an actual dividend-earning interest in the business, every participant would be prompted to individual efforts : (1) towards accomplishing more work in a given length of time; (2) in the saving of waste ; (3) in seeking and suggesting improvements in the manufacture and in the conduct of the business, looking to the advancement of the general welfare ; (4) in that it would naturally become the self-imposed duty of every employee to challenge a co-worker for laziness, or upon the commission or omission of any act through which a loss to the business would be the likely result ; and therefore (*c*) that capital in business is best secured when every employee is pecuniarily benefited through the enlarged success of the enterprise."

Mr. Purves puts the question : " Would the plan of letting the employees generally become part owners of the concern place them in a position to give trouble to the management of the enterprise, and would they not soon demand, as stockholders, the right to a voice in the direction of its affairs and in the shaping of its policy?" To this he presents the following reply:—"(*a*) That with the proper and timely guarding of the interests of the original investment through sufficient, clear, and undeniable limitations upon the rights and powers carried with the issues of deferred stock, such issues could not be used to the detriment of vested interests, but rather (*b*) that such a pecuniary interest in the enlarged success of the business would act as a guarantee of loyalty to the management, and as an incentive to the employees to further the legitimate business of the concern, and (*c*) that the employees with a money investment in the enterprise, if for no higher reason than the instinct of self-preservation, would realise the value and necessity for harmonious and sympathetic co-operation between the capital, brains, and energy of the concern."

To the further question: "Would capital be benefited by the operation?" Mr. Purves replies without reservation that it would, and for the following reasons:—"(*a*) That the net profits of the business would be largely increased, through the reduction of friction; the larger incentive of labour; the increase in the physical capacity of the workers to produce; the saving of useless waste; and through the absence of strikes and lock-outs; as in all of such increase in net profits the capital would be an equal sharer with its employees. (*b*) That the true loyalty and support of all employees would greatly strengthen the security of the capital in the business, and proportionately add to the real value of the investment. (*c*) That where adverse legislation may be easy of accomplishment, when it attacks the interest of one man or a small body of men, it would be quite a different matter where the interests of all employees are involved. (*d*) That the surplus profits would not be paid out and distributed, but would be held in the business, subordinated to the claims of the original investment, and so very materially adding to the security thereof. (*e*) That with a property interest in the business, the tendency of the operatives to shift from one concern to another without real purpose would be reduced to the minimum, and that the consequent advantage to the management would result in a distinct gain in the stability of the business."

All of which goes to show that while the labours of the pioneer may be forgotten, the result of his work lives after him, and becomes part of the influence by which social reforms can be brought into practical correspondence with the special wants and conditions of each succeeding generation.

CHAPTER III

PARTICIPATION IN PARTY POLITICS

To Mr. Sterne politics stood for the whole science of government, whose study must be undertaken with an open mind, and not at all in the spirit of partisanship. Believing, as he did, in the economic soundness of the principles of Free Trade, he was naturally attracted toward the party by which these principles had been espoused rather than to the party which had made the Protective theory its own. The conviction, which he early imbibed, that the country is governed best which is governed least, also predisposed him in favour of the party organisation whose traditions were identified with restraining the functions of the national government within the strict lines of the constitutional delegation of power. But with what came to be known as the Southern theory of State rights Mr. Sterne had no sympathy whatever, and on the question of slavery he was as radical as the blackest of Republicans. The following letter addressed by him in 1864 to Mr. Charles Dolfuss, editor of the *Revue Germanique* of Paris, outlines very clearly the nature of his convictions in regard to the issues of the war :—

In the Republic of letters introductions are unnecessary, and I can, without fear of rebuke, hail at the distance of 4000 miles a kindred spirit. All honour to the man who has advocated the cause of the North, and whose abiding faith in free institutions and free labour led him to the inevitable conclusion that in a struggle between the contending elements of freedom and slavery slavery is doomed.

It is with no little interest that we watched the course of the *Revue Germanique*, and we did so because we knew the weight of the opinions of Charles Dolfuss. A misconception in reference to the genius of our institutions has misled many European thinkers, and if by this letter I can succeed in partially dispelling that misconception, I shall not have written it in vain. Those who suppose that we are struggling for empire will discover their mistake, and find that we are really struggling for a lasting peace, and the restoration of that harmony which existed before the breaking out of this rebellion. Before the enactment of the constitution of 1789, the confederation of States, as it existed immediately after the recognition of our independence, was found to be ineffectual against the internecine feuds and strife which the men of that time perceived to be looming up in the distance. They therefore determined to form a more permanent union, founded upon the right of self-government on the part of each State, but granting to the central power the right, peaceably and amicably, to adjust conflicts which would in the course of time arise between the various members of the confederacy. And thus, to all intents and purposes, the thirty-four States now composing the United States of America are separate and independent of each other, with the full power to regulate their internal affairs as may best suit them, with the single reservation that they are bound to preserve the Republican form of government, and to submit their disputes to the peaceable adjudication of the Supreme Court instead of the arbitrament of force by means of war or restrictive legislation.

The General Congress elected by the various Legislatures, the Executive elected by the people, are merely means to attain that end. The rêsult, as experience has proven, has been most beneficial, and we have seen the unexampled spectacle of numerous separate and independent commonwealths residing together without the necessity of a standing army, without the thought of restricting the interchange of commodities as between each other. But the slave power, ever alert for its own safety, discovered that the march of free ideas and the prosperity of the North under the system of free labour would make the tenure of its position precarious, and that leaving the arbitrament of questions between the States to the peaceful settlement of a central regulating power, its system must vanish. The advancing stride of civilisation, armed with the power of machinery, which daily makes brains worth more, and muscle worth less, would, by the operation of natural law, supersede human bondage.

They, therefore, rebelled against that system which by leaving man free to his individual development permitted him to outgrow the trammels of power and restriction. They desired to withdraw the 4,000,000 of bondsmen from the eloquent hum of machinery and the instructive lessons of progress. The Southern States knew that force being the foundation of slavery, force alone can sustain it; that where the system of slavery ceases to rule it ceases to live. Hence the Rebellion. Our struggle has, therefore, a higher meaning than the desire of empire; it means that we cannot permit our country to be divided and subdivided, so that we fall into the same errors, into the same mistakes, from which Europe is suffering—standing armies, conflicting tariffs, and supposed antagonism of interests. It is that which we must avoid; it is that which we must at any sacrifice attempt to counteract.

But in times of peace rather than of war will our country be tried. The dangerous feeling is fast gaining ground that we must more and more centralise power, and that the individual has hitherto been too free. It is, therefore, with sincere delight that I read your article on Decentralisation, and I am convinced that it contains lessons of wisdom which it would be well for our countrymen to memorise. We are passing a tax bill, most unphilosophical in its provisions, and dangerous in its tendencies. We have sacrificed our writ of Habeas Corpus, and have ordained a censorship of the press. The necessity of the moment has perhaps been a sufficient excuse for our conduct in that respect, but it is necessary to awaken our people to the fact that their salvation does not lie in such sacrifices, but in the rigid maintenance of their rights and the reclamation of those natural prerogatives after the necessities of the hour shall have passed away. Believing that general progress is possible only through the progress of the individual, in order to reach the ear of the public we intend, at an early day, to organise a society for the promotion of a knowledge of political economy, an enterprise in which we hope to have the co-operation of European economists.

Trusting that you may continue in the good cause with the same force that you have hitherto displayed, and assuring you that you find many admirers on this side of the ocean, I remain, with the highest respect, yours truly, SIMON STERNE.

As above indicated, the measures adopted to silence the voice of the Northern press when it suggested sympathy with the cause of secession were alien to all his ideas of the sacredness of constitutional guarantees, and appear to have elicited from him more than one vigorous protest. The occasion of the following was the act of the Administration in forcibly restricting the circulation of the *Journal of Commerce*, *Daily News*, and *Day-Book of New York*. Like the communication to

Mr. Dolfuss, this plea for the liberty of the press is marked by a style and sentiment which are interesting as the product of what may be called the formative period of Mr. Sterne's intellectual growth :—

Within the last week a step was taken by our Government, the consequences of which are of the greatest importance to the American people. A censorship was placed over the press, and the indirect method of muzzling the same by forcibly restricting its circulation was adopted. We are denied the high privilege of seeing our ideas mirrored in the journals, and are robbed of the still higher liberty of giving free expression to our thoughts. So intent are we on the idea of preserving the Union and the Constitution—the forms in which our liberties were embodied—that we do not feel in attempting to preserve that form that the spirit for which we contend is fast slipping from our grasp, and that, on the tyrant's plea of necessity, we are rapidly being deprived of our liberties, and fast ceasing to be the representatives of those enlightened principles, the beneficent workings of which characterise our century, and are the surest test of our progress. The Habeas Corpus, one of the bulwarks of our liberties, has been suspended—that writ the suspension of which has never been attempted even in England. And the next great step in our enslavement is fast being accomplished—the suppression of the enunciation of public sentiment by means of the public press.

And upon what grounds are these infringements attempted to be excused, upon those liberties which but yesterday we guarded so jealously ; which but yesterday we regarded as the just pride of our people, the just pride of our country, the just pride of our system of government ? Liberty, in the broad sense to which we have been accustomed, was the result of our civilisation. That holy trinity—liberty of press, conscience, and speech—

was the flower which the tree of knowledge bore after the toil and labour of centuries. We have hitherto boasted of the proud pre-eminence of our nation in having established, almost a century ago, the fundamental law that the people are supreme. It was the success which attended the carrying out of that dogma that entitled us to the high esteem of nations, and not the fact of our territory extending from the St. Lawrence to the Rio Grande. And we are to be deprived of this distinction by one fell blow, without even the semblance of an excuse on the part of the Administration. It is idle to suppose that our liberties can be withdrawn and granted at pleasure. If our system and the principles upon which our Government is founded are right, then any of our liberties, be it of speech, press, or conscience, is an indefeasible right, as much as the right to hold and transmit property.

Now, let us examine the reasons given by some of the friends of the Administration for their act. They say in time of war we cannot regard law or rights. Indeed, not? Then, my amiable friends, suppose the people would learn that dogma by heart, and act upon it by turning out of power the whole Administration, rob the banks, or do some other equally lawless act, could you blame them? Would it not be a lesson which you have inculcated and instilled? It is true that in time of war measures must be adopted which would not be justified in times of peace, but the point to which these measures dare go is where indefeasible rights commence, and not one step farther. You cannot in consistency with our system of government confiscate my property to help you to carry on the war, and the right of the press to address itself, with perfect freedom to the masses, has hitherto been regarded in the same light as the sacred rights of property. If these journals whose liberty has been interfered with address themselves to a miserable minority they can do no harm; but if, on the other hand, they are the exponents of the opinions of a large class in the community, a blow has been struck at their rights for which the Administration can never sufficiently atone to an outraged people.

Have our politicians learned so little in the school of history that they do not know the oppression of a cause to be the surest way to benefit it, and that these journals which have fallen under administrative displeasure, in preserving a sullen and enforced silence, are really more eloquent than by filling their leaders with invectives against the war and the Administration? Do not intolerance and oppression make hypocrites of a large class of the community, and thus directly tend to lower public morality? It is advanced, on behalf of the Administration, that they know these journalists do not from conviction oppose the Administration, but from impure and corrupt motives. Who dares to judge of that? What man so pure or so exalted that he can with justice judge the motives of his fellow-beings? If the fact be true, as alleged, that one or more of the proprietors of these journals are base and dishonourable men, does it alter the right of the case? Have base and dishonourable men no rights, and can we the people be deprived of our liberties in consequence thereof.

You may be right, say the friends of the Administration, but it is a mere suspension of a certain liberty, the exercise of which is dangerous for the present, and we will grant it to you again as soon as present circumstances have altered. I do not want to enter into abstractions, but really, in my early years, I had always understood that the people, when they delegated certain powers to their governors, reserved to themselves some trifles, such as liberty of speech, conscience, and the press, and that it suited the whim and fancy of our prudent forefathers not to leave the exercise of these rights which they were absurd enough to suppose inalienable, to the arbitrary rule of any administration under any circumstances whatever. And can you really suppose that this, or any other administration, will not find an excuse, on the ready plea of necessity, to continue a domination the exercise of which is so pleasant and convenient to the rulers, and proportionately galling to the ruled? Are we so sure of our liberties that we can permit them to be trifled with by any Administration, however pure, or however just that Administration may be?

I feel that in giving expression to these thoughts, I but imperfectly express the feelings of a large class of the people who have hitherto earnestly, even zealously, supported the Administration in their attempt to put down rebellion, but who are now compelled to say: "In this labyrinth of complications and wrongs we cannot follow you." Nor is it penned with any ill-feeling toward the Administration, but from an earnest desire that in our hot pursuit to right our wrongs, we do not endanger those principles, the proper exercise of which has exalted us in the list of nations, and made us the beacons of light and of hope to the oppressed in the whole of the civilised world. It is not that I love my country less, but that I love liberty more.

Mr. Sterne's first taste of work closely related to active politics was in the organisation of the American Free Trade League. The fundamental principle of that organisation was, "That men should have the right to exercise their industry, to dispose of its fruits in any market which to them shall seem best, and with the proceeds to buy whatever and wherever they please." It protested against the paternal interference of Government with private pursuits, being convinced that the less Government is felt and seen, the better for all concerned. It believed "that 'Protection' to the Producer is Robbery to the Consumer, with the added hypocrisy of pretending to look after the latter's interest." Early in 1866 Mr. Sterne appears to have made a tour of the West, in his capacity of Secretary of the Executive Committee of the League, for the purpose of enlisting recruits and establishing branches for the organisation. His activity excited the attention of Horace Greeley, and drew from that vigilant sentinel on the watch-tower of protection, one of his characteristic tirades against the "doctrinaires" who were warring against the interests of American industry. He quotes Mr. Sterne as saying, in a speech at St. Louis: "I have been asked how is it possible with our heavy national debt to organise a system of free trade? Can we pay the interest on our national debt if we have the free trade system? My answer is, I believe, logically correct, that for the very reason of our having a national debt, it is necessary for us to inaugurate a policy of free trade—that is to say, a policy of revenue tariff interest, and not a policy of protective tariff. Any person who has reflected on the subject will see at once that a revenue tariff differs in every respect from a protective tariff. A protective tariff is levied for the purpose of prohibiting importations of foreign goods and other goods. A revenue tariff is levied for the purpose of courting the importation of foreign goods, for the purpose of getting the largest amount of revenue." All this was, of course, merely a new evidence to Mr. Greeley of the essential depravity of all free-traders, and of the truth of his persistent accusation that they were subsidised by British gold to compass the ruin of the American manufacturer. In this latter view, Mr. Greeley was doubtless greatly strengthened by an address issued in February

1866, by the Free Trade Association of London to the American Free Trade League of New York. Mr. Sterne had said that the League was composed of men of all shades of political opinion. This, according to Mr. Greeley, conveyed a false impression, and was intended to convey it, since, in his judgment, "there are not four persons connected with the organisation who are not either already in full communion with the Democratic Party, or preparing and expecting to be so before the next Presidential election." Thus, in addition to deriving its impulse and its sinews of war from Europe, the Free Trade League, according to Mr. Greeley, "looked for its votes to the Copperheads." And yet, not even Mr. Greeley himself could have been more fervid in his rejoicing over the triumph of the Union cause, than were the London Free Traders in addressing their American brethren. There is certainly nothing of the "Copperhead" sentiment about the opening passage of the address :—

> We congratulate the American people most cordially and sincerely upon the termination of that gigantic conflict in which they have recently engaged. Especially do we rejoice that slavery has received its deathblow, thus elevating labour from its degradation, and vindicating for all men the inalienable right of personal independence. We earnestly hope that every breach created by this war may be speedily and effectually healed, and that all your people, in whatever part of the Union they may be dwelling, may unite in the noble task of so reconstructing the social and political fabric, that the result of this fearful trial may be a national existence purified, elevated, and strengthened by the terrible ordeal through which the

nation had passed. We believe with you, that the present time is most auspicious for your undertaking. No work can be more worthy to supplement the one just completed than that of securing for free labour the right of freely exchanging its productions in the markets of the world. Indeed, this is the natural consummation of the task which was but commenced in the abolition of slavery. Free trade is the vital element of free labour; without the former, the latter cannot healthfully exist. The most perfect freedom of exchange is necessary to enable the labourer to derive the full value and advantage of his labour.

Nor was the editor of the *New York Tribune* or any of those who were at that time so loudly celebrating the virtues of a high protective tariff, and so recklessly impugning the patriotism of those who refused to agree with them, capable of the statesmanlike foresight which the following passage indicates, and with which Mr. Sterne and his associates were in thorough sympathy :—

It is, however, not merely in relation to questions of revenue and taxation that the necessity of Free Trade legislation is so apparent, as in relation to the urgent and herculean task now devolving upon your people, viz. the reorganisation of the trade and industry of the Southern States. We are firmly persuaded that the most potent ally you can summon to your aid in this great work is the principle of Free Trade. With a fertile climate of almost unlimited extent, producing articles which are required throughout the globe, with abundance of labour waiting employment and requiring organisation, the unnatural relations formerly subsisting between capital and labour being happily destroyed, the wisest course you can adopt is to throw down the barriers which prevent the world from becoming your customers to the largest possible extent. Adopt freedom of trade between the United States and the entire globe, and we confidently predict that not only will the task of restoring the industry of the South to its former productivity be comparatively easy, but that it will become vastly and widely extended.

The attitude of Mr. Sterne toward the political problems which remained to be solved after the war is fairly indicated in his preface to the *Constitutional History and Political Development of the United States*, written in 1881. He recalls the fact that European statesmen had doubted, and many thoughtful Americans at times had misgivings whether our institutions could bear the strain of the conditions in which, at the close of the war, the National Government was placed. But, looking back over the intervening sixteen years, he was able to say that while the ills of an improperly laid and collected revenue, a bad civil service, mischievous methods of taxation and corrupt municipal administration still existed, none of these evils could, properly speaking, be said to date from the war period, since the roots of them were planted many years before the slavery agitation was at its height. Nearly a million of men, who were under arms at the close of the war had been disbanded and reabsorbed by the agricultural and industrial activities of the country, and no appreciable increase of crime or lawlessness had been manifest. The Government had returned to a sound currency from a depreciated war currency, notwithstanding the fact that great masses of the people believed the return to specie payment would be the ruin of individual enterprise. A large proportion of the debt created by the war had already been paid off; and the remainder, by the establishment of a financial credit second to none in the world, had been refunded at so low a rate of interest as to reduce the burden of the debt, after taking account of the increase of population, to but a third of what it had been at the close of the war. The revenue of the country was so far in excess of its financial needs that, but for the ingenuity of politicians in devising jobs to absorb public funds, a bad civil service and governmental extravagance, the debt would have been reduced in a still greater degree.

Mr. Sterne recognised the fact that all these evidences of the elasticity of our institutions which enabled them successfully to meet unlooked-for emergencies, had elicited the admiring expressions of publicists the world over, and invited a closer study of a form of Government which, while securing on one hand individual freedom of action, did not appear to lack the power to produce certain results which were supposed to be among the special advantages of the more paternal forms of Government. But he insisted that it would be puerile in the extreme to attribute to their institutions the whole of the prosperity of the people of the United States. Any constitutional form of Government securing freedom of action in dealing with the practically inexhaustible resources of the country, among which he reckoned its vast treasures of mineral wealth, its fruitful soil and beneficent climate, coupled with a geographical situation which almost wholly excludes foreign competition, would have made for the inhabitants of the vast domain, known as the United States, a home filled with comfort, luxury, and wealth, and would have attracted seekers of fortune from every quarter of the globe.

Coming down to the purely economic aspect of the situation and prospects of the country, he goes on to say—

> That the institutions of the United States did, however, largely favour the growth of material wealth cannot be denied. Not to speak of other advantages afforded to individual enterprise, the entire absence of any interstate custom-house from Maine to Florida, and from the Atlantic to the Pacific, has given the inestimable and incalculable advantages of free trade in its most absolute form over a larger surface, and among more varied conditions of an industrial and agricultural character than unimpeded exchanges exist elsewhere on the face of the globe. While it is true that in more recent years (since 1846) European nations have let down the barriers of protection toward each other, both by treaty and more liberal legislation, yet in the United States the practical advantages of the system of free trade commenced almost synchronously with the teaching of the doctrine by Adam Smith in 1776. The errors of protection, which still govern the legislation of the United States in its relations with foreign countries, and to some degree counterbalance the benefits thus conferred, bring loss, but in the limited ratio that foreign commerce bears to a nation's internal exchanges; and as the ratio of foreign commerce is at best not one to twenty of domestic interchange, the benefits conferred by the freedom of exchange within the United States must have been out of all proportion greater than the injustice inflicted by the protective system inaugurated in 1861—a system which, if the

signs of the times do not mislead, is fast crumbling away.

The system has had a longer and more vigorous existence than Mr. Sterne was disposed to accord to it, but the fact that the opposition to it has been steadily growing in strength, and was never more aggressive than it is to-day, is very largely due to the work done by him and other pioneers of the revenue reform movement in educating the people into a comprehension of the essential incompatibility of high protective duties with the continued welfare of the very interests they were designed to foster. About the same time that the preface was written, from which the preceding quotations are made, Mr. Sterne was engaged in actively organising a State Revenue Reform League for the purpose of advocating a change in the unequal and unjust system of tariff taxation in the direction of a wider commercial freedom. To promote the formation of associations throughout the State to carry out the work of this body, Mr. Sterne drafted an address to the people in which he submitted certain reasons to show that the necessity for the proposed reform was imperative and immediate. Among these were the following:— Existing laws, by levying heavier duties upon the necessaries of life than the expenses of the Government require, impose a burdensome tax upon the poor, for the benefit of a small privileged class, and at the same time accumulate annually in the National Treasury a surplus to be squandered in extravagant, if not corrupt, legislation. The claim that so-called protective tariff laws enhance the wages of labour had repeatedly been shown to be fallacious, and was only advanced by those who sought to retain the existing system for the purpose of securing protection in the privileges which they enjoyed at the expense of the whole people. It was submitted that the system, instead of benefiting, worked a great injury to labouring men. It increased the cost of living, it so enhanced the cost of materials upon which their labour was expended, that the finished product could not hold its own in the markets of the world. Revenue reformers demanded, on behalf of American working-men, that taxes should be reduced or entirely removed from the materials used in their industries, in order to secure an enlarged demand at home for finished goods, and an outlet for the surplus product of their labour in the open markets of the world.

The plea was submitted to the judgment of the citizens of the State of New York that the exercise of the taxing powers of the general Government should ever be regarded with jealous scrutiny, and that when these powers are used in the interest of a favoured class to impose unnecessary burdens upon American labour and American industry, it is the duty of all men interested in the cause of good government, irrespective of party affiliations, to unite in an effort to secure the enactment of such measures of reform as would open the way to a more healthy commercial life. A reform in the tariff laws had been for some time demanded by the best opinion in the country, and the Chief Executive of the nation (President Arthur) had recommended such a reform to the favourable consideration of Congress. The time seemed thus to be ripe to make the politicians of both parties feel that the citizens of the State had a common cause in seeking to sweep away an unjust and vicious system of taxation.

Never recognising mere party triumph as an end in itself, Mr. Sterne continued to be all his life the steadfast advocate of what he regarded as the principles of pure Democracy without respect to the degree of acceptance which they received at the hands of the party organisation. He had nothing but scorn for those Democratic leaders who tried to dodge the tariff question, or who sought success at the polls by a surrender to the free silver lunacy. From the earliest efforts to debase the currency by an unlimited infusion of silver, Mr. Sterne was one of the most uncompromising defenders of the gold standard. In a letter to the *Nation*, dated February 7, 1878, after referring to the frequency with which reference had been made during the war to the latent powers in the United States Constitution, "which from time to time manifested themselves in most surprising forms," he went on to say—

> Now, let us call forth the reserve powers of the States and localise as much as possible the consequences of cheap money and dear commodities, and so let a fluctuating currency, uncertain values, and absence of commercial and financial credit—as chickens and curses are said to do—roost at home. The Constitution of the United States says: "No State shall make anything but gold and silver coin as tender in payment of debts." This implies that the States, not the United States, shall

have control of the subject of tender, as they have of all matters of contract, subject to the limitation that such tender must be "gold and silver coin." The extent to which either shall be a tender is not set forth.

Mr. Sterne's suggestion was that all the States not affected by the silver theory should pass a law whose essential provision should be that all debts, obligations, and contracts, expressed or implied, should be discharged and dischargeable only in gold coin of the United States, issued under section 3511 of the Revised Statutes, at their nominal value, and to the extent only of $20, should such debts be dischargeable in silver coin of the United States issued under section 3513 of the Revised Statutes (trade dollar).

And such gold coin shall be the sole legal tender in payment of all debts, public or private, at their nominal value when not below the standard weight and limit of tolerance provided by the United States Coinage Act, and, when reduced in weight below such standard and tolerance, shall be a legal tender at a valuation in proportion to their actual weight; and such silver coin shall be a legal tender at their nominal value for any amount not exceeding $10 in any one debt, and the minor coins of the United States shall be a legal tender at their nominal value for an amount not exceeding 25 cents in any one payment.

This suggestion evidently met the approval of the editor of the *Nation*, for the leading article in the same issue expands and applies Mr. Sterne's argument. The editor points out that it was folly to suppose that by accepting the Bland Bill, and making the best of it, the people opposed to them would be able to satisfy the silver fanatics. On the contrary, there was every reason for believing that they would be emboldened to try other experiments of the same sort. The silver movement had begun with rational bi-metallists; it had ever since been passing more and more into the hands of men who were burdened with no financial theories whatever, and whose ultimate aim was repudiation and unlimited Government money of some sort. Any sign of submission would lend this class more strength and enterprise, and spread the poison of communism, already very rife, farther through the ranks of the working-men. Should the Bland Bill be passed over the President's veto, the editor urged, as Mr. Sterne had done, that every effort should be made to localise the folly by State legislation. The sane States, which contain the capital of the country and most of its manufacturing industries, such as New England, New York, and Pennsylvania, should legislate promptly, making gold exclusively the standard of value, and, if thought desirable, making silver a legal tender at its bullion value in gold. This would meet the lunatics and criminals with the only argument which lunatics and criminals understand—the argument of impossibility. It would save the business of the country from a prodigious aggravation of the existing disorder, and would cause a restoration of confidence, by removing that dread of the wild-cat majorities in Congress, which was then so fatal to all enterprise.

Being interviewed about that time as to his attitude toward the question which threatened to divide the Democratic Party, Mr. Sterne said: "I am a Democrat who believes in the single gold standard. Any party that deviates from an honest money policy deserves to be beaten, and in my opinion will be." The principles of tariff reform which Grover Cleveland had adopted did not appeal more strongly to Mr. Sterne than the unyielding character of Mr. Cleveland's attitude toward the question of honest money. Mr. Sterne was one of the most ardent advocates of Mr. Cleveland's election in 1884; he threw himself, with characteristic energy, into the campaign of 1888; and he was one of the hardest worked of the Democratic campaign speakers in 1892. When the party organisation finally surrendered to Bryanism in 1896, Mr. Sterne promptly identified himself with the movement designed to rally the democratic supporters of the gold standard to the support of the Presidential ticket, headed by John M. Palmer and Simon B. Buckner. He believed that on the supporters of this movement had devolved the support before the American people of the doctrines and traditions of the Democratic Party, and the following declaration, issued under the imprint of the National Democratic Committee, was a thoroughly accurate expression of his views:—

In gross betrayal of the Democracy, the Chicago Convention proclaimed the gospel of hate between sections of the country, between labour and capital, between employer and workman. It demanded the debasement of our currency, which means the dishonour of the nation, the repudiation of private contracts, and the reduction of the pay of the labourer to one-half his present wage. It asserted in effect the right to pack courts of justice for the purpose of reversing the decisions which do not meet with popular favour. It denied the right of the Federal authority to protect the mails and interstate commerce, upon which depend the very existence of our great industrial centres and the markets of our farmers; it denied this right even after peace was broken, blood shed, and property destroyed. To all true Democrats these assertions are utterly abhorrent. Mr. Sterne was profoundly sensible of the fact that the Democratic Party did not perish with the triumph of repudiation and anarchy at the Chicago Convention, and he was equally impressed with the necessity, in the event of the election of a Republican President, that a powerful and genuine Democratic organisation should stand active and conspicuous before the country. Such an organisation would be of vital consequence to safe Federal administration, to the sound politics of the country, and to its security against an extreme and perhaps successful reaction in 1900 to excesses like those threatened by Bryan and Sewall.

The impression which Mr. Sterne's services in this campaign left on the minds of the men most competent to judge of their value may be inferred from the following letter addressed to him by Mr. Samuel O. Pickens, a leading member of the Bar of Indianapolis, and dated November 5, 1896:—

I am pleased to congratulate you on the result of the late election, and I want to thank you again for the services you rendered in this State. There is not a particle of doubt that the stand taken by Sound Money Democrats saved this State to M'Kinley. One of the gratifying things to me is that this election has proved that in times of great peril men can be counted on to lay aside their party affiliations for the time being, and take a stand against doctrines which threaten the honour and stability of our institutions.

To Mr. Sterne and many of those who acted with him, whether as Democrats or Republicans, in the cause of sound money, the result of the Presidential election of 1896 had also demonstrated the fact that, while a large majority of the American people were in favour of the maintenance of the gold standard, there was a dangerously heavy minority ranged on the other side. It was therefore deemed necessary that the united efforts of patriotic men of all parties for national honour and sound money should be continued, and Mr. Sterne's name appears among the signatures of a hundred thoroughly representative citizens of New York as in favour of the immediate formation of a nonpartisan association, to be named the "National Sound Money League." The Monetary Convention held at Indianapolis on January 12, 1897, was due to the influence of this body, and the work which was there formally initiated still awaits its final fruition in Congressional legislation. Mr. Sterne attended the Monetary Convention as a delegate of the New York Board of Trade and Transportation, and never ceased to labour for the principles of National finance, which it adopted, and of which the formal and final recognition of the gold standard by law was the most conspicuous triumph.

Mr. Sterne made, in the course of his speech delivered at the dinner of the Democratic Club in New York on January 28, 1896, a presentation of the duty of the Democratic Party toward the questions of the hour, which will remain a testimony alike to his courage and his sagacity. He began by pointing out that there is, in every party, a constant conflict between what is deemed to be expedient for the moment as against what is wise for all time. The temptation to sacrifice principle for expediency is greater in the case of a party than it is in the case of an individual, because a party lives by popular favour, and the advantage which is gained by the possession of power seems so controlling as to offer to a political organisation a great temptation. It was to hold up the standard of principle, and to admonish the assembled Democrats that nothing was to be gained by its sacrifice, that Mr. Sterne accepted the invitation to deliver this address.

He went on to say that many of the time-honoured principles of the Democratic Party had ceased to be questions of the hour ; that they had either become antiquated by the march of events, or by the decisions of the Supreme Court become imbedded in the Constitution, so that they were no longer living political issues. The party announced, through its spokesman, Mr. Cleveland, adhesion to the principles of a freer commercial policy, and antagonism to that perversion of the taxing power for private and individual gain, which is misleadingly termed "Protection." When President Cleveland was elected in 1892 on the issue, then squarely made, of opposition to the M'Kinley tariff and all that it stood for, the party was pledged to uphold the doctrine of revenue reform, and to apply it in practice by a revision of the tariff. The President was inaugurated while the country was still suffering from the effects of the crisis precipitated by the Baring failure. Mr. Sterne declared it to have been then his conviction that a reduced capacity for production, consequent upon the restriction of credit, made it wise to postpone, for a time, the new policy touching tariff legislation. He then felt on that question as a physician would toward a patient suffering from a tumour which, for the sake of safety, it had been determined should be extirpated. If in the interim between this decision and the time set for the operation the patient were seized with an acute disease, it would be wise to postpone the operation —however expedient in a normal condition—until the patient had sufficiently recovered his strength to enable him to bear it with reasonable hope of success. The Treasury needed revenue ; the change in the tariff threatened to, and did, impair its ability to obtain such revenue, and it was expected that the impairment would be made good by a direct tax on incomes. The Income Tax Act, then deemed of doubtful constitutionality, was passed, and had since been declared by the Supreme Court to be unconstitutional. The party was thus, at the very beginning of its progress toward revenue reform, confronted with an impairment of the National revenues, which were further reduced by the commercial depressson which lessened the whole productive capacity of the nation, and Democracy laid itself open to the charge—however unjust it might be—of unwise administration of the National finances. To all these causes of depression were added the failure of our cereal crops, and the abundance of the crops of Europe rendering the Old World, to a large degree, independent of the American supply. But the party leaders persisted in their determination to achieve some measure of revenue reform, and did produce a vastly improved tariff, based, to a degree at least, upon the principle that Protection, as such, was an abuse of the taxing power.

The country was at the same time suffering from another legacy of the protective system, which gave to the producers of silver a claim upon the National Treasury for the purchase of their output, and which was beginning to produce its natural result of threatening the gold basis of our currency, and thus placing us out of harmony with the financial systems of the great commercial nations of the world. This danger was met, and in part overcome, by the repeal of the Sherman Law, but the country was suffering then and continued to suffer from the consequences, not only of the silver purchases but of the mistrust incidental to keeping the Government of the United States in the banking business, by the issue of various forms of paper money with differing promises of redemption. All these had to be kept on a level so that the gold in the Treasury, pledged specifically for a redemption for a part of the currency, was constantly being withdrawn, and there was a steadily recurring liability to render the Treasury unable to meet its gold engagements in gold.

The enemies of the party and its policy charged

the decline in business activity to the revenue tariff, with which that decline had absolutely nothing to do, but which Mr. Sterne maintained, it would, under normal conditions, have had a tendency to remove. He admitted that they obtained a great many adherents by drawing attention to the difference in the conditions of prosperity under Republican rule, as compared with the preceding four years under Democratic rule. A great temptation was, therefore, presented to the Democratic Party, to compromise its position, and to make an effort, by the lure of some weak form of protection, to gain back its majority of 1892. Mr. Sterne held that to fall into that trap, to lower the party standard, was to abdicate the position of a great party. Its obvious duty between that time and the date of the election was to educate the people of the United States to understand that the tariff bore no relation to the existing depression in business; that to follow in the footsteps of its enemies was to surrender the reason for the party's existence. If protection were held to be justifiable, the Republican Party, which is responsible for it, and is wedded to it, and which has the confidence of all who profit by that system of taxation for private gain, is, logically, the party which is entitled to power. Mr. Sterne could see but one line of Democratic duty, which was to hold aloft the party standard of principles in regard to the tariff, while admitting that a mistake had been made in attempting to supplement by unconstitutional means, the decreased revenue consequent upon a reduction of the tariff rates—a consequence that would not have followed such reduction had not causes, wholly other than those relating to the tariff, conspired to continue and intensify the prevailing business depression. Relief must be promised to the community by persistence in revenue reform, and by the removal of the true causes of the depression.

Another temptation which would constantly beset the Democratic Party was to win over the silver producer and those people, some of whom wanted to use a debased currency to pay off their debts, and others who imagined that a debased currency gives them more dollars with which to supply their daily wants. Mr. Sterne pronounced the demands of the silver producer to be absolutely analogous to those of a producer of iron or of cloth, or of any other article of manufacture, to have the general public interest sacrificed to make a personal profit, and to enrich himself by levying and collecting a tax from his fellow citizens. It was to oppose such perversions of governmental functions to private ends that the Democratic Party had its great mission, and Mr. Sterne declared that when it ceased to have that mission, in every form in which it might manifest itself, he, for one, would cease to boast of being a Democrat.

After adverting to some of the cruder fallacies of free silver, Mr. Sterne cited some reasons why one metal should, and must, in every community having an extensively developed commerce, be the basis of the exchanges. In modern times loans are made for long periods, running, in the case of railway mortgages and Government bonds, from thirty to fifty, and even one hundred years. The creditor is willing to forego a high interest for the certainty of the return of the principal at the end of the period for which he lends his money. He is, therefore, not willing to give an option to his debtor to return the principal in one of several metals, whichever happens to be the cheapest when the principal becomes due. Mr. Sterne said that within the period of his own observation, interest had gone down from 7 to 3 per cent. The wages of capital had thus decreased over 50 per cent, while the wages of labour had increased over 100 per cent. It was, therefore, idle to say that a gold basis begat a tendency to make the rich richer and the poor poorer. On the contrary, the rich were content with less earning power on their riches, while the earning power of the poor had more than doubled. Thus, if there were any advance in the value of gold, from decade to decade, it was more than made up by the reduction of the interest rate, and many times more than made up by the willingness of the capitalist to lend his money for industrial purposes. The Democratic Party had stood for honest money and a stable currency, and Mr. Sterne uttered the warning that if it temporised with self-interested leaders and their deluded followers, who were willing to sacrifice the commercial and financial interests of the country for their own ends, it is doomed to destruction, because it fights against light, it fights against civilisation, it fights against the permanent interests of humanity. The warning did not prevent the folly of the Chicago Convention, but it clearly outlined the consequences of the surrender then made to the baser elements of the party. It is not too much to claim that this added warning is as relevant to the party conditions of to-day as it was to those of seven years ago.

> A party's only excuse for its existence is in educating the people on political questions. The party that has its ear to the ground for the purpose of catching the voice of its lowest followers, and which caters wholly to the political pit, is one that may achieve temporary success, but it will finally go out of existence, because public offices, with the large emoluments and advantages which flow from the possession of power, are given to them by the community only in return for that which it has a right to ask and will ultimately insist upon getting, namely, that its political education shall be increased and its general development and intelligence enhanced by the party to whom it has given so much.

Sincere admirer as Mr. Sterne was of the character and ability of President Cleveland, he found it impossible to give unqualified approval to the position which Mr. Cleveland had taken in his celebrated Venezuelan message. In this same speech he spoke of that message as committing the Democratic Party to uphold a principle of conduct toward the nations of Europe, which is a considerable development of the Monroe doctrine. As he understood that doctrine, it was a declaration that interference with the affairs of our sister republics on this continent should not be made by a foreign power, if the honour and safety of our own country should be endangered thereby. He regarded it as a somewhat startling assumption that the American Republic, with its 70,000,000 of people, should have its interests either impaired or endangered by a controversy about a boundary between a Government under a European protectorate, and one of the South American Republics. He proceeded to examine the logical effect of a claim that we are, in some form or another, without any proclamation or consent of the Governments affected thereby, the protecting sovereign of all the peoples of this North and South American continent. While such a position opened up a prospect of a magnificent and even beneficent protectorate of the whole American continent against injustice or wrong on the part of the Governments of Europe, it was accompanied by a grave responsibility which we must be prepared at all hazards to meet. In Mr. Sterne's judgment, such a claim would not be accepted by the nations of Europe, having possessions on this side of the Atlantic, without insisting that we assume the duty of seeing to it that our wards perform all their international duties. The legal doctrine called *respondeat superior*, which throws upon the master the responsibility for the wrongdoing of his servant, is one that would be applied if we insist that all the peoples of the South American people are our wards. When they refuse to pay their debts, when they fail to keep their pledges, when they make unjust reprisals, when they imprison or shoot foreigners or confiscate property, it is not only they but we who will be held responsible for such wrongdoing. Mr. Sterne took occasion to point out that it was a question for very deliberate consideration whether the Democratic Party was willing to accept this grave responsibility. Resolutions upholding the President, and hurling defiance at all the nations of the earth who refused to endorse our claim, were easily passed, and would meet with a ready response from the people of the United States. But these resolutions and the path which they indicated, should not be entered upon without taking into account the commitment of responsibility which they involved.

CHAPTER IV

ADVOCACY OF PROPORTIONAL REPRESENTATION

Speaking in 1893, Mr. Sterne said: "When a man has carried in his mind for twenty-five or thirty years a plan of reform upon a political subject, and has been in touch with the practical concerns of life during the whole of that period of time, if that idea has not been driven out of his mind, but on the contrary has been strengthened, it is proof either that there is something in the idea or nothing in the head." There is unquestionably something in the idea of personal, proportional, or minority representation, and there was a great deal in the head in which it found an early lodgment. In the first of those notable public deliverances which commanded the attention of the thinking public of New York in the later sixties, Mr. Sterne found the seat of the disease which affected the body politic in the failure to make our system of government a truly representative one, and, almost with his latest breath, he urged the adoption of some system of proportional representation as a means for the improvement of the municipal government of the city of New York.

Among the problems which the nineteenth century has bequeathed to the twentieth, there is none quite so elusive as this of making the opinion and will of every voting member of the community heard and felt in the body elected to represent it. And yet it requires no argument to show that, unless some adequate means is found of correcting the palpable injustice of the present majority system of representation, our scheme of free institutions must be held to be a failure. In a report on Personal Representation prepared in 1867, at the request of the Personal Representation Society, and submitted to the Convention then engaged in revising the Constitution of the State of New York, Mr. Sterne took the ground that if the doctrine of the sovereignty of the individual, and the arguments for the natural right of suffrage, are not an empty tissue of words, they mean that each individual of the body politic having the right of suffrage should, either immediately or mediately, have a voice in the framing of those laws, to which, as a citizen, his obedience is demanded. As it is impracticable to call the people together to make their own laws, the system of representation was devised, under which the representative is supposed really to voice the opinions and desires of the represented. If, at the outset, each vote of the constituent body had been regarded in the light of a power of attorney or proxy, and the representative, in casting his vote in the representative body, had actually, instead of constructively, cast the votes of the voters, and thus actually had represented the votes of his constituents, the taking of the vote in the representative body would be in fact what it is now only in name, representative. The indictment against our present electoral scheme is that it is not what it pretends to be, that it does not effect the representation of the people, but only of a part of the people. By the acceptance of the system of majority representation, we virtually disfranchise almost one-half of those who have concededly the right to vote upon public measures. In representing a majority only of the actual voters, and leaving the minority unrepresented, an act of injustice is done similar to that of excluding by main force the minority of the citizens of a free community from attending and urging their views at a public meeting convened for the purpose of making laws or deciding upon questions of public policy. Clearly, any act passed at the public meeting of such a majority, formed by the forcible exclusion of the minority, would not be an act of the people. The act passes, say, by a bare majority of that minority. Add to the defeated minority of the majority the excluded minority, who were not permitted to attend the meeting, and you have a measure to which the majority of those who were entitled to votes are opposed, which is nevertheless enacted into law by a minority in the name of all the people, and to which all are expected to yield obedience.

Mr. Sterne had no difficulty in showing that what is decided at the polls is not whether one or the other public policy shall prevail, but whether one or the other party shall be represented in the representative body, a widely different thing. Admitting the sovereignty of the people, the injustice remains the same, whether they are disfranchised by brute force, or by the operation of the law. In meeting the obvious objection that the majority will, in any event, have to make laws for the minority, even when all are represented, Mr. Sterne simply reiterated the right of the minority to take part through their representatives in the deliberations preceding, and finally to vote upon every measure, which, as citizens, affects their interest. When the minority in proportion to its numbers is fully represented in the representative chambers, he held that the majority of a majority —which is probably in point of fact a minority of the whole people—cannot pass and enforce laws which affect the whole community, on the pretence that it represents the people; but every measure would have to be in fact, what it is now in name—a majority measure—before it could become law. The reform to be promoted by the substitution of personal for majority representation is, therefore, one which rather tends to promote the better securing of a true system of government by the majority, and instead of aiming to supplant the rule of the majority by the rule of the minority, it tends to make our institutions more democratic, by placing power in the hands of a real, instead of a fictitious and sham majority.

In a lecture delivered in 1869, at the request of the trustees of the Cooper Union, Mr. Sterne made the broad declaration: "When you have decentralised your Government, when you have taken from the Legislature the power to pass special laws, when you have deprived the politician of the food upon which he feeds, when you have restricted government to its primary duties, the administration of justice and police duty, one thing more remains for you to do, and that is to make your Government what it is not now—a representative system of Government." By the adoption of the majority instead of the totality system of representation, we have virtually disfranchised all those who in any particular district do not belong to the dominant party. We have assumed that because the majority of the people, in their sovereign capacity, had the right to enact the laws, therefore, by a parity of reasoning, the majority of the electors of any particular district had solely the right to send a representative. The remedy for the patent injustice of this system was declared by Mr. Sterne to be the substitution of personal for majority representation. He proposed to accomplish this by making the representative the actual agent for the voters who have cast their ballots in his favour, he holding as many "proxies" as he has in his election received individual votes. Being, therefore, the embodiment of the votes cast for him, the representative's voice on each question coming up for decision in the Legislative Chamber would count for as many votes as he received at the polls. He explained the operation of such a system in New York State as follows:—The State of New York has (1869) about 800,000 voters. If it be desirable to have no more than the number of members which compose the present assembly, by dividing this number of votes by 128, the number of seats, you have a quotient of a trifle over 6000 votes necessary to elect a representative, as the minimum number of proxies or powers of attorney necessary to entitle a candidate to a seat. Every person receiving at any election for members of Assembly a larger number of votes than the minimum quota fixed by law, should be deemed elected; and each member should be entitled to cast in the Legislative body upon every measure or act coming to a vote, the number of ballots cast for him, and which he represents, be they 6000 or 20,000. The people then, in point of fact, would upon every measure vote through their agents, the representatives, as though they were owners of shares of stock in a railroad or mining corporation, and with like effect.

This differed very considerably from the plan of proportional representation which had been presented a dozen years before by Mr. Thomas Hare of London, in a pamphlet which took by storm that part of the intellectual world which devoted itself to the philosophical consideration of politics. In 1871 Mr. Sterne published a book on Representative Government and Personal Representation. This was an attempt to make Mr. Hare's work intelligible to American readers, but it consisted in the main of an entirely original treatment of the plans which had been suggested for the reform of the prevailing system of representative government. In his introduction to this compendious study of the subject, Mr. Sterne insists that representative government "as the one important fact of contemporaneous political history, is so pre-eminent that every examination of its basis, its development, and its proper application, cannot but be of the utmost immediate practical importance." The questions suggested by this examination are of such weight and comprehensiveness that almost all the political questions of the day find a solution therein, and the adoption of the suggested remedy would be, to use the language of John Stuart Mill, "a specific against almost all the ills of government which are inherent to our own system." To illustrate the importance to the citizens of the interests which, in our own country, are confided to representative bodies, Mr. Sterne cited the fact that in all matters pertaining to hygienic, criminal, and preventive police, he is dependent upon the representative body of his city or town; in all matters referring to his personal status, his property, and the laws which are to govern him therein, he is dependent upon the Legislature of his State; in all matters touching his relations as citizen, commercially, as belligerent, or as ally, to the inhabitants of other countries, he is dependent upon the National Representative Chamber. In practice, there are no rights reserved to the people beyond and above representative control. Our bills of rights in our constitutions are so many requests by the people to the legislative bodies, not to legislate upon certain subjects; but these requests have been generally disregarded when a strong tide of public opinion has made it safe to break the restriction. Waiving the question of whether or not this tendency to the consolidation of power in the representative chambers is for the good of society, Mr. Sterne argued, with obvious force, that its existence as a fact makes the inquiries into the proper formation of these bodies and the mode of election of their members the one transcendent political question.

While in the course of the evolution of free institutions under the limitations of monarchy and its cognate restraints, the growth of the representative system may be more or less irregular in a country like ours, whose government is based, theoretically, upon legal and political equality in the status of all citizens, it ought to be possible to arrive at the ideally best system of representation. Mr. Sterne recognised the fact that, in suggesting radical changes in the established methods of exercising the suffrage, he would run counter to the prepossessions of that numerous class who believe the Constitution of 1789 to be the highest embodiment of human wisdom, and who regard any one venturing to suggest an improvement on that instrument as guilty of an act of impertinent presumption. But he insists that while the members of the Constitutional Convention did a useful and important work, they were very far from creating an ideally perfect Government. That the framers of the Constitution did not foresee the extent to which party government would be carried in the United States is clearly evidenced by the electoral college clause. But it is this very party system which has corrupted, and threatens still further to corrupt, not only our Government, but, through it, the people; and to remove that yoke is a more difficult task than the thirteen colonies had before them when they rebelled from the mother-country, and the attainment of success therein a far greater step in the direction of human freedom than was gained by the successful issue of the War of Independence.

Adverting to the fundamental blunder of our representative system, Mr. Sterne proceeds to argue that we have confounded two independent and entirely different political ideas and processes —the right of representation and the right of decision. The principle of representation is based upon the assumed right on the part of the citizen to take part in the business of making the laws which are to govern him. As there are practical difficulties in the way of his doing so, he must appear by deputy—each man is entitled thus to appear by deputy. The machinery of representation, of voting, and of election is devised to accomplish this end. It does not accomplish it; it wastes from one-fourth to one-half the votes of a community. Even the majorities that are represented are unfairly and improperly represented, since the voter is compelled to sink his individuality, and oftentimes his best political opinions, for the purpose of belonging to the represented class. Two false conceptions have prevented the representative chamber from being what Mirabeau said it ought to be, a reduced picture of the people—their opinions, aspirations, and wishes: first, that the right of the majority to govern carries with it the right of the majority to sole representation; and, second, that countries, states, districts, and counties have, as mere geographical subdivisions, interests distinct from those of the people who inhabit them.

To make clearer the nature of the fallacies which underlie the popular view of majority representation, Mr. Sterne imagines the citizens of Athens met to consider the project of a representative body to take the place of the assembly of the whole people, and he puts into the mouth of Kleon, the demagogue, the advocacy of a plan embodying the details of our district system of representation. Against this he makes Thucydides speak in indignant protest, in an address of characteristic nobility of sentiment and elevation of view. The following extract from it has as direct a bearing on the political problems of to-day as it had on those of thirty years ago :—

Kleon artfully says that in cutting up the city into districts, all of the interests are sure of a hearing. This is a new idea in our politics. Districts, so many acres of land, have no interests as such; the freemen therein have, and these freemen come here and represent these separate interests in their own persons when there are such interests, a circumstance which seldom occurs, as it is fortunately not often that a part of our city has an interest different from, and antagonistic to, the interests of the whole ; and when such arise, no great harm is done if they are overridden, as they are generally dangerous. They are justly considered of importance in the scheme of Kleon, as that should be called a plan to foster and develop all the sinister elements of the worst elements of our body politic.

Then, again, let me cast for a moment your horoscope : If Kleon prevails, you flatter yourselves that the best men in Athens will be the representatives. Never! the most popular men will, and such are very far from being the best. The men who are the physicians of our souls, who tell us unpleasant but wholesome truths, who stem and breast the waves of popular opinion when they run counter to their highest conceptions of right,—such men, the most useful among us in political life, will be doomed to silence and inaction. The oily-tongued flatterer, the wily corruptionist, the superficial gabbler, the panderer to the greed and lust of the majority,—such and such only will you have to pass your laws. Then there will be an evil which will arise from this scheme, the consequence of which it is easy to foresee. You divide the people permanently into majorities and minorities—a division which is now but accidental, exists at the moment when we pass a law, is wiped out immediately thereafter. . . . Give exclusive representation to majorities, and you create parties whose opposition to each other will be permanent—one opposing, as a duty to itself, all that the other party proposes, however beneficial that proposition may be for the public weal. You divide the people into two hostile camps, struggling with varying success for the mastery; and that struggle, carried on, as it will be, with all the bitterness of party strife, with the use of every means, however unconscientious, will demoralise the whole community and destroy the Republic. Not only will the organised majority be a despotism, compared with which the despotism of one man is as naught, for the despot must needs fear a people in revolt or the assassin's knife; but a majority is acted upon neither by fear nor by conscience. That minority who are now free voters, who openly speak their mind, will then become, when the majority is very great against them, and they are hopelessly excluded from representation, conspirators who will sell themselves to different leaders of the majority. Parties, when about equally balanced, outbidding each other for mastery with corrupt bargains, or, when not evenly balanced, the one in majority an organised tyranny, overriding all constitutional checks, and the minority a band of conspirators,—

such is the not very distant future which Kleon's plan is preparing for you.

The plan of representation which Thucydides presents in place of the one which he assails with so much force is intended to represent the whole community, and be a miniature picture of the different opinions which, for the time being, exist in the minds of the people. It is that the number of representatives in the law-making power shall not be more than 200, and as there are about 200,000 freemen in the city, that would give one representative to each totality of 1000 voters, so that each opinion shared by the $\frac{1}{200}$th of the whole people would be sure of a representative. He offers another plan, calculated to achieve the same result, which is to regard each vote as a power of attorney, and allow none to enter the legislative body who holds less than 1000 of such powers, and then let the representative cast in the chamber either as many votes as have been cast for him or one for each totality of 1000 votes that he holds. The Legislature would thus never have more than 200 members, but might have many less than that number. Apart, however, from such matters of detail, the sum of the argument is that, in changing a pure democracy into a representative government, the whole people are entitled to representation, and only where the whole people are so represented can the taking of the vote in the representative body be deemed equivalent to taking the sense of the people in general meeting assembled. Unhappily, as Mr.

Sterne remarked, representative government as it is is the plan of Kleon, the demagogue. Representative government as it should be is one representing all interests and opinions of the community, in proportion to their numerical strength, by some such plan as is placed in the mouth of Thucydides.

A direct consequence of the majority system of representation is the necessity of creating a party, adopting a party name, and putting forward some party tenet or dogma. In Mr. Sterne's judgment, it is not usually the political tenet which has caused the party, but the party which has created the tenet. In none of these things, any more than in the choice of their representative, can the members of the majority usefully ask themselves what they ought to do—the only practical question is what will be successful. Thus, the process of creating a majority demoralises most of those who compose it, because it excludes the action of their higher moral attributes, and brings into operation the lower range of motives. They are compelled to disregard all that tends to individuality, and therefore all genuine earnestness of opinion ; to discard their political knowledge, their deliberate judgment, their calm and conscientious reflection. All these must be brought to a conformity with those who possess the least of these qualities. The same injurious influences operate in some measure on minorities whenever they make a decided stand for the purpose of contesting an election; the most intelligent will submit to the more numerous, except that in the case of minorities the greater apprehension of defeat may have led the more numerous element to raise their standard of choice in order to increase their hopes of success.

Simultaneously with this process of deterioration among those who compose the active parties, there is produced a result even more fatal to the design of true representation among another large, intelligent, and more scrupulous class of persons, who feel no disposition to make themselves the instruments of giving effect to the views of others with whom they have no common object or sympathy. These, therefore, take no part in the business of choosing those who are nominally to represent them. Mr. Sterne calculated that in 1869 only 71 per cent of those entitled to the suffrage cast their votes in the State of New York; in 1862 less than 78 per cent; and in 1861 but 64 per cent of the voting population were recorded at the polls. This voluntary abstention from exercising the highest duty of the citizen arose mainly from the fact that many men, not liking the choice of evils which party machinery presented to them, preferred to disfranchise themselves rather than become party to the elevation of unfit and improper men to political power. Countless exhortations of the party press, urging such men to take an interest in party politics, would, Mr. Sterne believed, ever prove unavailing so long as these men instinctively felt that the exercise of this right, under its present form, is a delusion and a snare. If they belong to the minority in opinion, they throw away their votes, as representation is denied to the minority. If they belong to the majority, they may be compelled to vote for men who turn uppermost in the machinery of party, and in whose professions of readiness to carry out the party principles they have no faith.

A system which divides people into adverse parties—arrayed under formal names, which are themselves exaggerations, calculated to excite hostility where none really exists—has thus, Mr. Sterne argued, the effect of preventing the expression of the true and individual opinions of the members who compose either party. It lowers the force of thought and conscience, reduces the most valuable voting elements to inaction, and converts the better motives of those who act into an effort for success and a mere calculation of the means to accomplish it. The infirmities of representative institutions are a natural result of the imperfections of the system which gives them birth. In addition to not representing the opinions of those whose votes elect its members, the representative body does not represent—first, those who abstain from voting; and, second, the minority, or possibly the majority, of those who have voted for unsuccessful candidates. By way of illustrating the limitations which our party system imposes on the freedom of choice of the voter, Mr. Sterne cited the following example:—A. is a voter in the State of New York, in sympathy with the system of reconstruction of the Southern States adopted by the dominant majority in Congress; he is also a free-trader, and therefore opposed to the fiscal measures of this same dominant majority. The Party places before him, as a candidate for the House, a Republican, who is a Protectionist; if he deems free trade of less importance than the question of reconstruction, he votes for one who, as he well knows, will, in the representative body, vote for measures which he firmly believes to be pernicious and immoral. B. is a voter in Ohio; he utterly detests the whole system of reconstruction which Congress has seen fit to adopt, and believes the tenets of the opposite party, upon all the questions relating to the status of the citizens who had seceded from the Government, to be the right ones; but this same party hints, in the campaign of his State, at repudiation, which may adversely affect his interests, or revolt his moral nature; he casts, therefore, his vote for a representative whose course in Congress he deems dangerous and vicious, in order that the candidate shall not prevail who is pledged to a course which he regards as still more dangerous. Thus, under the majority system, the voter is not free; his vote, or rather the possibility of making it effectual, is fettered with a condition which makes the act of voting cease to be equivalent to an expression of opinion.

Naturally, a reform which proposed to take from them their occupation did not commend itself to the professional politicians. Even in the realm of statesmanship it encountered powerful opposition. Gladstone's objection to it was: "We do not want to have represented immature, particular shades of opinion." Even John Bright thought that Hare's scheme was calculated to put in the nominees of little cliques; and it was the verdict of Disraeli that this and other plans of cumulative voting, having for their object the representation of minorities, were admirable schemes for bringing crotchety men into the House. There were occasions when the advocates of proportional representation seemed on the point of scoring a triumph. One of these was when the Honourable Charles R. Buckalew, of Pennsylvania, as Chairman of the Select Committee on Representative Reform, submitted to the United States Senate a report on the subject on March 2, 1869, accompanied by a Bill applying the system to the election of Members of Congress. Mr. Buckalew was accustomed to call the system one of "free voting," as opposed to the fettered voting which Mr. Sterne had so vigorously denounced. When a motion to provide for the election of Congressmen by the cumulative vote came before the House in 1870, representative reform found an unexpected ally in Mr. James A. Garfield, who delivered this remarkable testimony to its necessity :—

When I was first elected to Congress, in the fall of 1862, the State of Ohio had a clear Republican majority of about 25,000, but by the adjustment and distribution of political power in the State, there were fourteen Democratic representatives upon this floor, and only five Republicans. The State that cast nearly 250,000 Republican votes as against 225,000 Democratic votes was represented in the proportion of five Republicans and fourteen Democrats. In the next Congress there was no great political change in the popular vote of Ohio—a change of only 20,000—but the result was that seventeen Republican members were sent here from Ohio and only two Democrats. We find that only so small a change as 20,000 changed the representatives in Congress from fourteen Democrats and five Republicans to seventeen

Republicans and two Democrats. Now, no man, whatever his politics, can justly defend a system that may in theory, and frequently does in practice, produce such results as these. . . .

In my judgment it is the weak point in the theory of representative government as now organised and administered, that a large portion of the people are permanently disfranchised. There are about 30,000 Democratic votes in my district, and they have been voting for the last forty years without any more hope of gaining a representative on this floor than of having one in the Commons of Great Britain.

When the Proportional Representation Congress was held in Chicago in 1893, an address to the public was issued, in which Mr. Garfield's parable was taken up and continued to date as follows :—

Twenty-three have been added to the forty, and still the Democrats of that district maintain the forlorn hope. Iowa, with 219,215 Republican votes and 201,923 Democratic votes at the election of 1892, sent ten Republican Congressmen and one Democrat to Washington. Every 21,921 Republicans of that State has a representative, while the whole 201,923 Democrats have but one. In Kentucky the case is reversed. The Democrats have a Congressman for every 17,426 votes, while the Republicans have one for 122,308. In Maine the vote was 65,637 Republicans and 55,778 Democrats, but the Republicans got all the four Congressmen. In Maryland the vote was 21,762 Republicans and 113,931 Democrats, but the latter got the six Congressmen. The Republicans of Texas have not had a representative in Congress since 1882. The Democrats of Kansas have not had a representative since the State was admitted to the Union, though they have polled from a third to two-fifths of the vote of the State during that time.

The one important advance which had been made in this country by the advocates of proportional representation in these twenty-three years was the adoption in 1870 of what is known as the Minority Clause in the Constitution of the State of Illinois. This clause provides that "each voter may cast as many votes for one candidate as there are representatives to be elected, or may distribute the same, or equal parts thereof, among the candidates as he shall see fit, and the candidates highest in votes shall be declared elected." Under this provision the districts have been so formed that three members of the House of Representatives are elected from each district, and a voter may cast three votes for one candidate, or one and a half for one and one and a half for another, or one each for three candidates. The consequence of this is that any party in a district having more than a fourth of the votes, and uniting them on one candidate, may elect him in spite of anything that the majority can do. As a matter of fact, in nearly all the districts of the State both Republicans and Democrats elect either one or two representatives. In those where the Democrats are in the majority they usually elect two, and their opponents one, while in Republican districts the reverse of this occurs. It happens sometimes, though rarely, that the minority party, by more skilful organisation and management, succeeds in electing two members, but in practice the system has fully justified its main purpose of enabling a number of voters in a district, considerably less than a majority or a plurality, to concentrate their votes and make them effective. In this way the Illinois system has greatly helped independent voters in their struggle against the dictation of the professional politicians.

The conceded defects of the system are that it often results in a great waste of votes, because voters cannot tell beforehand whether they are casting more votes for a favourite candidate than he will need to be elected ; that it is calculated to make a nomination equivalent to an election, because each party usually nominates only as many candidates in each district as it is sure of electing, and thus the selection of representatives may fall into the hands of the political managers and bosses who control the primaries ; and, finally, that if a notoriously bad nomination is made, and an independent opponent is put up, he is more apt to take votes from the other worthy candidate than from the disreputable one. The Illinois experiment has had at least the merit of showing that to give the voter the required freedom of choice, larger districts than those entitled to return three representatives are necessary. In short, the real objection to the Illinois system is, that the principle has not been carried far enough in that State. Considering, however, the paucity of the results of the movement throughout the country, what had been accomplished in Illinois furnished ground for legitimate satisfaction.

In the summer of 1895 the Proportional Representation Society of New York, of which Mr. Sterne was president, called a conference to meet in Saratoga to take stock of the condition and prospects of the movement in this and other countries. In his presidential address, Mr. Sterne adverted to the fact that it was twenty-five years since he published his book on *Representative Government;* thirty-six years since Mr. Hare published his work on the *Election of Representatives, Parliamentary and Municipal;* thirty-four years since the publication of John Stuart Mill's work; twenty-eight years since an association, under the presidency of David Dudley Field, of which he was the secretary, knocked at the door of the then sitting Constitutional Convention of New York State for the acceptance of their ideas; and yet, while there have been here and there sporadic attempts made for the adoption of Proportional Representation in some of the States of the Union, with the single exception of the experiment in the election of both bodies of the law-making power of the State of Illinois, no great practical advance had been made toward incorporating into law the principles of Proportional Representation in the election of members of legislative bodies, and thus abandoning the single district system. Mr. Sterne admitted that the toiler after results, however remote, must have a stout heart if he does not feel discouraged when a retrospective glance shows such a meagre catalogue of achievement to crown a lifetime of effort, aided by such men as Mill, Hare, Courtney, Lubbock, and almost all the other publicists and writers in England, on the Continent, and in the United States.

Regarding, however, the progress made in countries other than our own, he found that decided advances had been made. In trying to discover the special causes which had so long delayed securing in the United States public attention for the far-reaching and beneficent reforms which are embodied in an adequate system of Proportional Representation, he discerned that other more absorbing questions had engrossed public attention. First, after 1865, the time when the underlying principles of minority or Proportional Representation became known to students of philosophical politics in the United States, there was the absorbing question of reconstruction. Next came the problem of dealing with the emancipated negro, and then that of reducing the burden of the national debt which the war had imposed on the people. After five years of exclusive attention to these practical problems, there came another ten years in which the financial question, the tariff question, and the resumption of specie payments were the paramount political issues. From 1880 to 1890 there came another ten years in which tariff legislation and the constantly recurring fight against the fallacies of the greenbackers, the silverites, and the numerous adherents of dishonest finance absorbed the attention of the people of the United States. During this period of preoccupation with the problems of practical politics, the one great triumph scored for the cause of progressive reform was the classification of the public service and the consequent placing of the minor public offices beyond the reach of the spoilsmen. The reform of the ballot, by the substitution of the Australian form for that in general use, was another measure of reform which was simple of explanation, and was readily accepted and accomplished within ten years.

Mr. Sterne was constrained to admit that, in some respects, it may have been fortunate that no substantial practical progress was made earlier in the history of the movement for Proportional Representation. He conceded that those who had given adhesion to the soundness of the principle in its earliest development were prone to accept it in its full logical significance; and that if they could have had their way they would have obliterated party by recognising nothing short of State lines or municipal lines, and electing national, State, and municipal representatives on general tickets and by the preferential vote. Political representation would thus have been given to small sections of political thought, with the result that there might have been injected into the representative chamber "faddists" instead of reasonable men, and the practical work of legislation might have been rendered impossible in the presence of a considerable number of impracticable representatives with vague ideas. He had become convinced that due account must be taken of the fear that legislative bodies might be impeded by fads under a system of minute party representation; and that, further, the fact had to be borne in mind that in our great cities there were considerable numbers of persons with chaotic and vitiated ideas on government, on property, and on human rights which five years of residence could not wholly dissipate. The main justification for the vast amount of money expended upon public schools is that they take the children of this heterogeneous mass of people, put them into the educational hopper, and grind them out to be American citizens. He had, therefore, been compelled to recognise the fact that until we have somewhat more thoroughly amalgamated into American citizenship, the immigrants untutored in our modes of thought, the thoroughgoing adoption of the true and correct principles of representation should be postponed for a while. It was necessary to disarm the fear of many, who otherwise would be on the side of the reform; that its application would give too much strength to separatist interests of religion, nationality, race, or sect. Further, however beneficial in other respects the destruction of party organisation, as now known, would be, it must not be carried so far as to embarrass legislation, and prevent—by the obstruction exercised by special interests—the common good from being enacted into law. Having due regard to such considerations, Mr. Sterne suggested to his fellow-workers at the Saratoga Conference that they should, for the present, be content to confine their demand for Proportional Representation to cities where its application would rather tend to the better representation of the best elements of the community, so that when accepted by the public there would be no reaction arising from consequences which can be foreseen, and therefore guarded against.

This train of reflection was doubtless in part prompted by the lack of success in inducing the State Constitutional Convention of 1894 to accept the plan of minority representation which had been offered in the form of an amendment by the Hon. John Bigelow. Under this amendment it was proposed to divide the State into five Senate districts and twenty assembly districts, and to elect therefrom one hundred and forty assembly-men and thirty-five members of the Senate by a method of minority representation, which would thus enable each district to elect seven senators and seven assembly-men, giving to each one-eighth of the population, plus one, direct representation. In the effort to secure recognition for this amendment, Mr. Sterne became aware of the causes which have retarded the extension of minority representation in this country. First in order was the obvious desire on the part of the politicians forming the majority not to divide political power with the minority. The, to them remote, consideration that they themselves may be in the minority within a year or two has practically little or no weight with them. They are still so completely in the thraldom of the spoils system of politics, which teaches them that the possession of political power enables them by means of the patronage it brings to consolidate and strengthen that power, that it appears to them that the accidental majority of the moment may be made, through the influence of patronage, a permanent factor of substantial political domination. He found also that even the leaders of the minority were not strenuous for the adoption of a system calculated to give their party a degree of political consideration and power justly proportioned to its numerical strength. In the first place, there was always the hope that the minority might itself become the majority. In the second place, there was in the Constitutional Convention a vitiating and corrupting theory at work based on a conviction on the part of the minority that it had perpetual domination and control over that small section of the State which represents more than one-half of the taxable value of the whole, and the monopoly of whose government was vastly more profitable to it than any acquired participation in the government of the State at large. The representatives of the minority did not propose, by any system of proportional representation, to be obliged to go shares with incongruous and disturbing elements in regard to this small section which they regarded as strictly their own field of exploitation. The scheme was opposed, too, by a number of pseudo-philosophical politicians who thought they saw in the idea something un-American, and these played into the hands of those who had selfish party ends in view, and who naturally desired to defeat a reform which they recognised to be fraught with ruin for themselves. Again, the adoption of the principle of minority representation would have meant to the party which dominated the Constitutional Convention an interference with that advantage which its members, as practical politicians, regarded as legitimately their own—the opportunity to use their power in the Constitutional Convention so to gerrymander the State as to make one party dominant in its elective force even if numerically weaker, and to maintain in control of the State Government the rural population, no matter how the population of the two great cities at the southernmost part of the State might increase.

When the Greater New York Commission of 1897 set about the work of preparing a charter for the consolidated cities, Mr. Sterne and his associates earnestly undertook the task of trying to have incorporated in it some provisions for the representation of minorities. A similar attempt had been made twenty-five years before in the charter prepared by Mr. Sterne, and adopted by the Committee of Seventy in 1872, and submitted by them to the Legislature. In that Act there was incorporated the principle of minority representation in the election of members of the Board of Aldermen as follows:—

Sec. 1 (Art. II.). The legislative power of the said corporation shall be vested in a Board of Aldermen, which shall consist of not more than forty-five members, one-fifth to be elected, as hereinafter provided, in each senate district of the city as now established by law.

Sec. 4. At such election each qualified voter in each senate district may give one written or printed ballot with the indorsement "Aldermen," which shall contain a list of not more than nine names. The voter may repeat on such list the same name nine times, or may make such list to consist of nine different names, or may repeat any one or more names on said list as often as he may see fit. After the closing of the polls on the day of election the canvass in each election district of the senate district shall be completed by ascertaining, assorting, and making returns to the county canvassers of the number of votes given for each candidate. Any ballot containing more than nine votes shall be rejected. From the returns so made the county canvassers shall determine the names of the nine persons having the largest number of votes in each senate district, and they shall be returned as elected. . . .

This secured to a minority of one-ninth or more at least one alderman, and of course, as the emancipation from party dictation continued, more and more representatives of the minority would have been elected. The Bill passed both the Senate and Assembly, but was vetoed by Governor Hoffman, on the sole ground that the provision securing minority representation was repugnant to the constitution, which gave to every male voter one vote. Mr. Sterne did not regard this objection as well founded, but he thought it a new reason for making a strenuous and persistent demand on the Constitutional Convention to change the organic law so as to permit of minority representation to its fullest extent.

In addressing the Greater New York Commission, Mr. Sterne urged that, whatever may be thought of the principle of giving to minorities representation in national or State legislatures, no reasonable doubt could be entertained that such representation in the local legislatures of our cities would be of great value. It would then be impossible for a careless or corrupt constituency of some political faction, comprising perhaps not much more than a third of the voting population, to elect an entire municipal legislature. He did not argue in favour of any particular plan for securing minority representation, but contented himself with the suggestion that some reasonable and constitutional method of giving representation to the minority in the municipal assembly should be incorporated in the charter, and that, if necessary, constitutional changes should be made in preparation for the introduction of the system. It was Mr. Sterne's own judgment, and in this he had the support of constitutional lawyers of the highest repute, that there was nothing in a system of minority representation or minority voting obnoxious to the Constitution of the State of New York. The conclusion of a carefully-reasoned opinion on the subject by Judge John F. Dillon is as follows :—

A change so radical as the system ot minority representation would undoubtedly meet with strong opposition, and the objection would be made that the failure of the Constitution to provide affirmatively for a minority system manifests a purpose to continue in its substantial features the ordinary system of representation by the majority alone as distinct from a system which permits minority representation. That objection, in our judgment, would not be well founded provided the system of minority representation adopted recognised the right of all electors to vote for every office to be voted for, and to have effect given in every case to the majority vote. Our best judgment is that an Act providing for minority representation, in which the right of all electors to vote for every elective officer is provided for, and which gives effect to the voice of the majority, would not violate any provision of the Constitution of the State of New York.

On the statement, of which the above is a part, being presented to Judge Benjamin F. Tracy, of the original Charter Commission, he stated that he concurred in the views which it expressed.

The Commission, however, failed to incorporate in the charter any provision for minority representation, and adhered to the system of electing all the members of the municipal assembly by districts. Resolutions proposed by Mr. Sterne, and passed by the Committee on Legislation of the City Club, were offered in protest, on the ground that experience had demonstrated that a municipal legislature, composed entirely of men elected from small constituencies, would tend to represent not the best citizenship of the community but the petty politics of localities. If the local legislature is to have considerable powers, it becomes important so to dignify membership in it that men of character and ability will be induced, as they have been in England, to become members. The election of at least some of the members on a general ticket from the whole city would contribute to this end, and would also make the political parties less likely to nominate notably bad men than under the district system. Tammany Hall has never ventured to nominate candidates so ignorant and corrupt for executive offices as many of its candidates for the Board of Aldermen.

The results of the City election of 1897 fully sustained the soundness of the position taken by Mr. Sterne. As he afterwards showed, in applying to the Charter Revision Commission of 1900 to give some recognition to the principle of proportional representation, Tammany and the Democrats elected twenty-three of the twenty-eight members of the municipal council, or 82 per cent of the entire number; and the Citizens' Union and Republicans together, with 48 per cent of the voters, elected only five, or 18 per cent, of the council men. In the argument submitted to this Commission Mr. Sterne declared that, while the system of proportional representation, if logically carried out within New York, would totally abolish the districts, yet in recognition of the fact that there are separable interests as represented by certain constituencies which were welded together by the charter forming the greater city, he would propose to make three large divisions—one representing the boroughs of Manhattan and the Bronx, one representing the borough of Brooklyn, and the other the borough of Richmond—and to divide these into equal constituencies, so that on the whole there shall be, as near as possible, ten great subdivisions electing nine from each of these subdivisions, and giving each one-ninth quota of voters within such district the power to elect a representative. This would give a fair representation to all parties, and in large parties of voters freedom of choice within party lines.

Mr. Sterne directed attention to this peculiar phase of the political situation in New York that there are usually five or six separate parties or groups of voters, each with its separate ticket. There is no one of these groups which generally numbers a majority of the voters. They are all minority groups, but Tammany being the largest minority elects its candidates by a plurality. The only way in which Tammany can be defeated is by a fusion of the opposing parties. Now, fusion is usually difficult, and sometimes impossible. Against the solid constituency of Tammany Hall, held together by many ties of self-interest, there are other groups of voters, with more or less ideal platforms and programmes of reform, united by no predominating self-interest, and indisposed to yield what each considers an important plank in its platform for the sake of fusion upon a single candidate. Yet all of these parties and groups are at one in their opposition to Tammany, and if they all could elect each its own leading candidates without fusion, it would be found after election that they would eagerly unite on many lines of resistance to the syndicate of politicians in control of Tammany. Proportional Representation is exactly suited to this plan of action. It enables each party or group to put up its own ticket without fusion, and to elect just as many candidates as those to which its numbers entitle it. Altogether this means, in fact, a majority of the council. Indeed, it may be expected that with the increased opportunities for electing independent tickets the proportion of anti-Tammany voters would be greatly increased.

Speaking as President of the Proportional Representation Society, and for a Committee of that Society appointed to present their views to the Charter Revision Commission, Mr. Sterne declared it to be the conviction of himself and his associates that Proportional Representation is the next step which should follow in the line of policy along which the city of New York, under the direction of the State Legislature, has been moving during the last thirty years. The plan which they submitted was based upon a frank recognition of political parties, but, in the earlier days, neither the Constitution nor the laws recognised the existence of parties. A voter was supposed to vote not for a party but a candidate on his personal merits, and the actual dominance of party was not recognised by the Legislature until the year 1870, when the bi-partisan police and election boards for New York and Brooklyn were created. In 1880 the Boards of Registration were also made bi-partisan; in 1882 the Legislature, for the first time, enacted a law protecting party primaries. In 1891 a long step in advance was taken when the Legislature adopted the present ballot arranged in party columns. Here, for the first time, it was legally recognised that the voter selects first his party and then the candidates within that party. That law gives the first legal definition of a party and authorises nominations made by the party authorities. Finally, in 1897, the last and most radical step was taken, in the Primary Election Law of that year, when the State completely legalised the political parties as agencies for nominating and electing the officers of Government, and proceeded to frame a careful definition of a party, defining the qualifications for membership and providing State officials for conducting the party elections and certifying the result. Proportional Representation is apparently the next step in the same direction. The plan proposed by Mr. Sterne and his associates is fitted to the party column ballot. It is based on the acknowledged legal status of the parties. But it is a correction of a flagrant inconsistency which comes into view with this new importance of parties, namely, that the voters do not all belong to one party, and yet only those who belong to the largest party are permitted to govern the city. They proposed that the legislative branch of the City Government should be a thoroughly representative body; that it should include the recognised leaders of all parties in the same numerical proportion as the party voters, and should thus be a reflection of the opinions of the constituency which elects it. And since the people choose necessarily to act through political parties, and since those parties are now the legal organs for such action, it follows that the next step is a measure like proportional representation which will secure justice to every party so long as it is numerous enough to form a substantial quota of the qualified voters of any district. Proportional Representation in this way would afford a reconciliation between those who would concentrate all power in the hands of a dominant party and those who would eliminate party.

Mr. Sterne had no illusions as to the effect of this or other measures of reform in effecting any radical change on the character and purposes of the mass of humanity. What he did expect is very fairly outlined in the following extract from an address delivered two or three years before his death, and which, incidentally, furnishes an interesting revelation of his mature opinions on the subjects in which he was most deeply interested:—

> When one arrives at my years, he feels how dangerous it is to prognosticate the effects of any particular reformatory measure on the body politic. Many of our citizens expected great results from the Australian system of voting. It is true that in its entirety it has not been

established, butat all events greater secrecy has been accomplished, and it was supposed that a large number of people who were willing to follow the machine so long as it was known how they would vote, would, on complete emancipation by the secrecy of their vote, abandon it and come over to the side of the good people. We all of us have experienced very serious disappointment that such has not been the result. Secrecy of voting enables almost as many people who, under the eye of popular censure are deterred from voting on the wrong side, to exercise their selfish small interests when protected from the eye, as would quite outweigh the number of people who, under the domination of fear and possibly bribery, exercise their vote in conformity with the wishes of the machine. Many of you, and I may say of us, anticipated great things from the adoption of civil service reform. Civil service reform has made great headway within the last fifteen or twenty years, but the institutions of America remain pretty much as they were then, notwithstanding such reform. Although some little progress has been made, it has been so slow and intermittent a one that its effect on the general tone of politics has been so slight, that none of us feel as though we were in a strange country when we look back on what was and see what is.

Hence I do not venture upon any promise of supreme good if minority representation were once adopted; all that I can promise is, that the balance of good will be in its favour. What I know is this, that wherever adopted —in Denmark, in Geneva, in Neuchatel, in France, and in Illinois, in a tentative and half-hearted sort of way—it has never been abandoned; that if adopted with us, it will, in the first place, make public affairs, or in other words, a political career, a reasonably certain career for the bold, upright, honest, right-thinking man to enter into. It would create freedom from party ties, and make success possible notwithstanding such freedom; it would destroy the balance of power parties and the corrupting influence that they exercise; it would represent, for weal or woe, the community just as it stands, and would make the representative body a reduced photograph of the whole body politic.

Under these circumstances I concede that the vilest and the basest in the community could send their representative, but he would be known as the thieves' representative, and there would be no disguise as to his position, and he could not by any possibility affect the rest. He would probably be an outspoken advocate of all the sinister interests in society without disguise, which is very much better than the disguised representatives that we have now, many who are sent by constituencies that are vile, but in consequence of their being mixed up with the rest of the community the true character of their representation is not known.

It would be a return in a more liberal form to the old class representation, where each particular important section in the community, the merchants' guilds and the trades guilds, sent their representatives to the common council chamber, where they met to discuss their respective interests, and each man represented precisely what he claimed to represent, a special class interest, and from the whole the general public will was furthered and welded together. And it certainly would bring the foremost minds, the best purposes, and the highest intellects of the country once more into political activity, by enabling them to achieve success in a just and proportional strength to the effort put forth, and not setting before them the seemingly hopeless task of persuading the majority of their fellow-men of the usefulness of their purposes, and the beneficial results of their aims, when those aims seem far distant, and those purposes are wofully misunderstood by people who want direct benefits from the immediate dispensation of patronage by the public powers and food from the public crib.

Surely it is not unreasonable to expect that when each vote will tell to some purpose, the men who now, by reason of the hopelessness of the struggle, abstain from political activity, will return to it. There will then be no majorities which are overwhelming, and no despairing minorities. Then we shall have for the first time truly representative bodies. The permanent machinery of party will be unnecessary, because a temporary coalition will produce representation, and the majority of the representatives will represent a corresponding majority of constituencies, only that the particles, no longer under coercion to fly together mechanically, will seek their natural affinities, and different groups will form themselves, and the majority will therefore not be a haphazard mechanical combination held together by the whip of the boss and fearing rebellion against the boss lest the party may be disintegrated and destroyed. There will be a general and quick representation of every new and important political idea, which will be ventilated and answered. If, then, representative institutions fail to secure good government, it is because mankind is not fit for it and there is an inherent defect in the organisation. Under the present system our legislative machinery has so utterly broken down that there is not a conservative interest in the country that does not look to the meeting of legislative bodies with apprehension and hail their adjournment with feelings of relief from a constant menace; and that arises from a consciousness dimly expressed but genuinely experienced that the successive Congresses and annual Legislatures do not represent the people but coteries of politicians, who interpose themselves between the people and the voters and keep up a government in the name of the people, just as the Roman emperors long after every vestige of liberty departed from the Roman Empire promulgated their laws in the name of the people of Rome. We have thus far in our efforts at reform treated symptoms and not the disease itself. We tried to escape from the consequences of evil legislation by suggesting bi-annual legislatures, on the theory that, inasmuch as the meeting of the legislatures is an evil, having it sit but half the time lessens the evil. Let us reform our legislative body by making it truly representative; reform the methods of legislation (which, however, is the subject of another address), and make our representatives truly representative, and we may hope for a change in the spirit of the people through the freedom of choice given to them, and an entire change in the character and capacity of the members of our legislative bodies.

CHAPTER V

REFORM OF THE METHODS OF LEGISLATION

As indicated in the address quoted at the end of last chapter, Mr. Sterne regarded the reform of the methods of legislation as not less necessary than a change in the system of electing legislators. In the notable address on Representative Government, delivered in 1869, he declared that the right to pass what are called private Bills should by one blow be entirely and completely abrogated. "If any person is in a position to require relief for which our laws are inadequate, and the legislative power must be called into play, then pass some general law which shall not only relieve the person aggrieved, but all others who may be similarly situated." He was deeply impressed by a remark made by Chief-Justice Church in 1875, in delivering the opinion of the New York Court of Appeals, in the matter of Kiernan, to the effect that it was not safe to speak confidently of the exact condition of the law in respect to public improvements in the cities of New York and Brooklyn, because the enactments in reference thereto had been modified, superseded, and repealed so often and to such an extent that it was difficult to ascertain just what statutes were in force at any particular time. This statement prompted Mr. Sterne to make a detailed study of the methods of legislation, and the imperfections of these appeared to him so glaring and so numerous that for twenty-five years he missed no opportunity of directing public attention to their causes and remedy.

In an address before the New York Municipal Society, on January 6, 1879, he made the first public statement of the convictions he had reached on this subject. He began by contrasting the conditions which existed when the Government of the State of New York was organised and a general grant of legislative power conferred upon the Legislature, with the conditions which existed at the time of his discourse. Forty pages of general and special statutory enactments recorded during the early years of the independence of the State the whole of the legislative work of a session; and even the active lawyer, leader of the Bar though he may have been, the leading merchant or the large landed proprietor, could spare time to go to Albany as a representative to supply the legislative wants of a homogeneous, contented, and simplicity-loving people. Mr. Sterne pointed out that the methods which were considered sufficient for the poor, simple, agricultural population in 1789, were, with very slight modifications, the methods of ninety years later. No distinction is made between public and private Bills; there is no ministerial or party responsibility in reference to public measures; private and local Bills are not subjected to any scrutiny, to any trial, to any safeguard, as to their passage, which distinguishes them wholly from the public legislation, and which would afford reasonable guarantees that the rights of individuals have been protected in the drafting of the Bill before its introduction and the amending of the Bill during its passage, and that such private, special, and local legislation is not in conflict with the context and purposes of the general law. He argued, with obvious force, that when we take into consideration the fact that modern society has been reorganised within these ninety years, that the growth of wealth has advanced at a rate fiftyfold as compared to its growth anterior to this century, while population has shown an increase fourfold greater than that of any previous period of similar length, and corporations have multiplied a hundredfold within the same time, that all this brings upon the legislative body a pressure for special rights and a corresponding disregard of general rights previously without example. Under such circumstances, it seemed quite inexplicable why that differentiation which has taken place in every well-constituted factory, in every well-constituted department of human industry of any description, has not taken place in our legislation, and our community has not deemed it necessary to erect bulwarks against this pressure of special interests.

Reviewing the conditions which went to the making of a legislative session, Mr. Sterne pointed out that the members of the Senate and of the House arrive at the State Capitol respectively pledged to their parties on party measures, but free upon other subjects to constitute our legislature for the year. The only contest at the beginning of the session is the election of a Speaker with a view to the formation of commitees, and the Speaker, although he has the important function of appointing committees, and can manipulate their membership as he pleases in special interests, has no responsibility in the way of suggesting, framing, shaping, or conducting the legislative course of the session. If bad laws are passed, he is held blameless, if good laws fail in their passage, unless through the direct interference of his ruling, no responsibility attaches to him. When the committees are organised, any member can introduce Bills, and that right is practically without limit, until toward the close of the session. Whatever the nature of the Bill may be, whether it be to frame a new code of procedure for the State, a new system of commercial law, a village charter, or an act to secure the better application of funds to relieve the poor in some remote town, it takes the same course ; it is referred to what is supposed to be its appropriate committee, is scarcely ever drafted at the Capitol, is suggested as a general rule by some special or private interest behind it, and its success depends mainly upon the pertinacity and skill with which this interest or its lobby sees fit to push it.

Under such a condition of legislation, the cynical statement that skilled talent is necessary for the purpose of securing the passage of a Bill, and that it is idle to expect a Bill to be turned out as law unless such skilled talent is employed, contains a considerable amount of truth. Unfortunately, the skill which is invoked is generally unscrupulous in its character, instead of being that of a body of men whose duty it is to supervise and become responsible for the legislation of a given session. The members of the Legislature, when they convene, expect Bills to drop into their hands upon which they are to act, and there are always private interests throughout the State sufficiently alert and active in asking for legislation from year to year to occupy most of the session, whatever may be its term. A Bill that happens to be the order of the day occupies it to the exclusion of more important measures, and it seems to be nobody's business to see to it that such a Bill, if it is unimportant, be postponed until the important Bills of the session are disposed of. The committees meet at hours when members usually consider it a hardship to be compelled to attend, and those composing them have neither the sense of responsibility attaching to a judicial inquiry, nor do they feel themselves in any degree occupying the position of judges. No formality is observed, no decorum, no order or method of inquiry. The Railway Committee will hear an argument upon the same day upon a suggestion to change the general body of the railway law, and upon a proposal to compel milk trains on the Harlem Railroad to run at a certain rate of freight. The Committee on Cities will hear an argument upon the question of changing the organic law of the city of New York immediately after or before an application to alter the line of the opening of a street in the city of Hudson. Local, special, and private laws jostle public laws, and the order in which they are heard, and the time given to them respectively, is very much dependent upon the pressure which is brought to bear upon the individual members or the clerk. And when at the end of a session a volume of laws is brought forth, two-fifths of which are mere administrative regulations, one-fifth private acts, and one-fifth local laws, and only the last fifth laws of general public utility, and the whole incongruous, inharmonious, and adding additional confusion to an already confused mass of legislation, no one member nor any officer or officers of the Legislature or State executive Government may be said to be responsible for this evil. The committees work independently of each other; there is no drafting committee; there are no examiners; there is no council of revision; there is nothing, in short, to secure order except the necessarily hurried and perfunctory examination that can be given in the Executive Chamber, the incumbent of which at best can only prevent by his veto the most outrageously unconstitutional Bills from becoming operative.

In setting about a reform of the legislative methods thus outlined, Mr. Sterne was acutely conscious of the fact that in the effort to cure existing abuses, new ones might be created. He recalled that when the pressure of private interests had created a lobby so powerful that our legislative methods had become a scandal and disgrace, it was thought advisable to erect a barrier by limiting the powers of the Legislature in certain directions, and particularly those in which the lobby influence had been most perniciously exercised. But the provisions designed by the Constitutional Commission of 1872 against private, local, and special legislation had been circumvented by the practice of making special grants under the cover of general legislation. It only required a few years of the operation of the constitutional amendments, which went into effect in 1875, to demonstrate that the great danger of such limitations of legislative power lay in the fact that wherever the restrictions were clearly applicable, the special private interest which felt itself hampered by the existence of the constitutional limitation would strain every point to have the general law so amended as to meet its special case. Hence the little harmonious legislation that was left was thrown into the arena of private interests to be hacked at and torn to pieces as they might dictate.

Mr. Sterne proposed to go to the root of the evil, and give form and method to our legislation by distinguishing clearly between matters of public and private concern; by providing that all private or local Bills which it is desired that the incoming Legislature shall act upon shall be filed with the Secretary of State sixty days before the opening of the legislative session; and that no private or local Bills should be introduced during the session unless so filed, except with the consent of the Governor and two-thirds of both Houses entered upon the journals by ayes and nays. After the Bill has been filed, its object and a synopsis of its contents should, at the expense of those interested, be advertised in the State paper before the opening of the Legislature, and if it affects private interests by the proposed occupation of or interference with the surface of any street or highway, or in any way involves the right of eminent domain, owners of property along the line of the street or highway, or proposed improvement, should be individually notified before the opening of the session. Objections to Bills should thereupon be filed within the first ten days of the session, and after they have elapsed, these several private Bills should be referred to joint special committees of members of the Legislature, and experts to be appointed by the Governor, who should sit as though they were courts of justice, and after a proceeding analogous to a trial, report from time to time the Bills with their amendments to the Legislature. The Bills and these objections thereto, all duly filed, should be considered in the same light as the framing of an issue at law. A calendar should be made for the Bills in their respective committees, and notice of the time and place of trial and hearing given to the parties interested. Then at the trial of these issues all interests could be heard through counsel, testimony could be taken, and the question whether the Bill should become a law would partake of the nature of a judicial inquiry into rights, instead of a mere legislative inquiry for the information of the legislators.

To the objection that this was investing legislation with the character of judicial procedure, Mr. Sterne replied by the statement that private and local legislation, according to the principles of the Roman law and the fundamental principles of the English law as well, is not, strictly speaking, legislation at all, but partakes of the nature of a grant by a legislative court of the same validity as a judicial decree, allowing or establishing special exemptions, privileges, or monopolies, in derogation or in alteration of the common right which is established only by general law. It was pointed out that the English Court of Chancery felt itself at liberty to enjoin a party from promoting a private Bill before Parliament when such a Bill would be in violation of a contract, and when it was suggested, on argument, that such an injunction was an interference with the constitutional right of petition, the answer was made by the Court that the passing of private and local Bills is not, strictly speaking, legislation at all, but is an exercise of the parliamentary right to grant a petition for special privileges, and thus is an exception to general legislation. As the exercise of this right is never undertaken by Parliament except by the promotion of private parties, who, through counsel, attend and follow each legislative step of the Bill —steps which are never continued when it is abandoned by such private parties,—a court of equity has the right to prevent the promotion of such Bills, the effect of which would be practically to operate as violations of contract, express or implied.

Mr. Sterne scouted the idea that party responsibility existed as a fact in connection with the administration of our Government. Addressing a body of men, more than usually interested in all the legislation that affects the State, and specially interested in the legislation affecting the city of New York, he asked them whether either political party had advanced or proposed any scheme of legislation for the coming year of a public nature; whether either or any party was pledged to any scheme of legislation for the coming year as to this city; whether any of them knew what measures were likely to be introduced and to prove successful which were of a public nature; and whether there was any one to be charged with the duty of promoting such measures in the halls of legislation. As it was manifestly impossible to answer any of these questions in the affirmative, it was impossible to resist the force of Mr. Sterne's statement that, even as to public measures, we are remitted entirely to haphazard legislation, such as may be suggested by private interest or by private ambition, and that in the absence of leadership, even public legislation is thrown into the arena of the lobby to be fought over, to take its chance with private legislation, and to depend upon the accidents of the conduct of chairmen of committees, engrossing clerks and committee clerks, whether it is to be adopted and come in the shape of a Bill into the hands of the Governor. The conclusion was certainly irresistible that, in a community in which legislation plays so important a part, there should be no longer tolerated a state of affairs which annually gives us laws without plan, and enactments without examination.

It was eminently characteristic of Mr. Sterne

that once he had convinced himself of the public necessity of some great measure of reform, he should immediately set about finding the agency most appropriate for carrying it out. This usually involved the education of a number of men, all of them busy, and most of them constitutionally sceptical of the value of any counsel of perfection in matters affected by practical politics. On this question of the prevention of defective and slipshod legislation, the legal profession was, naturally, the constituency most likely to have an intelligent appreciation of the importance of the appeal. We accordingly find Mr. Sterne addressing the American Bar Association at its annual meeting at Saratoga on August 24, 1884, on the subject with which his name had already become identified, and a year later we find him making a report as chairman of a committee appointed by the Association of the Bar of the city of New York, on a plan for improving the methods of legislation of this State. In this report, a special appeal is made to lawyers to bestir themselves in correcting the radical defects existing in the methods of legislation, because they are thereby cheated of a boon common to all other professions, that increasing years bring rest in labour. But the hasty and prolific legislation of the time, and withal the entirely irresponsible methods of law-making, render the lawyer's experience and knowledge of much less use to him than it would otherwise be. He went on to show that the constitutional restrictions of 1875, in restraining the Legislature from passing special laws in a large number of enumerated cases, had not brought about the beneficial results which were anticipated from them, as even the number of laws which are annually enacted had not been materially reduced by these restrictions. In 1874, before the constitutional amendments took effect, the annual number of laws was little more than 600, and in 1884 the Acts of the year amounted to 550. These constitutional restrictions had, however, brought with them an evil in many respects more dangerous than that which they were intended to cure, namely, that of creating a large body of laws having special and local objects in view, but which are disguised under the form of general legislation, so that it has now become wellnigh impossible for a lawyer, without the most recent volume of Acts before him to give his opinion upon any legal point, as it is within the range not only of possibility, but even of probability, that the Legislature was, at the instance of some private or special interest, induced to change the old landmarks to meet some special case. He cited as one of the most recent illustrations of this fact, the general law passed in 1884, authorising corporations organised under any general or special law of this State, for any kind of manufacturing business, to consolidate into a single corporation, which Act was devised specially for the sinister purpose of enabling the Gas Companies to consolidate their separate corporate entities.

The report in question, which is obviously the work of Mr. Sterne, declared it to be safe to say that one-half of the changes in the general law are moved and brought about by some special or personal interest, and with the specific purpose of meeting a special case. No adequate machinery exists in American legislative bodies by which these motives can be scrutinised and a test afforded of whether the law should be enacted, nor is there any responsible machinery organised in our State Governments either to protect the general body of the law from encroachment and change of this character, or to compel the promoters of special and local Bills demanded by private interest to establish the necessity or expediency of granting the privileges which they involve. Attention was directed to the well-known fact that members of the Legislature are, with very rare exceptions, not the authors of the Bills which they introduce. The legislative committees cannot give, after their introduction, the time required for their consideration, and have no machinery, even if there were time, by which the objects and purposes of the Bills, and the effects they are likely to have upon the interests which are to be directly or remotely affected by their passage, can be definitely ascertained. Under such conditions, it was hardly to be wondered at that the lobby should have continued as powerful an agency for evil as ever. So long as legislators are compelled to rely upon *ex parte* statements for information in regard to any proposed law, an organised lobby became as necessary a concomitant to such a condition as a trained bar is a natural incident to the due and proper administration of justice.

The profound distrust of the results of legislative activity had become such that the most popular remedy for existing evils was that of biennial legislative sessions. The desire for these arose from the widely-diffused conviction that the legislative session was on the whole an evil, and to diminish the activity of that evil by one-half would be to confer a benefit on the community. But as the author of this report went on to show, such a remedy deals merely with the symptoms of the disease and not with its source. If the evil arise from an insufficient examination of the Bills before the legislative body, and the absence of responsibility for their preparation and enactment, this proposed remedy will not alone fail to obviate the existing difficulties, but the attempt to compress within the short period of a legislative session once in two years the work which is now performed in twice the time by annual sessions would have a tendency to decrease the present inadequate scrutiny and care, and thus necessitate greater haste, and therefore intensify rather than diminish the existing imperfections of the system of law-making.

Having considered the character of the evils, whose existence was undeniable, the Committee announced as their conclusion that the cure for these evils was to be found in following the principle which has operated successfully in English parliamentary procedure, for more than a generation, as to local and private as well as general laws. Mr. Sterne had pointed out in his address before the American Bar Association, that the English statesmen of the preceding generation had wisdom enough to see that successfully to cope with the ingenuity of the captains of the modern industrial era, it was necessary to arm the Legislature with additional and better means of sifting legislation, so as to separate the useful from the mischievous. At an earlier period, but subsequent to the foundation of our own Government, the British Cabinet had been converted from being merely personal advisers to the Crown to occupancy of the position of the Chief Executive Committee of Parliament. As part of the responsibility which attached to the party in power, the guardianship over the law and the changes to be made therein to meet public exigencies, was assumed by the ministry in office as part of its duties. We, on the other hand, have adopted party government without attaching to it this grave party responsibility. Our public laws and the changes made in them are not committed to the care of any official body.

This important change in the English Constitution was the first step in a process of legislative development and reform which culminated in the adoption of the standing orders of 1848, and completed the separation between the method of treatment of public from private and local Bills. The former are placed under the wing of the Cabinet. The latter are no longer treated as legislation, strictly speaking, but as petitions to Parliament for special immunities or privileges which are conducted by private parties, subject to a strict rule of procedure, tried as a lawsuit, the petition and Bill being filed before the beginning of the session, and opposed at every step, as a whole and in detail, by the Board of Trade, and by every private interest which may be menaced or affected thereby. Counter-petitions, attorneys, counsel, and a trial, a standing and a day in court to all parties in interest before the Bill can become a law, prevent wrong to individuals; counsel for the ministry for the public Bills, and special counsel for the private Bills, committees to aid them in the intelligent discharge of their work, prevent the possibility, by collusion, of working a public wrong.

By virtue of this system of standing orders, no private or local Bill is considered by Parliament unless deposited in the private Bills office sixty days in advance of the session. If it be a railway or canal project, a deposit of 5 per cent of the estimated cost of construction must be made at the time of filing the Bill. If it involve the exercise of the right of eminent domain, evidence must be given that notice of intention to file the Bill has been served on all the persons whose interests are likely to be affected adversely by the legislation. Accompanying these documents, as to the contents of which the most precise instructions are given in the rules, there must be deposited a sum of money to cover the expenses of preliminary examinations of the Bill, in order to ascertain, officially, whether the standing orders have been complied with.

The opponents of the Bill have, until fifteen days before the opening of the session of Parliament, to file their objections to the Bill, and to point out wherein the standing orders have not been complied with by the petitioners. If, either by the unaided investigations of the official examiners, or at the suggestion of adversaries, it becomes apparent that the promoters have failed to give the requisite notice by advertisements and by personal service, or that the map is not in conformity with the Bill, or in any other particulars they have failed to comply with the standing orders, the Bill is indorsed "standing orders not complied with," and Parliament is relieved from its consideration during that session. If there be a question whether the standing orders have been complied with, the parliamentary agent is heard upon the subject. If he can explain a seeming neglect, the examiners may allow the Bill to be entertained, but no substantial deviation from the rules is tolerated, and non-compliance means non-consideration. If the Bill is entertained, a further payment is to be made by the promoters to pay its way during its consideration in committee. Each of these payments is about £50. Bills are then separated by the Chairman of the Ways and Means Committee and the Chairman of Committees of the House of Lords. Those that involve railway or canal projects, or which involve the exercise of the right of eminent domain, are referred for special scrutiny to the Board of Trade. All are examined by the Chairman of the Committees of the House of Lords, who makes his suggestions and amendments, which are generally accepted by the parliamentary agents, who are the attorneys for the promoters of private and local Bills, in filing and conducting them until they come to be considered by the parliamentary committees in open session.

The Bills are then referred for trial. The trial committees are composed of chairmen who are members of Parliament, one or two additional members, and several experts thoroughly conversant with the technical elements of the subject-matter of the Bill, and who need not be members of Parliament. A calendar, analogous in character to calendars of trial causes in a court of justice, is then prepared, containing a list of the Bills, and a trial is had in which the petitioners as well as the adversaries of the Bill are represented by counsel. The question of the expediency of the passage of the proposed measure is determined first as a whole, on the preamble, and then by sections; and every injury, direct or indirect, is presented for the consideration of the Committee, to be avoided, if possible, by amendments to clauses of the Bill, or by the award of proper compensation. The adversary who succeeds in defence of a property right, to secure by amendment the insertion of a clause which in all fairness should have originally been inserted in the draft deposited by the promoters of the Bill, mulcts the latter to pay the contestant's costs. If the Committee determine in favour of the Bill, they so report, together with their amendments, to the House, and with but very rare exceptions the House regards the findings of a committee on a private or local Bill as final. This method of ascertaining the merits of a measure is so complete, the examination of witnesses and experts is so thorough, every element that can enlighten the mind of the legislator has been brought to bear with so much accuracy and forensic skill, that the margin of human error, after such a trial, is very small. The amount paid to Parliament for considering a private or a local measure is, on an average, $1000 a Bill. By these payments, which are somewhat in excess of the cost of the service of examination, the expense of private legislation is not only avoided to the English Parliament, but even the expense of public legislation is defrayed.

The difference between that system and the no-system of the United States was obviously enormous. The English system places the business of drafting proposed legislation (both public and private) in the hands of skilled specialists, all parliamentary draughtsmen. The services of the parliamentary draughtsmen and counsel are employed by the Speaker, by the chairmen of committees, and by the ministry; and they are consulted by the parliamentary agents in important cases of private legislation. This system has caused the lobby virtually to disappear, a fair trial and no favour being secured for private Bills. A member of a committee of the English Parliament regards being button-holed or talked to in the interest of a measure before his committee almost with the same disfavour with which a self-respecting judge would regard a like attempt to entrap his judgment, or influence his opinion. In place of the lobby as we know it, England has a trained bar analogous to the Common Law bar; the parliamentary agents take the place of attorneys, and parliamentary counsel take the place of barristers. A division has been made between the treatment of public and private legislation, which recognises the fundamental distinction between them to the advantage of both. Another important fact was recognised by this change; that in the pressure of modern society for development, the general body of the law cannot possibly keep pace with its ever varying features and necessities; no attempt, therefore, was made to restrict private legislation, but it was subjected to rule and form, submitted to scrutiny, and surrounded by safeguards. Thus, while the system meets the demands for legislation of a private or local character to vary the general law, it does not inflict any injustice on other private and local interests, and the general body of the law is not allowed to be torn to pieces at the demand and under the pressure of such interests.

Mr. Sterne steadfastly maintained that the remedy for the acknowledged evils of our system lay in the adoption of the English practice adapted and simplified to accord with the traditions of American legislation. As chairman of a special committee of the Board of Trade and Transportation, charged with the duty of proposing amendments to the legislative articles or the Constitution of the State of New York for presentation to the convention of 1894, Mr. Sterne prepared certain sections on legislation calculated to introduce greater deliberation into the treatment of public Bills, and to stamp all private and local Bills with the character of petitions subject to public hearing and quasi-judicial examination. He succeeded in having the Convention accept a single provision out of the whole scheme of constitutional reform submitted by him to bring order and method into legislation. This was the provision requiring the submission to the Mayor of Cities of local laws relating to their municipalities. No more important contribution has, of late years, been made to municipal home rule in this State, and none whose good results have been so conspicuously manifest. Later, after it had been demonstrated to the author of these amendments that his views were still considerably in advance even of the progressive opinion of the time on such questions, Mr. Sterne was appointed one of five commissioners to recommend changes in the methods of legislation. In this capacity he made the most careful and painstaking study of the legislative procedure of most of the States of the Union, and his hand is very clearly apparent in the report of this Commission, addressed to Governor Morton on November 30, 1895. Being an eminently practical man, and not prone to insist on what was manifestly unattainable, he indorsed in this report the opinion of his associates that—

> So elaborate a system as that which England has developed to guard its legislation from becoming mischievous to the community, it would not be practicable to recommend for adoption in the State of New York. Progress must be taken cautiously in that direction, and such steps in legislative reform must be taken from the experience of sister American Commonwealths, rather than from a highly-developed form of European procedure; making advances beyond such experience only when the greater pressure of business upon the Legislature of the State of New York, as compared with the legislative bodies of other States, imperatively demands a treatment differing from their own.

The Commission, therefore, while recognising

the great superiority of the English system over those which are in vogue in American Commonwealths, also recognised that such changes as they contemplated must be gradual in their adoption to secure permanence, and be in conformity with the spirit and habits of the people adopting them. A beginning had, at least, been made by the requirement that Bills should be printed, and on the desks of legislators three days before their enactment, and by the further amendment to the Constitution by the Convention of 1894 relating to laws which affect cities. Nothing had, however, been done to afford an opportunity to improve and perfect proposed legislation while on its passage by compulsory timely notice of intention to apply for its passage, and by proper hearings while the Bill is on its way to become law. The Commission had the benefit of the opinions of men of large legislative experience, and a general agreement was reached that to secure better legislation in the future it was necessary to methodise and improve it in the following particulars :—

First. That all private and local Bills, including Bills which relate to municipalities, shall be filed either before the beginning of the legislative session, or within thirty days before their presentation to the Legislature, unless the Governor of the State takes upon himself the responsibility of making a special recommendation of urgency ; and that each Bill shall be accompanied with proof that a notice was duly published or personally served, or both, as the circumstances of the case may require, on every interest which may be affected by such legislation.

Second. That the petition for such legislation shall set forth its general scope, object, and utility. This petition may be answered in writing by any adverse interest. Such petition and one or more answers, which partake of the nature of pleadings in a civil suit, shall be filed with the Bill, and these petitions and counter-petitions, duly signed, shall accompany each Bill of this character during the whole of its legislative progression.

Third. That Committees of Revision, both Senate and Assembly, should have their powers enlarged for the consideration of all measures, both public and private, or local; and that each of such committees shall be assisted in its labours by a lawyer of, at least, ten years' standing, with an adequate salary to ensure proper talent, who shall have such assistance as may be necessary. These committees to act as advisory committees for re-drafting Bills, and for recommendations as to their effect, with suggestions as to their operation upon the general body of the law, and to point out constitutional or other defects. Such counsel to be appointed by the Governor, Lieutenant-Governor, and Speaker of the House for a fixed term.

Fourth. That a day calendar shall be printed one day in advance, and distributed among the members.

Fifth. That general public measures should be referred, before passage, to the Commissioners to Revise the Statutes, to report upon the effect of such measures and their place in the body of the statute law.

Sixth. That Committees of the Legislature should be empowered to take testimony.

Seventh. That every Committee should be required to report the private and local Bills which have been submitted to it, with the reasons for its action, within a certain number of days after the Bill has been committed to its care.

Eighth. That some of the Senate committees should be enlarged, particularly such committees which have imposed upon them the most onerous duties of the legislative session—such as the Committee on Cities, the Committee on Finance, and the Committee on Judiciary.

Ninth. That a proportionate share of the printing expenses incident to a legislative session, which amounted during the last session to the sum of $200,000, should be borne by the parties interested in the Bills, and in whose interest and at whose request legislation is considered—particularly moneyed corporations, stock corporations, or private individuals.

Tenth. That the general laws should be completed as rapidly as possible, and all public statutes should be incorporated into them or into one of the Codes.

Eleventh. That all Bills amendatory of the general laws, or of the Code, should refer briefly in their title to the general subject to which they relate.

Twelfth. That all amendments to city charters, or to the general, municipal, and corporation laws should briefly state in the title the subject of the sections of the statute which are proposed to be amended.

Thirteenth. That with reference to every Bill affecting any department of the State Government, or the general administration of the law, subject to the supervision of such department, notice thereof shall be given to the head of the department having the administration of such subject under his supervision, and an opportunity afforded him to be heard before the Bill is reported or passed.

It was explained that most of these propositions had been considered in other States of the Union, and that the more important of them have been adopted in some of those States and work well. Attention was particularly called to the provision relating to the giving of notice of intention to apply for the passage of special and local Bills, and also to the requirements that applicants for Bills shall pay the expense of printing them, and that committees shall report within a certain time upon private and local Bills. The States of Rhode Island, Pennsylvania, New Jersey, North Carolina, Georgia, Florida, Alabama, Texas, Arkansas, and Louisiana have constitutional provisions on the subject of publication of notice of intention to apply for certain Bills before they can be considered by the Legislature.

The constitution of Pennsylvania provides that no local Bill shall be passed unless notice of the intention to apply therefor shall have been published in the locality where the matter or thing to be affected may be situated, which notice shall be, at least, thirty days prior to the introduction into the General Assembly of such Bill in the manner to be provided by law, the evidence of such notice having been published shall be exhibited in the General Assembly before such Act shall be passed. This has been followed by an Act substantially incorporating the constitutional provision, and amplifying it for the purpose of making it more effectual.

The report went on to point out that although other States have embodied either in their constitutions or by statutory enactments, like provisions to those of Pennsylvania, that State affords in its characteristics and legislative necessities a closer analogy to the State of New York than any of its sister States with the possible exception of Massachusetts. It was thus assumed that a legislative reform which has worked well in that State could not but prove beneficial in the State of New York. Hence, the Commission directed inquiries to be made of public men and leading lawyers of the State of Pennsylvania, and received from them the unanimous assurance that the requirement of timely notice of intended legislation and of the publication of the general purposes of the Bill, in advance of the session of the Legislature or the consideration of the measure, has prevented the introduction and passage of a large number of Bills like those which had previously encumbered the statute book of that State ; that it has prevented ill-considered measures, diminished the evil of over-legislation, and been fruitful of unmixed benefits to the inhabitants of Pennsylvania.

Assembly Rule 15 of the State of New York provides that "No Bill affecting the rights of individuals, or of private or of municipal corporations, otherwise than as it affects generally the people of the whole State, shall be reported by a Committee unless it is made to appear to the satisfaction of the Committee that notice has been given by public advertisement or otherwise to all parties interested without expense to the State." In case the Bill affects the rights of a municipal corporation, such notice shall be given to the Mayor in cities, and to the President of the Board of Trustees in villages. This rule is scarcely ever observed, but both the law (chap. 121, Laws of 1818) and the rule are a recognition that notice of some kind is essential to good legislation. No requirement to secure adequate notice, nor for the publication of the intention to apply, is embodied in the Rule, and if legislation is effected without the required notice, it is questionable whether there may not be an impairment of validity by reason of the absence of such notice. The Commissioners, therefore, prepared a Bill which provided, with great precision and stringency, for such notice and the filing of Bills considerably in advance of their consideration. In addition to this Bill the Commission recommended that a constitutional amendment on this subject, similar to the provision in the Pennsylvania Constitution, be adopted in this State so as to carry out adequately the proposed reform.

It also appeared to the Commission that a long step in the right direction would be taken, if Bills, before their third reading, and while yet capable of amendment, could be submitted for scrutiny and revision to one or more trained lawyers, whose only client in the matter would be the State, and for whose conclusions, if satisfactory, a carefully selected committee of the best men in either House would become responsible. This part of the system of improved legislative methods which the Commission decided to recommend, had already received substantial recognition in legislative procedure, in the form of the Committee on Revision of the Assembly. By Rule 16 of that body, this committee is charged with the duty of examining and correcting all Bills prior to their third reading, "for the purpose of avoiding repetitions and unconstitutional provisions, ensuring accuracy in the text, and references, and consistency with the language of the existing statutes." It is also part of its duty to "report whether the subject sought to be accomplished can be secured without a special act, under existing laws, or without detriment to the public interests, by the enactment of a general law." Changes in sense or legal effect and material alterations in construction are guarded by the provision that they shall be reported as recommendations, and not as amendments. It is the testimony of those familiar with the facts that some good has been accomplished by this committee since 1890, the time of the adoption of the present rule, but that much more might have been done by the aid of counsel of experience and ability, and by enlarging the duties of the House Committee, and equipping the legislative machinery of the Senate, with a similar committee, equally provided with proper counsel.

The Commission, accordingly, determined to advise the amendment of the legislative law so as to make statutory provision for committees on revision in each House, with counsel therefor, who shall be lawyers of experience, and receive sufficient compensation to secure the grade of talent required. The fact was recognised that, in 1895, the Legislature had charged the Commissioners of Statutory Revision with certain duties which would ordinarily be performed by legislative counsel, and that such duties have ever since been discharged by those Commissioners during the session. But it was felt that there was urgent necessity for the completion of the collection of general laws which was the specific purpose for which the Commissioners of Statutory Revision were appointed, and it was anticipated that to this burden was likely to be added the herculean task of a scientific revision of the Code of Civil Procedure. If the Commission of Statutory Revision were to be, in addition, the only legal adviser of the Legislature during many months of each year, the reduction of the general statute law to anything like system would have to be considered as indefinitely postponed. Besides, the great majority of Bills do not reach the Commissioners for examination until they have passed both Houses; and to render revisory powers of any considerable value, they must be exercised before the third reading.

How slender were the results attending the painstaking labours and well-considered recommendations of the Commission of 1895, may be inferred from the following letter addressed by Mr. Sterne to Governor-Elect Roosevelt in regard to the changes which were urgently required in the methods of legislation, — a letter containing his last words on a subject about which he had thought, written, and spoken with unwearied assiduity for twenty-three years, and whose adequate treatment will be one of the testimonies which posterity will bear to his far-sighted sagacity :—

December 21, 1898.

Hon. Theodore Roosevelt,
Governor-Elect of the State of New York.

Sir—A recent paragraph in the papers indicating that you were at work upon your message to the Legislature, which doubtless will outline your policy as Governor of this State, made me feel that if I had anything to say with reference to such policy, I should express it before the message is completed.

Although in different party ranks, I have during my whole adult life striven to be, as a Democrat, as independent as you have been, as a Republican, and have not hesitated, either by silence and inactivity, or by positive revolt and opposition, to indicate or to express my convictions when I thought my party was in the wrong, and was misleading the voters of the city, state, or country.

I address the views herein contained to you, because I am thoroughly impressed with the conviction of the sincerity of your opposition to the sinister interests which control party policy, whether such interests are labelled Democratic or Republican. You have proved yourself a brave soldier, as well as shown that you are imbued with the proper civil courage; and I therefore venture to draw your attention to certain basic lines of policy which must be pursued if the enemies of the political welfare of the Commonwealth are to be successfully suppressed for many years to come.

We claim to be a practical people, and are very impatient with the theorist so-called. As in medical science it is not practical common sense to deal with the symptoms of a disease instead of constitutionally, and the man who treats only the outward signs of a diseased condition is regarded by the practical medical fraternity as a quack, so in politics the hue and cry against the boss, the personal abuse of Mr. Croker and of Mr. Platt, and the warfare against them, instead of fighting the system and causes which produce them, and of which they are merely the exponents, is quackery. No amount of admonition to legislators that they shall not allow themselves to be bribed, coerced, or controlled by personal or political considerations to perform their duties in accordance with their conscience and their oaths of office, and no amount of pointing directly or indirectly at Croker and Platt as the evil geniuses to be avoided by them, will produce the slightest effect, and is only quackery.

Mr. Platt's strength and position at the head of the Republican organisation of the State of New York arises from the fact that for a century and more the State of New York has made no improvement in its methods of legislation. I speak of this as a whole. I am well aware of the few constitutional efforts that have been made during the past fifty years to curb and bridle the Legislature, and put safeguards around legislation; but these efforts were misconceived in theory, and produced little or no good results in practice. Indeed, some of the supposed reforms produced practical results of a most mischievous character. With few exceptions, every successive Legislature has increased the number of Bills enacted into laws over those that preceded it, and has had under consideration a correspondingly increased number of Bills which have failed to become laws. So that year after year a great mass of statutes, scarcely any of which are prepared by any public body, and almost all representing some private interest, emanate from the Legislature of the State, and in such bulk that it must be incontestably true that none of them receives proper consideration, and that most of them receives no consideration at all. Thus a vast mass of undigested matter, unfortunately having the force of law, is every year dumped upon the community to work out its mission of evil. It is in this situation that the skilful manipulator, the adroit manager of men, the guide who is willing to take the responsibility upon his shoulders, and relieve the individual members of the Legislature from a responsibility which he cannot help but feel, and for which he is neither adequately equipped nor fully competent, becomes a source of danger to the community. The position of such a chieftain is such that he can reap a great profit for himself, and for the organisation which he represents. That this is not only true of the condition of the legislation of New York State, but also applies to the Congress of the United States, is shown by the fact that Senator Edmunds, as presiding officer of the Senate of the United States, at the conclusion of the session of 1885, said: "It may not be improper for me to say that, in view of our recent experience, it may be doubted that Congress can congratulate itself on being the best example of a legislative body conducting its business with that deliberate and timely diligence which is the inseparable handmaid of wisdom and justice, as well in the making as in the administration of laws. It is, I think, an evil of large and growing proportions that measures of the greatest importance, requiring much time for proper examination and discussion in detail, are brought to our consideration so late that it is not possible to deal with them intelligently, and which we are tempted (over-tempted, I fear), to enact into laws in the hope that fortune, rather than time, study, and reflection, will take care that the public suffer no detriment."

Mr. Carlisle, the Speaker of the House of Representatives, in the same year and at the same hour, and surely without consultation with the President of the Senate, as he belonged to a different political party, expressed the same sentiment in different words :—

"It is evident that unless some constitutional or legal provision can be adopted, which will relieve Congress from the consideration of all, or at least a large part, of the local and private measures which now occupy the time of the committees and fill the calendar of the two Houses, the percentage of business left undisposed of at each adjournment must increase. It is not reasonable to suppose that an alteration of the Constitution could be effected ; but it is worthy of serious consideration whether a general law might not be enacted which would authorise the Executive Departments and Courts of Justice to hear and determine these matters, under such rules and regulations, of course, as would amply protect the interests of the Government and secure to the citizen, doubtless, a more expeditious and appropriate remedy than is now offered."

Private and local legislation had increased to such enormous proportions from 1865 to 1871 that it was felt that something must be done to relieve the legislature of the burden and the corrupting influence of such legislation. Instead of following the example of Great Britain which methodised its legislation by its parliamentary standing rules, and subjected all private and local legislation to proper trial, when a half century ago it met with the same difficulty arising from the growth of corporate interests and particularly the development of the railway system which caused much traffic in franchises about 1842 and 1843, it was determined in this State to amend the Legislative Article of the Constitution. This amendment went into effect January 1, 1875, as the result of the recommendations made by a Constitutional Commission appointed by Governor Hoffman. Henceforth, the legislature was prohibited from passing private or local Bills, for a large number of specified purposes, which it was supposed could be better accomplished by the enactments of general statutes. It was thereby expected to remedy the evil of traffic in franchises, and careless and over-legislation from which this State was then suffering. The legislature of 1873 which had enacted 874 laws was then regarded as a record breaker of reckless and useless legislation, and was held up as a warning example of the result of permitting private and local legislation where general laws could be enacted upon the same subject. Notwithstanding this constitutional amendment, the output from the legislative mill at Albany has in recent years steadily increased, so that notwithstanding the constitutional provision of 1875, instead of 874 acts which had been passed in 1873, 1045 were passed in 1895, while in 1896 the number increased to upwards of 2000, and in 1897 to upwards of 1592, thus showing that this constitutional amendment did not produce the expected result of diminishing the number of legislative enactments. The constitutional amendment did, however, produce a most mischievous result which greatly aggravated certain evils. After its adoption, the practice of concealing under the guise of general laws legislation designed to affect private interests and to meet individual cases became general. This practice tends to destroy and has already very considerably destroyed the symmetry of the laws, and has substituted fickleness and changeableness for certainty and stability. It unsettles judicial construction and precedent, and in many cases deprives citizens of vested rights without giving them an opportunity to be heard in their own behalf.

Whilst on one side there is a board of statutory revision for the purpose of codifying existing miscellaneous statutes upon the same subject-matter, there is a constant process of disintegration going on in the legislative halls, tearing, under the impulse of the constitutional provision of 1875, the body of our laws to pieces to serve special and private ends. The state of the law in relation to so important a matter as public assessments in the cities of New York and Brooklyn was in 1875 so lamentable, that the then Chief Justice of the Court of Appeals of this State in a deliberate opinion delivered by him in a case pending before that Court, admitted that it was not safe for the Court, after oral and written argument of counsel, to speak with any degree of confidence on the State of the law upon that subject. Matters have become worse, instead of better, since that time; and it is therefore not surprising that in this mass of proposed legislation which is put before the legislature each year for enactment into law, and in the mass of Bills which are actually enacted into law—a bulk so great that the statutes of 1897 and 1898 embraced respectively 2563 and 1616 closely printed pages—it becomes perfectly evident that it is not within human possibility for the most astute and conscientious member of the Senate or Assembly even to read during the brief session of the Legislature the mass of material that is placed before him, much less to deliberately consider and wisely to act upon measures which are expected to become law. Under these circumstances, it is but natural for the average legislator to look to some one for guidance, and he feels himself helpless in consequence of the mass of material with which he has to deal, and the lack of all machinery to winnow and examine it preliminarily, and knowing that the great bulk of the Bills are dictated by personal interests, he turns to some one, and to whom more naturally than the leader of his party, to whom, more or less, he is indebted for elevation to power—to ask, what of this mass shall I pass? That such leader finds his profit in the position which is created by this lamentable neglect of proper organisation of the law-making machinery, and that the party supplies a kind of machinery where the Commonwealth has failed to provide any of any kind, is a natural consequence. It is the neglect of the community, of its lawyers, of its law-makers, of its constitutional advisers, and its methods which has created the situation. Mr. Platt and Mr. Croker are the effects and not the creators of the general demoralisation, corruption, and confusion which attends our law-making and which, if not put a stop to, will soon undermine our institutions.

At the present time the greater part of the Bills which are presented to the Legislature are drawn at the dictation of private and local interests without any regard to their effect upon the general body of the legislation of the State, or how they will affect adverse interests, or touch the general public weal. They are introduced at any time during the session. There is a slight time limitation, but that can be evaded. The Bills are considered by committees who have not the benefit of process of trial for their proper sifting and the critical examination of their respective provisions. The committee-men are dependent for information upon assertions of one side or the other, and not upon proof, when they give hearings upon Bills. The pressure upon the committees is so great that it is practically impossible for even the best informed and the most industrious legislator to understand what changes are being made in the existing laws or to keep himself even superficially informed as to half the legislation during its passage in the Senate or Assembly, or to exercise any deliberate judgment before he votes on any question.

Much of what I say is a condensation of a report submitted to the Governor of this State on November 30, 1895, and made by me as a fellow-commissioner with such practical politicians in the best sense as Charles T. Saxton, Danforth E. Ainsworth, John J. Linson, and John S. Kenyon. The Commission was appointed by Governor Morton to make recommendations as to changes in the methods of legislation in the State of New York. A copy of that report is attached to this letter in confirmation of the views herein expressed. Allow me to quote from this report the opinion of the Commissioners on the subject of biennial instead of annual sessions of the legislative body. This has by some people been proposed as a remedy for the evils mentioned, and the public mind has been agitated to look favourably upon the proposition, and your co-operation has been asked to promote the final passage of a constitutional amendment authorising biennial sessions. The report of the Commission, which has my approval now as it had then, says on this point :—

"The Commissioners have considered, only to dismiss, the suggestion that any relief from over-legislation and careless law-making is to be found in biennial sessions of our legislative bodies. It is obvious that when it is impossible under the existing system to secure, even with annual sessions, the time necessary for careful, deliberate and painstaking work, and when the pressure for legislation, even with annual sessions, is beyond the capacity of the legislature to deal with it adequately, such pressure and the number of Bills would manifestly be largely increased by biennial sessions, with a consequent decrease in the possibility of passing carefully and deliberately considered statutory enactments. The undersigned Commissioners have, therefore, determined from the outset to see whether the methods of legislation could be improved, instead of seeking for a remedy in a less frequent meeting of the legislative body."

I draw your attention to the wide difference in method with which the same subject has been treated in England. From 1840 to 1845 a condition existed in Parliament which caused Francis, the historian of the English railway, to say that at that time a serious doubt prevailed as to the freedom of the British Parliament from pecuniary corruption. This doubt has since that time been entirely removed, mainly because a clean line of separation was made by the Standing Orders of the House between private and local Bills on one side, and public measures on the other. For public measures ministerial responsibility is imposed on the government in power. Private and local Bills are not treated any longer as legislation, but regarded as petitions to Parliament for special privileges or for immunity from the operation of the general law, which, as a condition to receive parliamentary consideration, must be filed before the session opens; all interests adverse to or affected by the petition, or any clauses of the Bill, have to be notified. A very rigid and formal code of procedure has been enacted as to the manner in which the Bills must be drafted, the scrutiny they must be subjected to by public officers, the proof which has to be given of service of notice on interests affected before they even enter the parliamentary doors. If permitted to enter, the whole expense of the consideration of the Bill is borne by such private interests. This is fixed by a schedule of charges which accompanies the Bill through all its legislative steps, and which must be discharged and paid into the public treasury before further steps are permitted to be taken. Counter-petitions may be filed to any petition for legislation; the committees are courts which may examine witnesses and call for books and papers; their deliberations are aided by a competent bar of parliamentary practitioners; the pleadings are, in so far as compliance with the standing orders as to form and notice are concerned, all disposed of before the parliamentary session opens; and if the promoters of the Bill have failed properly to protect the parties whose interests are adverse to the Bill, they are mulcted in costs. The parliamentary committees examine, at the expense of the promoters, experts on the various subject-matters of the Bills; the whole work of legislation and consideration whether the matter preliminarily is ripe for action is done at the expense of the promoters, the nation is at no charge for such expense, and no Bill can be smuggled through of a private or local character without a most careful scrutiny as to its effects on other interests and the public weal, and sufficient warning is given to the community of its purpose. The adoption of such a system of publicity, notice, and trial, would dry up corruption as the sun destroys the vermin hidden under cover of a stone at the banks of a brook, when the stone is turned over. The traffic in legislation now carried on in the State of New York, consisting in large part of guarantees of immunity from adverse measures—immunity, if meritorious, which full investigation and publicity can give more effectually than the protection of the party chiefs—would for ever end. Close the sources of food upon which our political leviathans feed, destroy the business which makes them prosper, and you have ended their careers. This end will never be brought about by abuse of the persons who now represent the system. There is no more intelligence displayed in the usual mode of fighting these symptoms of diseased conditions than there is in the act of the anarchist who kills a Czar, assassinates an Empress, or explodes a palace. There will inevitably be after such removal of Czar, assassination of Empress, and explosion of a palace, some other ruler of the same character or mansion of the same kind to take the place vacated or removed by the insane act of destruction.

After adverting to the importance of securing

a reform of methods of representation for the purpose of diminishing, if not destroying, the evils of boss rule in cities, Mr. Sterne went on to say :—

The two reforms I take the liberty to suggest will produce a fundamental change and peaceful revolution in the class that comes uppermost in political life in our State and municipal politics. All other measures that have hitherto been suggested or devised to accomplish the same purpose are mere palliatives. Even Civil Service Reform, of which you are one of the foremost exponents and which is the most beneficial spur to administrative reform in our country, does not and will not touch the marrow of our political evil. Although not generally introduced, great progress has been made in the adoption of the principle of Civil Service Reform both in the nation, State, and, in some lesser degree, in municipalities. It is, however, painfully manifest that at no time in the history of American politics have political parties been so well organised, so regardless and so defiant of the highest public opinion, and so absolutely secure in their domination. We must, therefore, look to some other source for emancipation from a tyranny which, whilst it preserves the forms of freedom, saps its foundation.

To you, whose past history shows us that you have the courage necessary for the occasion, I hope may be reserved the great credit of bringing forward and inaugurating measures of relief to the community which will produce permanent instead of temporary victory over misrule for the people of the State and city of New York. By adopting scientific methods in our legislative procedure you will be following the precedent, step by step, of the parliamentary reform inaugurated in and carried through by England. In adopting minority representation, you will be following the precedent of our sister republic, Switzerland. It is to be expected that the same beneficial results which have attended the adoption of these measures in the countries named, will attend their adoption in this State. Our community is by no means inherently corrupt; its commercial credit is sound, and its manufacturing industries produce as good and trustworthy machinery as that of any other people upon the face of the earth. It is only in the political field that we are behind the foremost nations of the world in the practical application of our advantages to the intricate situation created by modern conditions, and we are so because we have failed to make the progress in the machinery of politics commensurate with that which we have made in all other fields of human activity. —Respectfully yours, SIMON STERNE.

To this Mr. Roosevelt made the following reply:—

OYSTER BAY, L. I., *December* 24, 1898.

My dear Mr. Sterne—I have read your letter with the greatest care. As regards excessive legislation, I am inclined to agree with you, although I think that Biennial Sessions would also be of some service, as Judge Earle believes. I am by no means clear on the minority representation plan. We had an approximation toward it in New York once, as regards aldermen, and it worked badly. I should regard it as a misfortune if, under Mayor Van Wyck, we had an anti-Tammany majority of the aldermen and council, and this majority composed of groups. The group system is shown by the experience of France and Germany, to be far more objectionable than the party system, in the long run. I shall have to consider this group business very carefully, before going into any measure that would be likely to promote it.—With great regard I am, very sincerely yours,

THEODORE ROOSEVELT.

CHAPTER VI

THE RELATIONS BETWEEN THE RAILROADS AND THE STATE

It was beginning to be recognised thirty years ago, that the question of the relations between the railroads and the State was one affecting not less vitally the health of the body politic than the material interests of the people. To the influence of no one man was the perception of this fact so largely due as to that of Simon Sterne. In March 1874, we find him addressing the Joint Committee of the Legislature on Railroads in favour of a Bill providing for the election of railroad directors by a system of minority representation, and for the appointment of a State Railroad Commission, and already showing the possession of so thorough a grasp of his subject as to suggest the devotion to it of years of previous thought and study. It is plain that the subject is one which early engaged his attention. Lecturing in 1869, he quoted the remark of Judge Sharswood of Philadelphia to the effect that this country is the paradise of corporations, and added: "It is fast becoming more than that, it will soon be a Government by corporations. Our railway companies, which originally were mere creatures of our legislative bodies, are now their masters." He quoted the opinion of another observer, as expressed in a recent pamphlet, to this effect: "Moneyed men, associated under various titles, have gradually bought up, under the name of corporate privileges, the more important prerogatives of taxation and administration. A generation ago, they approached the leading politicians as suppliants; now they hold them in pay, and use them not only to extort further immunities, but generally to control the entire machinery of the body politic."

It was a fundamental conviction with Mr. Sterne that our existing constitutional restraints were entirely inadequate to deal with the new power which had been called into being by the modern organisation of capital. He pointed out that written constitutions can protect the community from such evils only, which are, at the time of their enactment, experienced or immediately anticipated. The evils which lie in the remote future, it were vain to expect any community to erect safeguards against. Against the dangers of centralised power we erected the barrier of jealous State organisations, sovereigns in all things except the delegated power conferred upon Congress, a Supreme Court, and the President. Against the sway of social snobbishness and unjust discrimination, we erected the barrier of no patents of nobility; to obviate the dangers of power exercised by great wealth, accumulated in families and continued therein, we abolished in all our

States the right of primogeniture; we prohibited entail; we have forbidden perpetuities; and we limited accumulations by will to a life in being. We have substantially, as a people, said, that here by the general polity of this community there shall be not only no hereditary nobility, but there shall be no vast accumulations of ancestral wealth. We have said that death, the natural limitation of life, shall practically be the natural limitation of accumulations, acting upon the wise theory that all great accumulations of wealth tend, at best, to a social tyranny, to class interests, and to the creation of a body of men in the community with feelings, pursuits, and purposes distinct from the general welfare of their fellow-citizens; giving a power to purchase immunity from the just consequences of wrong-doing, and thus creating in fact, if not in name, a nobility.

But, as Mr. Sterne went on to show, in all this we forgot that, by the device of corporate longevity and perpetuity, all the preventatives we have applied against those evils of entail, perpetuities and accumulations, are set at nought. The simple expedient of unlimited corporate existence, corporate property, corporate accumulations, and corporate activity serves to neutralise precautions which are upon the statute-books of every State, and which have represented, from the very origin of our institutions, our settled purpose and polity. A natural person who, through entail, acquires vast landed estates, or, through perpetuities and accumulations, great values in personal property, is hedged in and circumscribed, at all events as to its use, by personal fear, by personal honour, and by a spirit of caste, which finds expression in the phrase of *noblesse oblige.* But the artificial person known as a corporation has no such limitations of a moral character ; it uses its accumulations or its property, which may be the results of hundreds of years of earnings, without scruple, without conscience, and, in the legal phrase, without a soul.

These figures were cited to show the suddenness with which railway corporate wealth had increased. In 1830 there were but 23 miles of railway in operation in the United States ; in 1840 there were but 2818 ; in 1850, 9021 ; in 1860, 30,635 ; while in 1876 there were 77,470 miles, representing a gross capital somewhere between five and six thousand millions of dollars. This vast accumulation of property, representing a special interest, was not foreseen by the men who framed the government of the United States. As Mr. Sterne argued, even had they foreseen it they could not have foreseen that it would be controlled by comparatively few men, and that the great trunk lines would have a constantly growing tendency to consolidate and combine. This tendency was not anticipated even by the statesmen who witnessed the birth and early growth of these enterprises, else they would have devised some plan by which, in reference to corporations, something analogous should take place in the way of a dispersion of influence and of wealth to that brought about by the death of the individual, or else a concentrated element of sovereignty would have been lodged somewhere in the community to make head and front against so formidable a growth of power and influence. It was admitted that the settlement of this country would have been impossible at the rate at which it had been settled; that the development of its wealth could not have taken place at the rate it has; that our community could not have sprung from a few sparsely-populated States into a nation bearing equal rank with the foremost peoples of the earth, within the short period of forty years, if it had not been for the railway. But the power that made us great had become tyrannous; and Mr. Sterne addressed himself to the suggestion of ways by which the abuse of this power might be prevented without detriment to its continued usefulness.

It was because of the fact that he had for a number of years made a special study of the relations existing between the railroads and the public with reference to the adoption of such equitable legal measures as would protect the public interest, and because he had repeatedly and disinterestedly urged upon the legislative committees of the State the passage of a Railway Commissioners' Bill, that he was asked by a number of representative men and firms of the great commercial interests of the city to deliver an address on this subject on April 19, 1878. In the course of that address, after enumerating the arguments above summarised, he entered into an examination of the conditions to which the commerce of New York was subjected by the so-called capitalisation of its roads. The system of railways throughout the State of New York was built anterior to any system throughout the United States. They were built at the cheapest possible rate. They were built under the most advantageous circumstances, and when the New York Central system of railroads was consolidated in 1869, its capital stock represented a par of $28,000,000; its bonds were represented by a par of $12,000,000; being a total of $40,000,000. The Hudson River Railroad at that time had a share capital of $7,000,000, and a bonded debt of $7,000,000, or $14,000,000 in all—making the combined stock capital of these two roads $35,000,000, and their bonds $19,000,000 or a total of $54,000,000. Mr. Sterne went on to recall the fact that 1867, 1868, and 1869 were the years of the highest prices of every commodity, land included, that this country has ever seen. It was a period when property in the City of New York had risen three times its value, when every pound of iron was worth $3·00 to $1·00 as compared with the price of ten years later, when every car was worth $2·00 to $1·00 by the same standard of comparison. At that period of inflation it got into the heads of the owners of the New York Central Railroad and of the Hudson River Railroad that they would take the cheap united road of these corporations, costing $54,000,000, and capitalise it upon an entirely different basis—that of the then valuation of its property and franchises. They accordingly declared upon the Hudson River Railroad a scrip dividend of 50 per cent; and at the time of consolidation another dividend of 85 per cent of the then outstanding stock of

$16,000,000, making an issue of $13,000,000. And the New York Central, in 1868, made a stock dividend of 80 per cent, being $23,000,000, followed by one of 27 per cent, making $7,000,000 additional at the time of the consolidation. Thus these combined roads were capitalised at double their value, even as represented by stocks and bonds, and it is a violent assumption that the roads cost anything like the sum which the stock and bonds represented.

The consequence was that the law of 1850, which authorises the legislature to step in whenever the dividends of a railway rise above 10 per cent on the actual cost of the road, and declares what shall be done with the surplus, was, by this process of capitalisation, made absolutely nugatory. The dividends of the railway between 1869 and 1878 had been, on the actual cost of the road, something above 16 per cent—in all probability something over 20 per cent. Because these roads were capitalised at $80,000,000, they insisted that they must pay the interest on that sum, when it was notorious that their cost did not represent $80,000,000—represented, in fact, less than $40,000,000, the other $40,000,000 representing no more labour than it took to print the scrip dividends. Mr. Sterne contended that if the New York Central Railway, holding, as it does, the cheapest line of rail to the West, could, by a combination, persist in getting 8 per cent on its watered capital, it imposed a tax on the people of the City and State of New York precisely in the same way as though the debts of the counties of this State and the debt of the City of New York had been improperly increased $50,000,000. He illustrated the injustice done to the City of New York by assuming that New York, in 1869, had first built its main line of rail at the enormously inflated prices then existing. In such a case New York would have been at a perpetual disadvantage with other cities that had built their railways in cheaper times. Instead of this, however, New York State did build its main line of rail during the cheap time, from 1835 to 1850, and had the additional advantage of securing for its through line of rail an enormously large local traffic contributed by cities previously built up by the canal; and had, further, a gradient far superior to that of any railway to the west in any of our sister States. All these great natural and special advantages, which should have enabled the City of New York to maintain and continue the start in commercial supremacy which the canal had given it, and which were really the property of every citizen, were absorbed by this capitalisation for the benefit of a few private individuals.

Another illustration which Mr. Sterne was accustomed to cite of the subserviency of the State Legislature to railroad influence was its placing on the New York taxpayers of half the cost of the Fourth Avenue improvement. When the Harlem Railroad was permitted to come within the limits of New York City in 1833, it was required by its charter to make a contract with the City of New York as to the conditions under which it might use the public streets. The terms which were imposed by the then city government were that the railway might have the use of Fourth Avenue on the condition that, if at any time thereafter, by the growth of the population of the City of New York, the use of the surface of the Avenue by the railroad should become dangerous to the lives and detrimental to the property interests of the citizens, then, as the city authorities might direct, the railway corporation was to viaduct or tunnel the Fourth Avenue from its then depot at the City Hall to the Harlem River at its own expense; and from time to time, if the city so directed, the railroad was to remove, in whole or in part, its tracks farther up town, and finally go to the north of the Harlem River. The terms and conditions of such removal or the building of such structure were left wholly optional with the city, and the expense wholly upon the Harlem Railroad, the city having at all times the right to determine the nature and character of the occupation which should thenceforth be permitted to exist upon the streets of New York by that corporation. No other compensation was asked from the railway corporation for the use of the great city highway, and no other compensation was paid.

For almost forty years Fourth Avenue was occupied by the railway, and then, when by the growth of the city the running of a steam surface railway along Fourth Avenue had become extremely dangerous to the lives of its inhabitants, and it had killed many people, a general demand went up for the enforcement of the contract of 1833. Thereupon the Tweed Board of Aldermen of 1871, at the instance of the Harlem Railroad, passed an ordinance requiring the present structure to be made on Fourth Avenue, and imposed one-half of the cost thereof, in defiance of the contract of 1833, upon the City of New York. But popular sentiment, largely influenced by Mr. Sterne's public utterances, was too much for even Mayor Hall, and he promptly vetoed the ordinance, which the Board did not attempt to pass over his veto. The Legislature of 1872, however, notwithstanding the fact that a great reform movement had swept over the City of New York in 1871, passed, precisely in terms of the resolution of the Tweed Aldermen, the Bill known as the Fourth Avenue Improvement Act, imposing half the expense of creating a great viaduct and roadway for the Harlem Railroad and its lessees, the New York Central and New Haven roads, upon the city. In other words, it exonerated the Harlem Railroad from the payment of about $4,000,000, under the contract of 1833, and imposed that expense upon the city.

What Mr. Sterne contended for in his advocacy of a railway commission like that which already existed in Massachusetts, was to enforce absolute publicity of, and uniformity in, accounts, publicity of contracts, the abolition of special rates, the prohibition of pooling, and a tariff of rates which, though framed by the railways, shall be advertised in advance, and not permitted to be increased or lowered except upon a long notice, and that the tariff shall be the same to every person standing upon the same plane. He was willing that the railways might make, if they pleased, a car-load a unit of freight charges, and thus draw the line between wholesale and retail, or make a further distinction, based upon the unit of a train shipment. But every shipper who ships by the car-load, or ships by the train-load, or ships but a pound, should be placed upon precisely the same footing as every other shipper who ships a train full, a car full, or a pound. In other words, the common carriers should not be permitted to build up one individual and pull down another, or build up one town and pull down another; and there should be a strict limitation of the rates of profit, based on an actual, not nominal, cost of road which should be permitted to be earned in the way of tolls upon a public highway. The Bill which he drew at the request of the Board of Trade and Transportation, and which had at that time been for four years in the hands of Committees of the Legislature, provided for the organisation of a Commission composed of three members, to whom the reports previously made to the State Engineer's Department should thereafter be made, and who, instead of being compelled to publish whatever reports the companies chose to send, could ascertain their truth by personal investigation; could compel the filing of all contracts with railroad companies, with directors, corporations, and individuals; could compel the report of all delinquencies on the part of the railways in meeting the just expectations of the public, keep them within the bounds of their chartered rights by actions at law, and report to the legislature the results of their investigations, with suggestions of such remedial measures as they might deem required. He held that publicity is the one great remedy in this country against almost all its ills, and that though not a very satisfactory nor a very quick remedy, it was one which involved the least danger in its adoption.

This line of treatment obviously suggested the query, What control could be exercised by a New York Railroad Commission over the railroads of other States; and in default of such control, how discriminations by these railroads against the commerce of New York were to be prevented? This brought up the larger question, which he admitted he would rather suggest than attempt to solve. But he left no room to doubt that he had already given careful consideration to the plan of railroad regulation which, some years later, matured into the Interstate Commerce Commission. He said that if the transportation monopoly of this country had become too powerful for the control of a single State, and held each one in bondage, the only remedy might be, as to railways, to wipe out State lines, to enlarge by implication the meaning and scope of the words "regulation of Commerce" in the constitution of the United States, and to obtain control of our great railways through national legislation. The cry that this is centralisation did not frighten him, because, whether centralisation is objectionable or not, depends on whether it is good or bad, and whether it supersedes a better or a worse system. He had long ago felt that the railway and the telegraph had made this country one nation, and that State lines were, in many instances, as much hindrances as they are promoters of true liberty. Every suggestion of governmental control of the railway interest was looked upon with disfavour because when our western farmers felt the pressure of railway mismanagement, or the pressure of taxation resulting from bonding their counties by the railway interest, they struck at it boldly but blindly, by enacting what is known as Granger legislation—legislation which, as Mr. Fink said, attempted arbitrarily to "guess at freights," and guessed wrongly. It was doubly unfortunate that the Western States should have attempted this interference with the railways on the eve of a period of financial depression which was general throughout the United States, and, indeed, throughout the world. This depression affected the railway interest precisely as it did other interests. Yet the railways have not hesitated falsely to charge that the depression was mainly due to the Potter legislation and that this was mainly responsible for the misfortunes which had overtaken the country as the result of general, commercial, and financial distress. Mr. Sterne argued that no danger could come from such a species of control as he and those working with him suggested, because of the success which had attended the appointment of a very powerful railway Commission in conservative England, and had also attended the work of the Commission appointed by Massachusetts.

The Assembly Special Committee on Railroads, usually known as the Hepburn Committee, which honestly and seriously addressed itself, as none of its predecessors had done, to providing remedies for evils, which the entire mercantile community of New York was at one with Mr. Sterne in condemning, was greatly indebted to him for a luminous exposition of the conditions of the problem with which it had to deal. He appeared before the Committee as counsel for the Chamber of Commerce and Board of Trade and Transportation, and his opening statement contained a very instructive review of the development of the railroad legislation of the State. He showed that in the early stages of these new roadways they were regarded only as improved highways; and it was in contemplation by the legislative bodies which chartered them, as well as by those who received the franchise for their operation, that the province of the company owning the road would be to build and construct this highway in the same manner as it is the province of a canal company to construct a canal; and that although they might supply motive power, the cars and the business of transportation that was to be done along this highway should be in the hands of private individuals. The early charters, both in England and in this country, contained provisions analogous to those contained in the Canal Companies' Acts, by which persons and corporations, other than the company owning the line, were permitted to run their own cars over it, on payment of certain tolls for motive power. All the early Acts contained carefully prepared schedules of both freight and passenger charges down to the minutest details. Thus, the fixing and regulating of freight, as well as passenger charges, were not only not considered confiscation or invasions of the right of property, but were necessary deductions from the fact that the railways were regarded as improved public highways, and that such conditions were, therefore, essentially proper and inseparable from the concessions when made.

Mr. Sterne made the following highly suggestive quotation from a report of a special committee of the legislature in 1843, the language of which is no less relevant to the conditions existing to-day than it was to those of twenty-five or sixty years ago :—

> Combinations and confederacy of any magnitude and extent, even among natural persons, are looked upon with suspicion, and except some good reason, not inconsistent with the public good, and based upon necessity, is apparent for such combinations and confederacies, public sentiment will not tolerate them ; and every such combination and confederacy by which the rights of others are to be and may be injuriously affected, is a misdemeanor, and punishable as such ; and the committee can see nothing which should entitle incorporated companies to greater confidence from the public or milder treatment, when they, by their officers and agents, combine for purposes which may, and to some extent must, necessarily affect injuriously the public interest as well as the rights of individuals.

The various links of the New York Central system, and the New York and Erie Railway, were first prohibited by law from carrying freight in competition with the canal, and were subsequently, by modification of their charters, compelled to pay toll to the canal fund equivalent to what the goods, had they been carried on the canal, would have paid to it. In process of time, however, this restriction was first modified, and in 1851, was removed, the railways being left free to charge on freight what they saw fit. The passenger traffic was, however, subjected from the outset to strict regulations ; and the reason why the freight traffic was not so subjected was because in the infancy of these enterprises, it was not supposed that the freight traffic would be of any value to railway corporations, but that if they carried freight at all, it would be confined to mere passenger baggage or articles of luxury which could bear the expensive tolls that it was supposed railway companies would be compelled to charge as transportation rates. It would have been regarded as the wildest sort of visionary forecasting for any one to have suggested that the time would come when all but a small fraction of the eastbound freight would be transported by rail.

Down to 1848 every railway charter was a special concession derived from the legislature in each particular case, and before the power of eminent domain could be exercised, the legislature had to be satisfied that the enterprise was one of public utility. The constitution of 1846 required the Legislature to pass general laws, under which corporations should be formed, and as the special railway legislation was a source of much corruption, it was deemed advisable to enact under this constitutional direction a General Railway Act. In 1848 an Act was passed under which railway corporations could be organised, but which still provided that, before the companies could exercise the right of eminent domain, they should obtain a special grant of authority to that effect from the

Legislature. This law remained on the statute book just two years, when a new law was passed to take its place—the General Railway Act of 1850—which, with its amendments, substantially is to-day the general law under which railways of this State have since been built, and under which all have been operated. State supervision and control as to passenger traffic were maintained by Section 28 of this Act, the amount to be charged therefor was not to exceed three cents per mile, but this law left the railways without control as to the charges to be made on freight which was rapidly growing into the more valuable and more important branch of their traffic. This was done under the impression that the law of competition which had operated so efficiently in the supply of almost all commodities and services, and which had in all other matters produced the most beneficial results, would in the case of the railways be also operative to secure the lowest possible rates of freight and the highest standard of public service. It was not foreseen that the natural law of competition cannot apply to such a case, unless railways were multiplied to such a degree that they would be too numerous to combine, since possible combination excludes competition. The fact was also lost sight of that competition could come only from an expenditure of so vast a sum of money that its investment was not likely to be made. The economic law that a service, which must be consumed on the spot, and the supply of which can be indefinitely extended by the same person or class of persons, excludes competition, was also lost sight of or was not known. Hence, at the end of almost thirty years, from the passage of the general railroad law, the people of the State were confronted with a railway problem of the first magnitude, involving not only one, but almost all questions with which other people had to deal in relation to these corporations.

The growth of the railway system of the State in those thirty years may be inferred from the fact that in 1845 New York had only 721 miles of rail; in 1876, 5550. In 1845 the capital represented by the New York railways was $18,000,000. The capital, stock, and debts in 1879 were about $500,000,000—representing an average cost of about $80,000 per mile. The aggregate gross earnings of the railroads in New York State in 1845 were about $2,000,000; their gross receipts in 1875 were about $70,000,000, and in 1879 they were very close upon $95,000,000. It was Mr. Sterne's contention that this vast power had been permitted to grow up and overshadow almost every other interest in society, without responsibility for its management to any one, except, perhaps, a very illusory responsibility to its stockholders. The State had ceased to control it; the control of the stockholders has been practically evaded. It constituted itself an *imperium in imperio*, overshadowing and overwhelming in its character; permeating every county and every town in the State; employing the best legal and administrative talent; exercising a constant influence on elections; often determining the composition of the Committees of the Legislature, and, at critical moments, dictating the personnel of the State Government. When in 1850 there were in the State of New York, with a mileage of 1230 miles, twenty-six operated railways, the average number of miles controlled by each company was about 45 miles; but, thirty years later, with almost 6000 miles of railroad, the number of roads had increased to but fifty, and half this mileage and half these companies were controlled by the Erie, the Delaware and Hudson, and the New York Central Railroads. Split up as the interest was, in its early years, without a comprehensive plan of operations, without a systematic method of conducting its affairs, there was scarcely any danger to be apprehended from our then railway system. But amalgamation is one of the laws of railway being, and this had already proceeded in New York with gigantic strides. The smaller railways, anterior to 1850, wherever they competed, were constantly at war, and low local rates were the consequence. With the era of large corporations, controlling thousands instead of hundreds of miles, the waste and destruction incident to a war of rates were so great that alliances, defensive and offensive, were entered into under the form of freight contracts, culminating in a great pooling system.

Hence, at the date of Mr. Sterne's address, even the pretence of competition was abandoned between the great railway corporations of the country. This was largely due to the discovery made by the railway corporations in regard to the limits to which a war of rates could safely be carried on against each other. Disastrous experience had demonstrated the fact that this must stop short of driving a rival line into insolvency, since an insolvent road, relieved from any present hope of dividends on stock or interest on bonds, carries freight for anything that will yield an excess over operating expenses. Therefore the New York Central enters into a combination with the Baltimore and Ohio and Pennsylvania Roads to sustain these lines against its own natural advantages, and those of New York Harbour to prevent its rivals from unloading themselves by insolvency of the responsibility of paying dividends and interest on bonds, because the moment they become insolvent they are, by reason of that fact, more formidable competitors than before. If, on the one hand, making railways insolvent by competition would compel them to take up their rails and retire from business, and if, on the other hand, so many lines could be competitively built to distributing points that their managers could not combine on the rate of tolls, the law of competition would apply in railroading as it does in most other forms of business. But as none of the results accomplished by competition in the ordinary vocations of life takes place in the case of railroads, it is clear that to attempt to apply the general law of competition to phenomena so exceptional would be, to use Mr. Sterne's phrase, an exhibition of doctrinaire pig-headedness.

He was quite willing to concede that the railway system had conferred enormous benefits upon society, of which the State of New York had enjoyed its full share; but he insisted that in our gratitude to the railway system for the benefits that it has conferred, we must not overlook the shortcomings of the men who manage railways, and who, as he claimed, prevented the commercial community from reaping as large a benefit therefrom as they were entitled to enjoy. Whatever might be the disposition to praise those great minds to whom we are indebted for the steam engine and the application thereof to locomotive purposes, Mr. Sterne insisted that we must not confound Vanderbilt with Watt, or Jay Gould with Stephenson, because at the time the men who derive their splendid incomes from railways entered the business, these enterprises had for a generation proved assured successes, and there was nothing in transportation by rail of a problematical or doubtful character.

He proposed to show the Committee that the diversion of trade from New York and the growth of rival cities was mainly due to the peculiarities of management of our railway lines, by which through rates to and from Liverpool and Western centres are almost as low as the ocean freights alone would be from New York to Liverpool or Liverpool to New York. He further proposed to prove that the railway companies of the State had shamelessly evaded the provisions as to ten per cent dividends, in the watering of their stock and the issuing of their bonds. They had, indeed, capitalised the future prosperity of the community, capitalised the supposed value of their franchises, capitalised the non-interference of the legislature and the neglect of duty on the part of the State, so as to make it almost impossible to tell what the cost of railway construction and equipment has been ; and how much, from time to time, of the amount which has gone upon the books into the construction accounts had actually been invested in the road. He also proposed to show that the whole system of railway accounts was delusive in the extreme, and was a system by which both the public and the stockholders were grossly and egregiously misled. Further, he made it part of the same indictment that these common carriers dealt unequally with localities, and individuals in the same localities, making by special contracts and special rates, unjust and special rates, unjust and oppressive distinctions, preferring one man to another, in a particular town, one locality to another, and all this quite independent of the commercial considerations of wholesale and retail, and independent of the considerations of mileage, volume of traffic, or facility of handling at termini. Another point made was that the interior of the State is discriminated against in favour of citizens of far Western States at most distant points, and that such discrimination had resulted in the decay, if not the destruction, of the agricultural interests of New York. Still another was that wherever the monopoly power exists without check, and points not touched by any competitive railways are to be found, the tariff rate is grossly unjust and oppressive. Even at such points it was charged that special rates are made of an arbitrary character, preferring one man in the same community to others, exempting one man from the general tyranny, and adding the burden of his exemption to the load already carried by his neighbours. Moreover, many of these rates were made on contracts, by which the shipper agreed not to use the canal, thus making a discrimination by special contract against the property of the State, for the protection of which the provision was inserted in all the earlier railway charters that these same corporations should not carry freight which might be carried upon the canal, or that if they did carry it, that they should pay a toll to the State equivalent to that which the canal would have earned by such carriage.

All this had a very practical relation to the conditions of railroad business as they affected the commerce of New York twenty-three years ago, and is not without relevancy to the conditions of to-day. The character of the legislation which it inspired has been already explained. Mr. Sterne had correctly apprehended the character of the abuses of railway management, for which the Interstate Commerce Law was expected to provide a remedy. The conclusions reached by the United States Senate Committee, of whose investigations that law was the product, were very much on the lines above indicated, and were substantially identical with the general tenor of the conclusions which Mr. Sterne had reached years before. In an article on "Monopolies," prepared for Lalor's *Cyclopædia of Political Science, Political Economy, and Political History of the United States*, he gives, in a very brief space, a compendious statement of the railroad problem, which, for clearness and comprehensiveness, it would be difficult to match in the copious literature of this subject. In this article Mr. Sterne points out that railway enterprises have, from their very nature, a tendency to become monopolies. The proportion of fixed charges to mere operating expenses, dependent upon the rate of business, is so great in the railway that it may almost indefinitely increase its business without any proportional increase of expenses after it has once been constructed. The existing line can, therefore, almost always outbid a competitor for business as to the rate at which it sees fit to do it. As the service is consumed at the spot where it is created, and is rendered without a relative increase of expenditure for the purpose of rendering it, there is, in the nature of things, a monopoly created, which demands the constant exercise of legal restraint.

The article goes on to show that although railways may be increased in number from given points, yet even when an active competition for a time prevails, the number of those railways will necessarily be so few that their interest to combine, as against their tendency to compete, will outweigh competition, and combination become the general result of almost all competitive railway building. After combination has been effected, the community is confronted with the fact that its service is no cheaper than it was before; that its business is done by two or three lines instead of one which previously rendered the service; that one line would have sufficed to do the whole business, and that there is a loss of capital to the community represented by the building of the second or third line. This capital is lost because the community has failed to do its duty in limiting the charges of these corporations which are enabled to earn extravagant rates of profit upon a limited business, by the growth of the community. So large is the income as compared with the investment that new capital is tempted into the same field for the purpose of dividing the business with the existing line, not because there is any necessity for the rival line, or because of the incompetency of the existing line to perform the work, but simply because of the profit made by the existing line upon its traffic. Thus, upon a given amount of business yielding, on an expenditure of $10,000,000, a million and a half a year profit, it will pay capitalists a fair rate of interest to expend another $10,000,000 for the purpose of taking $750,000 net profit out of the existing line. Mr. Sterne argued that if the community were to reduce the profit of the existing line by legal enactments, $10,000,000 would not be invested in the building of a second line, but would be available for other purposes. No service is done to the community by the building of the new line between two given points, if prices remain the same to shippers and the business is subsequently divided between the two roads, but the ten millions of capital are diverted from other employments. If in consequence of competition between the two lines the price of carriage is reduced, the community is the gainer to the extent of such reduction; but if, after the new line is built, a combination is made between the two roads to maintain prices, so that both may earn dividends upon their capital, the community has lost for other purposes the ten millions unnecessarily invested. At the time this article was published (1883) the illustration above given had ceased to be a hypothetical one, and rested on facts within the knowledge of every one who had observed the course of railway construction, railway wars, and railway combinations in the United States. If it were sought to qualify the conclusions reached by insisting that a competing line does touch, at intermediate points, territory which is not touched by the previously existing line, and thus incidental benefits are conferred, these benefits by no means outweigh the enormous waste of capital which has been occasioned by railway construction for the mere purpose of dividing business, with combination as to rates.

Two or three years before the widespread bankruptcy in 1893 illustrated the correctness of Mr. Sterne's inductions, he had pointed out, with his accustomed clearness, the way in which things were drifting. In an article in the *Forum* of September 1890, he starts out with the declaration that the wastefulness of both capital and energy, and the unnecessary costliness of accomplishing very simple ends are among the most prominent of the manifestations observed in tracing the causes and consequences of the insolvency of railways in the United States. Between 1823 and 1850, the denser centres of population east of the Mississippi River were connected by rail under a financial system which provided for primary construction by actual subscriptions and contributions in cash to capital stock. Since 1850 the building of lines at first in part and finally almost exclusively, has been carried on upon the basis of bonded indebtedness for primary construction. It is approximately correct to say that the first mortgage bonds, on the many lines of rail west of the Mississippi, represent in par value the average cash investment which originally brought these roads into existence, and that the junior mortgages and stock represent in part a capitalisation of the anticipated future development of the country and of the profits of the projectors. It can also be said that, as the actual market value which these junior liens and stock realised was often but a small percentage of their par value, the profits of the projectors were, in many instances, no more than a fair return upon the risks of the enterprise.

As Mr. Sterne goes on to show, while the road is in the hands of the original projectors and constructors, the amount of the capitalisation and its subdivision are matters of no consequence. When, however, through sales and transfers of the securities to third parties, the management of the road passes exclusively under the control of the holders of the stock, the effect of the capitalisation which makes its par value out of all proportion to any representative value originally invested in the enterprise, is soon felt. The result has been that, with the exception of the trans-continental lines subsidised by Congress, almost all the railways constructed, and operated beyond the Mississippi

River, had for over a quarter of a century been managed by the holders of securities which represented little or no value in actual construction, and upon which the railway could not pay interest or dividends. Thus the seeds of that insolvency were planted which, beginning with 1873, had produced a bountiful crop of defaulted railway securities.

Railway construction is generally undertaken when there is considerable activity in the money market, and when capital commands a high rate of interest. While the line is under construction interest is generally paid out of money raised for that very purpose. The capital which should go into the road is thereby diminished, but the credit of the company during building is maintained. After the railway is nominally finished, and particularly during the first two or three years of its operation, when many parts of it should be renewed, and when its roadbed and rolling stock should receive the benefit of a large proportion of its earnings, the road, in consequence of the necessity of meeting the requirements of its creditors, is pinched and starved as to necessary betterment. Thus, at the end of a few years, the deterioration of the line is such that there is little earning capacity left, and this condition continues until the volume of the floating debt is so great that the road must pass into the hands of a receiver, or be dismembered by sales under judgments. When accumulating debt does not produce the catastrophe, other causes do. Legislative inquiries within the States through which the line is operated, and mandatory demands on the part of the State Governments to keep the road in better order, must be answered and complied with. A year or two of bad crops intervening, the insolvency which was planted in its very organisation by the system of construction becomes open and declared.

The junior liens are the first on which default is made. Usually money enough is earned to pay interest upon the original cost of construction, represented by the first lien. Cases are rare, even under the adverse circumstances of over-competition and successive bad crops, when there is not a surplus, over mere operating expenses, sufficient to produce at least some interest for the first lien. Upon default of the payment of interest on the junior lien, its trustee institutes proceedings to foreclose; and the curious result is then brought about that, instead of a sale under foreclosure, followed by a distribution of the proceeds and a fresh start by the purchaser, with a smaller capital, a reorganisation of the railway takes place, which differs wholly from that which occurs in ordinary cases of insolvency. When a merchant or manufacturer, whose stock-in-trade or whose property is subject to mortgages, becomes insolvent, the mortgagee forecloses his lien without the slightest reference to those who may come behind him, sells out the property at the best price it will fetch, pays himself out of the proceeds in part or in full, and, if a surplus remains, turns it into court to be distributed among those whom it may concern.

In practice, this simple process of foreclosure

has been found, when applied to railway enterprises, to be destructive of vast pecuniary interests, harsh to the holders of junior liens, and inconsistent with the public right to have a highway continuously operated. Those who are subordinate to the first lien have opposed it bitterly, since they believed their expectations to be of the nature of a vested interest which should not be interfered with so long as they are willing to bear some sacrifices for the realisation of those expectations. In the endless litigations which have resulted from this contention, courts have leaned against the strict forfeiture of equities of redemption, cutting off for ever such contingent but vast pecuniary interests. An unwritten law of adjustment, depending neither upon statutory sanction nor upon direct acknowledgment in the opinions of courts, has come into existence, based upon the recognition of what may be called an ethical patriotic sentiment,—that it is a hardship to disappoint expectations resting upon the faith of the development of our common country. The absolute right of foreclosure, while admitted in theory, is made so difficult of accomplishment in practice, that it amounts to almost a denial of a contract obligation of the railway mortgagors. Therefore, there is a semi-enforced acquiescence by first mortgagees in almost every case where the junior lienors and stockholders exhibit any willingness to place, by assessment on their own holdings, the property in proper repair and efficient condition; adding thereby to the security of the first lien, and either paying or finding the defaulted interest on prior liens.

Thus, with additional capitalisation, the corporation starts afresh on a career of drawing drafts on the future, based on the expectancy that at some other time the junior liens and the stock will be lifted out of the non-interest-paying and non-dividend-paying condition. The machinery of this adjustment, for the very reason that it is not recognised by the law, and therefore is not regulated by it, is extremely wasteful and expensive.

Inasmuch as interest upon the defaulted bonds of a railroad accumulates during the time that it is in the hands of a receiver, and the road is generally improved during that period, the stockholders are invited to participate in the reorganisation, and are required, as a general rule, to pay an assessment varying from five to twenty dollars a share, for the purpose of providing first, payment of back interest on the first lien; second, an additional fund for betterments after the road passes out of the hands of the receiver; and, third, a guarantee fund for the payment of interest for a year or two. The holders of the junior liens are generally content that they have not been cut off by the prior lien; are willing to waive their back interest and take new bonds for their former ones; and, if they are not required to pay an assessment, regard themselves as having safely escaped the danger of foreclosure on simply receiving new pieces of paper for those they formerly held, and a nominal increase of the principal sum to which they may regard themselves as being ultimately entitled. Additional securities are issued to represent receivers' certificates, if there are any, and to provide for the outlays of committees and the expenses of the operations of a guarantee syndicate to take at a fixed price the securities to be issued; so that all parties in interest may feel confident that the money necessary to take the road out of the hands of the receiver will be furnished. All this produces the further anomaly in the history of insolvent railways that, instead of emerging from a condition of insolvency with a lower capitalisation, as it normally should, by reason of not having paid interest upon the original capitalisation, the railway is reorganised with a higher capitalisation, and, therefore, it would seem, with less capacity to pay interest upon its issues or securities. The apparent absurdity is explained, and the practicability of the scheme is made clear by taking into account that since 1872 the rate of interest upon prime securities has fallen from 7 to 4 per cent. This condition has aided and fostered this method of railway reorganisation, and the wastefulness of its procedure is largely hidden by the decline of interest.

When a time of stationary interest shall have arrived, the method of reorganisation which had been adopted since 1873 would, in Mr. Sterne's judgment, become impossible. The enormous expensiveness of receiverships, the fees of large numbers of committees and their counsel, the adjustment, by heavy payments, for services of all sorts during the process of reorganisation, would be a burden too onerous to be borne, when it could neither be hidden nor counterbalanced by a drooping rate of interest. Mr. Sterne held that in many States, more especially of the west and south-west, the causes and consequences of the false capitalisation of railways had been wholly misunderstood by their people, and therefore by their legislators. Laws retaliatory, instead of repressive, had been enacted; and the courts, influenced unconsciously somewhat by popular opinion, had rendered decisions of a confiscatory tendency, which neither punish the offending parties nor right any wrong, but which simply add to the difficulties and embarrassments of the confiding purchasers of railway securities in the eastern markets, who in all probability acted in entire good faith in making their purchases. The legislation of these States is based on the idea that, by the excessive capitalisation of railroad property, some wrong is done to the community through which the railway runs. Mr. Sterne had reached the conclusion that the wrong done is to the purchasers of the stocks and bonds, who are misled into the belief that the printed values have some correspondence to the actual values. He pointed out that many things are done in the world of finance which it is entirely proper to prevent before they are accomplished, but which it is entirely improper to punish after the acts have been committed if there were no law prohibiting them. A legislative body composed of wise legislators, would seek to repress, or at least to limit and control, artificial capitalisation; but a community which fails to do so by the exercise of the necessary foresight in the law authorising corporations of any character to be formed, and which indirectly obtains a benefit by the wrong-doing, has lost the right to punish for past offences of that character.

When the penalty of past recklessness came in 1893, and about one-sixth of the total mileage of the railways of the United States, between January 1893 and February 1894, passed from the control of the proprietary interest into the hands of the courts, to be administered by receivers, Mr. Sterne contributed to the *Forum* a thoughtful article under the title of "Recent Railroad Failures and their Lessons." Here was a sum of bankruptcy represented by a capitalisation of bonds and stocks of about $1,750,000,000, which was not chargeable to a long series of crop failures, nor to diminished earning capacity of the railway companies themselves from the over-construction of new lines, nor to any such general collapse of business as to make the misfortune to railway investments merely part of a general disaster overtaking the country. As Mr. Sterne pointed out, while there had been a severe and even serious depression in all departments of trade, to none had the result been so ruinous as to the railway enterprises of the United States. No sixth part of any one of the numerous commercial and industrial branches of the activity of the country had come to grief; nor, indeed, had anything akin to it occurred. Even during the great strain in the months of July, August, and September 1893, commercial credits were, as a rule, maintained, and engagements, with rare exceptions, met, and this, notwithstanding the fact that in large mercantile businesses bills fall due almost every week, and not, as in the case of railways, at long intervals and on fixed interest days, and the payment of which can, therefore, be provided for months in advance.

In examining the peculiar conditions affecting railway enterprises to which the disasters of 1893 were to be attributed, Mr. Sterne scouted the idea that they were wholly or even partially due to the Interstate Commerce Law. After showing in detail the results of the application of that law to the conduct of railway business, and citing some of the decisions of the courts which had reduced the powers of the Commission to a very small compass, Mr. Sterne put on record this opinion :—

> A Commission, therefore, consisting of reasonable and intelligent gentlemen who are not even clothed with the power of a court ;—who are without authority to make any arbitrary rulings, or of enforcing them by direct action if they should make them ; whose investigating functions have, in large proportions, been nibbled away by the judicial interpretations of the last three years ; whose decrees are disobeyed ; whose mandates have in several instances been set at defiance, and who, since the enactment of the law, have, year by year, been deprived, by decisions of the Federal courts, of almost the whole of their controlling moral force,—cannot be held responsible ; nor can the Act which it is their function to interpret and cause to be observed be held, in any but a very remote and to an almost inappreciable degree, responsible for the extraordinary calamity which has overtaken the railway enterprises of the country.

The first explanation which Mr. Sterne offers of the phase of the railway problem presented by the events of 1893 was that the railways have outgrown the ability of the community to furnish men of the high moral and intellectual order necessary for their proper administration. Most railway presidents and chairmen of boards came from the ranks of other professions, or from branches of employment in the railway, the business of which is wholly foreign to the financial administration of the road. The capacity, industry, and knowledge required for the successful handling of the budgets of railway properties which have a gross income ranging from $12,000,000 to $40,000,000 are as great as are required for the balancing of a nation's expenditures and receipts. Whether the net earnings will suffice to meet the fixed charges, not to speak of dividends on stock, is largely dependent upon a profound knowledge of the internal administration of the railway and the development of its earning power, and also to a great degree upon a prevision akin to genius, of the condition of markets and crops, and of the general financial situation. Quoting the statements that between the calamity year of 1893 and the normal year of 1892, there was a difference in the total gross earnings of 183 railroads in the United States of only $25,000,000, or less than 3 per cent deficit, Mr. Sterne remarked that even conceding that the companies which were driven into the hands of receivers showed a greater average of loss, nowhere was any such percentage shown as would account for their insolvency were the railroads conducted upon any safe and sound business principles. In all but a few cases the railway corporations of the United States literally live from hand to mouth, and have no working or reserve capital whatever. A railroad usually starts with a bonded indebtedness which, taken at par, represents a value in excess of the cost of the road, and upon which fixed interest is compulsorily payable. As interest runs on the bonds long before the completion and during the construction of the road, a part of the bonds are issued to cover payment of interest. Then, years after the road has been in operation, the original bonded indebtedness, representing ties that have rotted, rails that have been sold, cars that have been broken up, bridges and engines that have disappeared, remains a charge upon the road. For all additional capital invested, new equipment bonds are created or other obligations issued, and finally a floating debt is incurred. All these again bear interest, until the large total represents, not what the road is worth as it stands, but the whole capital which from first to last went into it, much of which has wholly disappeared, and some of which has been stolen, and therefore has no interest-earning capacity. Nothing is written off from the capital account, and no substantial part of the earnings is set aside for replacement. All this vicious financing produces the result that large floating debts are constantly accumulating, and the shock of a single bad year, affecting either income or credit, produces insolvency.

For the financial resuscitation of the railway system of the country after the calamitous events of 1893, and to prevent their recurrence, Mr.

Sterne believed that a uniform and conservative system of railway legislation, simultaneously enacted by the States of the Union and strengthened by federal legislation, was imperatively necessary. He insisted that the trustee relation of the majority of the stockholders toward the minority should be recognised and enforced. The minority should, in proportion to their strength, perpetually have a voice in the management; the crude confiscatory and communistic legislation of the Southern and Western States on these subjects should give way to scientific and conservative measures. Railways should be secured a field of operations until public necessities require the construction of additional lines, and in that field held to a strict public accountability so as to prevent oppression; reasonable facilities for the development of a fund to meet the public requirements for additional safety and accommodation to railway servants and the public. Pooling should be permitted under the control and supervision of a public body like the National Railway Commission, and the evils of receiverships and the waste of reorganisations limited, if not wholly prevented; an official accounting should be provided for, and some safeguard found against the secret accumulation of floating debt. Mr. Sterne conceded that these reforms could not be accomplished without work and sacrifice, but, as he remarked, without them no good things in this world are accomplished.

One of the latest important public utterances of Mr. Sterne on this subject was in the form of an address on "Railway Pooling," before the

Convention of the New York Board of Trade and Transportation, on October 26, 1897. He prefaced this address by the statement: "As a student of political economy; as the counsel who conducted, for the Board of Trade and Transportation and the Chamber of Commerce before the Hepburn Committee in 1879, the investigation of the abuses in the management of railways in the State of New York, which resulted in the appointment of the Railroad Commission; as the draftsman of the Railroad Commission Bill, and other remedial measures which have become implanted in the policy of the State of New York; as one who was consulted by the Cullom Senate Select Committee on Interstate Commerce in relation to the proposed congressional legislation of 1887; as counsel of Railway Corporations, and as counsel of the Interstate Commerce Commission in some of its important cases, there is scarcely a phase of the matter involved in the question whether pools or division of traffic agreements should be allowed or not, that has not in some way or another been presented to my mind." He said that he had been a witness to the condition of things brought about in the State of New York between 1876 and 1878, by the fierce railway war which then prevailed. A rate was made on flour to the Minneapolis miller without a corresponding reduction on the carriage of grain from the West to the miller of Rochester and Black Rock, so that the mills of the State of New York, with a single exception which enjoyed the benefit of a special rate, were as effectually shut out from the market as though they had been destroyed by the torch of the incendiary. Goods were carried to Boston from the West at lower rates than they were carried to New York, and goods were shipped to Boston and carried from Boston to the West at lower rates than they were carried from New York. The New York Central Railroad had practically no rate for local traffic within the State of New York. Every rate, on application, was made special, and was made one rate to one man and another rate to another man, depending upon the caprice, friendliness, or sense of propriety of the local traffic manager. It was then boldly claimed, and the claim was acted upon, that the business of railroading was a private enterprise, with which the State had no concern. As the result of the investigation instituted in 1879, and lasting over nine months, the duty of conducting which devolved on Mr. Sterne, there was a complete reversal effected of the legislation which had hitherto prevailed in the State, and railway managers themselves were educated as to their true interests and duties in the performance of their function, by being enabled to grasp the idea that their interests and duties were harmonious.

When the United States Congress in 1887 took up the subject of regulating the commerce which could not come within the purview of each State, the question of permitting or prohibiting pooling was actually mooted. Mr. Sterne then advised that pooling should be permitted under strict Governmental supervision; that the absence of any arrangement for the maintenance of rates resulted in a fluctuation and inequality of railway charges far more injurious to the community than the slight increase of rates due to their being kept uniform. In other words, his position was that the rates of railroad transportation resemble taxation, in this respect, that even a higher rate of taxes is better for a community than irregular, partial, and preferential taxation, although the average rate be lower. It was therefore his conviction that the inhibition upon pooling in the Interstate Commerce Act, as passed by Congress in 1887, was a mistake, and that the inferential inhibition against agreements to preserve rates in the anti-trust legislation of 1890, as interpreted by the supreme court, was almost a misfortune. He held that in lieu thereof any arrangement between railroad corporations looking to the maintenance of the rates reported to the Commission, so long as those rates were in themselves reasonable, should have been favoured on the condition that the Interstate Commerce Commission should pass judicially upon any such arrangement before it became effective, and that for the purpose of informing the Commission, and of enabling it to pass with intelligence upon the pooling agreement, the schedule of rates agreed upon be simultaneously subject to its scrutiny and acceptance. Mr. Sterne pointed out that it is not of the slightest public consequence, so long as the railway company itself agrees to the terms, whether a particular railway shall have 10, 15, or 20 per cent of a given total of through traffic. It seemed to him, therefore, that the scrutiny of the Commission should be devoted wholly to the rate and the other public matters which are the result of the pool, and that the Commission's approval or disapproval should be to the questions thus submitted. He believed it to be also reasonable that the approval or disapproval should not be left as a finality to the Commission, but should be subject to review by the Appellate Divisions of the United States Circuit Courts and by the Supreme Court of the United States.

In his article in the *Forum* of March 1894 Mr. Sterne touched a point likely to become of growing interest, and on which the following correspondence, from which names are, for obvious reasons, omitted, throws an interesting light :—

I have read with much interest your article in the March *Forum* on "Recent Railroad Failures and their Lessons."

I regret that you saw fit to give the weight of your name to accusations against trust companies as trustees under corporate mortgages, and I cannot allow such accusations as you have made to go by without entering my personal protest against them.

It is true that my association with the —— Trust Company may, in your opinion, disqualify me for exercising independent judgment in such a matter. Nevertheless, I think I am capable of forming an opinion free from interested motives.

When you say that "the trustee has no personal sense of responsibility, and no personal character for zeal and discretion to maintain towards his *cestuis que trustent*, the bondholders," you are, I think, gravely in error. When you charge the trust companies with being mere instruments of the railroad companies, and their managers controlled by a desire to derive profitable business from the railroad companies, you are, so far as the —— Trust

Company is concerned, unjust, and I deny the truth of the statement. In my association with Mr. —— and his company, I have never in a single instance known of their yielding to such influences as those to which you refer. On the contrary, I have always observed an eagerness to do everything possible for the bondholders without reference to the wishes and desires of the people from whom the business came. Wherever in the opinion of the counsel for the trust company it was necessary or proper for the trustee to take any action for the protection of the bondholders it has been invariably taken, and the motive attributed by you to the officers of these companies, viz. the desire not to offend the concentrated power from whence their profitable business is derived, has never been permitted to influence the decision in the slightest degree.

In all the cases where we have had occasion to recommend to a court the appointment of a receiver we have never, in my recollection, asked the court to appoint any receiver except upon the recommendation of bondholders, and usually of a majority of the bondholders, and I do not remember to have had any complaint made of us or our action in that respect. It is strange that in the course of more than ten years of very active foreclosure business there has never been any complaint of the —— Trust Company in the matter of the appointment of receivers, if as you say the rule is that "trust companies have special, and sometimes sinister, and oftentimes conflicting interests, and are administered by persons in sympathy with the railway officials."

The officers and managers of our trust companies here are among the best of our citizens, and I think they have reputations to maintain, and a personal responsibility with reference to their trusts.

I do not mean to say that the —— Trust Company has always administered its trust to the entire satisfaction of every bondholder. In the battle between minorities and majorities it has sometimes happened that the

Trust Company has been compelled to take sides—sometimes with the majority against a factious minority, sometimes with the minority against an oppressive majority—but their decision in this respect has always been in favour of what they conscientiously believed to be right, proper, and just, and not that which would be merely profitable in a pecuniary sense.

You ask: "Who has ever heard of any one of these trust companies calling the bondholders together to prevent dishonesty, waste, and mismanagement before their result in the shape of a default of interest was upon them?" You know as well as I do that the trusts are those which are devolved upon the trustees under corporate mortgages in the usual form. The trustees are not appointed to prevent dishonesty or mismanagement. In order to charge upon them the duty of watching over all the mortgaged properties with an eye to the prevention of any mismanagement, they should certainly be provided with some means of discharging such a function. The payment of a trustee of 50 cents or 1 dollar a bond for certifying is not expected to furnish a fund to enable them to employ experts and detectives to examine their mortgage properties from time to time, and I never before heard that any reasonable person entertained any expectation that they would perform that duty. Railroad managers, as a rule, do not exhibit their dishonesty, waste, and mismanagement in a very public way, and to constitute the trustees under mortgages a superintending body to insure honesty, economy, and proper management in railways, would be essentially to vary their sphere and duty from that which now prevails. It would be more pertinent to ask whether there was ever a case where any one called the attention of a trustee to dishonesty, waste, and mismanagement, and called upon the trustee to take proper steps to prevent it, where the trustee refused to do so.

You railway attorneys who draw these mortgages limit the powers of the trustee in every way possible.

You give them a mere naked mortgage title, and hem them in by every possible restriction. You tie them down so that they can come into court only under prescribed conditions and in fixed cases. You are, as other railway attorneys are, vigorous in opposing any action of the trustee except where the letter of the contract authorises the proceeding. But no bondholder, to my recollection, has ever complained that the —— Trust Company refused to act when it should have acted.

There are many things in your article which meet with my cordial approval, and some of the evils of which you complain are undoubtedly great evils which should be corrected. I believe that there should be legislation which would prohibit the appointment of any person as receiver who was connected with the insolvent company as an officer, director, or otherwise; but in your strictures upon trust companies as trustees I think you have gone altogether too far, and I cannot refrain from expressing my regret at what you have done.—Yours very truly.

To which Mr. Sterne replied—

My dear Mr. —— I suppose I must allow myself to be quite seriously criticised for the pleasure of having your cordial approval of the many things in my article; but lift yourself to an elevation as much above the interests of the Trust Companies as I do above the administration of railways to get at a proper point of view. I admit that your Trust Company, the ——, and our mutual friend Mr. ——, and all the officers, are as free as circumstances will permit from all the evils of Trust Company administration or railway trusteeship, and if it had been possible to make a special reference of exemption to them or it, and one or two other companies in New York City, I would have done so. But I have had an experience with so many, whom I could not single out by name, which justifies every word of my criticism; and you may remember one or two incidents which bear out, to your own personal knowledge, the strictures that I made in my article.

My first impulse after receiving your letter was to go over and have a talk with you, but I shall probably follow this letter within a few hours.

The railway situation is one to which every right-thinking man connected with the administration, directly or indirectly, of those great properties should give some thought in the way of correcting the evils attending their administration. It is becoming a scandal of great magnitude, and which, for your own credit in the eyes of the world, we should rectify. If you were not so busy and hampered by interests, you would probably be able to make a very important contribution towards our enlightenment. As you forego doing so, you must let us lesser lights stumble along as best we can, and take the good that we can offer with the mistakes which we will inevitably make; but always believe me to be both sincere and fearless—you might regard me perhaps as reckless—in my willingness to oppose the wrongs I see, and, at all events, always believe in my esteem for you and those that surround you in your own office and the office of your leading client, the —— Trust Company.—Ever yours faithfully, SIMON STERNE.

CHAPTER VII

CORPORATIONS AND CORPORATE RESPONSIBILITY

MR. STERNE had ample opportunity to study the relations between the modern corporation and the community on all its sides. In a lecture delivered in 1880, he considers "The Corporation: its Benefits, its Evils; as Benefactor, as Monopolist." In this discourse he claimed that the corporation had neither beginning of years nor end of days. It is not a growth of this century, nor even of modern civilisation. It is older than what is known as ancient civilisation. It even ante-dates written history. As each corporation has, as lawyers define it, perpetual existence, aggregate corporations will, in all probability, be the last thing to be frozen to death when the earth shall have cooled, and the sun no longer give us heat enough to maintain animal and vegetable life.

To the corporation as it exists to-day he assigned a rôle essentially beneficent. The timidity of capital is proverbial; and in all probability nothing short of the limited liability offered by the shareholding interest could have secured the necessary funds to realise for practical purposes the mechanical and chemical discoveries and inventions which within the past century have changed the relations of peoples toward each other, and stimulated the production of wealth a hundred-fold. If, in each case, the application of the discovery and the experiments necessary to test it would have imposed an unlimited liability, it is extremely doubtful whether capitalists would have been found to risk their all upon ventures which, in their early stages, must have appeared to the cautious investor as hopelessly chimerical. It was only by the tempting bait of unlimited profits, with a positive limitation of liability, that capital could be allured from safe ground to embark upon a dangerous sea of uncertainty and experiment, which, however, turned out more fruitful of wealth than all the sources of profit from which it was tempted. Taking into consideration the enormous profits which have been derived from the application of steam, of electricity, of gas, from the power-loom, from the Whitney gin, and from thousands of appliances owned and operated by corporations; the opening up of mines, the development of mines, an industry so subject to fluctuations and conditions of uncertainty, that upon a large scale it is scarcely ever found in the hands of private individuals. Mr. Sterne thought it safe to say that the direct and immediate economical advantages of limited liability have been largely in excess of the losses which have come in its train.

The debit side of the account of the joint stock corporations, from an economical point of view, is the tendency to bring upon us recurring financial crises. The share is not only a legally recognised divisible proportion of a whole, but it is a draft upon the future expectations and hopes of the individuals who organised the enterprise. It is in concrete form a discounting of the future, and represents in an aggregate sum the expectations of a generation. A mining enterprise is started, or a new invention is made, which promises success, lures capital to secure its development; and the capital stock of such an organisation is very likely to represent not merely the present value, but the anticipations of the projectors as to its prospective value. Thus an enormous quantity of fictitious representatives of value are created, quite out of proportion to actually available assets, and having for their foundation no other basis than human hopes. When these enterprises are successful, and these hopes are in a fair way of being realised, we have what is called a time of inflation. A speculative feeling pervades the community, and this large shareholding interest affords an indicator as a thermometer does of the weather, of the existence of such a feeling, but, unlike the thermometer, to some degree stimulates it. Large fortunes are made not because any particular share has increased in value, but because the expectations indulged in yesterday by a few are supposed to-day by many to be nearer realisation. And therefore the difference may, and frequently does, represent an actual market value in stocks, based on hopes, out of which actual fortunes are made. Of course, since it is possible to realise fortunes on the Stock Exchange from the different grades of hopefulness and confidence that may exist in the human breast from time to time, there must be a corresponding possibility of loss and ruin arising from depression of spirits and distrust which may, for the time being, pervade the community. And yet the actual earnings or property represented by the shares which, in the one case, secure fortune's smiles, and in the other bring penury and ruin, may not in the least have changed in intrinsic value.

So long as the law, in the ordinary and industrial pursuits of society, simply allows people to combine and to limit their liability by giving adequate notice of their intention to do so, and the function and activity of the combination do not partake of a monopoly character, or do not attach themselves to what are substantially State functions, there can be but little injury or danger, other than that adverted to, latent in such a combination. In such a case the function of the State is properly limited to insisting on the utmost publicity of financial administration, in order to protect the shareholding interest as much as possible from being exploited by the directors. When the function to be performed by the corporation partakes of a public character, is one that involves the exercise of the right of eminent domain, or is affected by a public interest, either because of the large capital necessary for the construction of the work or because the locality of the corporation or the kind of business in which it is engaged partakes of a monopoly character, then such a corporation becomes a child of the State. That is to say, in such a case, the State exercises part of its duties through the instrumentality of a corporation, inviting private capital to aid in the performance of these functions on the promise of giving to such capital the whole or the greater part of the profits derived therefrom. In such a case the supervision and control of the State should be obligatory, because their absence leads to complications and disturbances of a most dangerous character.

Whenever the Government in inviting capital to perform what substantially is its own function, acts under the belief that, in delegating its right to exercise eminent domain for the purpose of creating these corporations or companies, it creates and stimulates competition contemporaneously with their endowment, it sooner or later discovers that such competition does not prevail; that the absence of personal responsibility to the people for the exercise of quasi-governmental power by these corporations leads to tyranny, and that badly as the governmental machinery may work, it is better to accept its function than the more perfect machinery, but diminished personal responsibility of the substituted corporate enterprise. Eight years later, Mr. Sterne became painfully aware of the extent to which this tyranny might be carried, and we find him asking in the *Railway and Corporation Law Journal* of November 17, 1888: "Is it not the experience of every practising lawyer that, when he is brought in contact with one of the great combinations of capital and its doings, when he sees the reckless manner in which it deals with the stockholding interest, the artifices connected with its administration, and the misrepresentations and positive frauds in relation to such administration, coupled with the entire immunity from responsibility accompanying the building up of huge fortunes by manipulation of values and their representatives by unscrupulous but extraordinarily gifted individuals, that the weapons of the law break down when directed against or brought in conflict with these novel devices of capital to escape legal responsibility, which absorbs, without rendering a compensating service, a vast proportion of other people's goods?" He cited as examples the manner in which the guaranty of the Manhattan Elevated Railroad Company to pay 8 per cent on the stock of the Metropolitan Elevated Railroad was defiantly broken, and this breach maintained; the decisions which have upheld the absorption of rival lines by the Western Union Telegraph Company in defiance of limitations on corporate authority and in defiance of the general laws of the State, and the facilities which have been afforded to street, steam, and cable railway companies, in disregard of constitutional limitations, to lay tracks and confiscate private easements.

Mr. Sterne went on to ask whether it was not true that a stock manipulator and manufacturer of the United States may put out issues of securities of all kinds by artfully contrived representations publicly made through others, of expectations of continued earnings, and after the investments are made, take the very opposite position, showing that the earnings which had been represented as made, were illusory, that rival lines made the earnings of the same amount impossible, and that the stocks and bonds were issued upon expectation that had proved false, and were substantially over-issues as compared with the amount that could be realised out of the property, and then he himself become the largest purchaser at the low prices, after having sold at the highest, and reorganised companies thus wrecked, upon a new basis of interest bearing securities lower than those which had been issued by himself and his coadjutors a few years before, making money by inflation, making money by ruining the inflated property, and again making money under reorganisation, all engineered and manipulated by himself under the cover and by means of the law. That so monstrous a transaction, yielding enormous sums of money to its projectors and resulting in disastrous losses to the investor, could succeed, and yet that the law should be powerless to attach thereto a well-defined responsibility by way of restitution, could only, in Mr. Sterne's judgment, arise from the fact that the courts were acting on a new legal maxim (which he described as "de maximis non curat lex") without knowing it. The very magnitude of the transaction makes the individual as weak and powerless against the perpetrators as he is against the Government. He cannot assert his rights without spending a sum larger than that of which he has been deprived. When he does get a hearing, his case comes under one of the exceptions to the general principles of law or equity on which he relies, and which, therefore, ceases to make the case at bar applicable to such a manipulating potentate, and he finally abandons his case disheartened, or gets an adverse decision in the court of last resort on a question of practice. Or, if the courts grapple with the question on its merits, they find themselves lost and amazed by the financial difficulties, and fail to apply to so intricate and complex a situation the plain principles of law and equity, so that we have an illustration that when a fraud or wrong takes on colossal proportions in figures, the litigant has no remedy.

Mr. Sterne gave two reasons why the law has no remedy in such cases : (1) The intelligence of our administrators of the law is not equal to the intelligence of our leading bankers and railway magnates. The industrial development of this age has been far beyond the juridical development. The law has made in recent years no such progress as every useful art and science has made. The consequence is that the applied arts and sciences have attracted into their field the strongest and best intellects of the community, and they are better equipped than the administrators of the law in ingenuity and intellectual alertness. Nimbleness of mind is more readily met with in the bankers' and railway presidents' rooms than on the appellate benches of the courts of the land. There is learning on the one hand, and a preternaturally developed instinct of gain and the seizing of opportunity on the other. The slower-footed animal, therefore, cannot overtake the fleeter organism. Before the nineteenth century the government and the law had absorbed the strongest intellects of the community. The nineteenth century widened the field of activity for intellect, and offered greater attractions and more profitable results in directions other than the law or government. Whatever of strength there is in the law is retained by the stronger interest to be turned against the rest of the community. The law itself becomes thereby an element of oppression, instead of the benevolent mother of Justice. (2) The law in the machinery of formation has not kept pace with the general development of the community. Our law-making is still in the colonial period. There is no division of public from local law. No notice is given of local laws to those interested in their passage or rejection, and at the end of each year Acts are either purchased or smuggled through the legislative bodies without any knowledge on the part of the many affected thereby, and unfortunately without any responsibility being attached to such loose and slipshod legislation by the political party in power.

Four years later, in the course of a philosophic examination into the general question of the responsibility of the State to see to it that monopolies created through its agency do not become oppressive, Mr. Sterne remarked that an adherent, however blind, of the *laissez-faire* doctrine, cannot insist that the State should let alone monopolies created by law. He held it to be the constant duty of the law-making power to circumscribe the special organisms which it calls into being. Where a business has grown to such proportions in the hands of certain individuals or of a combination of individuals, that they can crush out competition by losses deliberately incurred by them, and which they can easily bear by reason of their enormous accumulation of capital, and which, therefore, drives out of business those who, though equally capable of rendering the service of supplying the commodity, are incapable of bearing the losses thus imposed, a problem is presented which has not yet been solved by modern society. He instanced the Standard Oil combination as the most flagrant and the most conspicuous instance of this in the country. Originally, a corporation with a capital not larger than that of many of its competitors, its managers, by securing special freight rates from the great trunk lines to the seaboard for their crude petroleum and the refined article, obtained so great an advantage over their competitors that they had, on the one hand, the producer in their toils, and, on the other, so effectually destroyed their rivals in the business of refining, that 90 per cent of that business was engrossed and monopolised by the combination. Mr. Sterne declared it to be idle, because it is wide of the truth, to say that they were either superior refiners or superior producers. They were simply less scrupulous or more alert than their neighbours in making combinations with the railways, who, in violation of all proper business interests connected with transportation, and of their duty to the State, entered into a compact to deprive of a market others equally favourably situated for production and refining. The result was that the Standard Oil Company could purchase other refineries at any price they saw fit to pay, and in many cases purchased them simply to dismantle them and curtail production. When, by such methods, the combination became so powerful as to control a capital variously estimated from ten to twenty millions of dollars, they openly dictated terms to the railways with which they had previously been in collusive combination, and obtained exclusive control over their transportation facilities from the producing points to the seaboard. Not content with that condition of affairs, they determined to abandon the railways altogether and constructed their own pipe lines to tide water. Here, then, is an industrial monopoly not created by law, which has no legal sanction for its performances or exaction, but which, nevertheless, operates precisely in the same manner as though a law had been passed placing the consumers of oil in their possession, to be taxed at their own will, requiring the railway companies to charge them only such rates as they see fit to pay, prohibiting other people from engaging in the same business, and dismantling and destroying the works of those already engaged in it. Were such a law proposed to be enacted, the community would cry out that it was monstrous, far exceeding, in tyrannical outrage upon the community, anything ever attempted by the Tudors. Yet in this free country, where all trades and occupations are supposed to be open to competition, this mischievous result has been achieved. Mr. Sterne insisted that it was clearly the duty of the law-maker, under the principle of *salus populi suprema lex*, to insist that it is no part of the law of competition that men shall use their capital deliberately to ruin other people, and the legislator should prevent the existence of conditions which enable such unfair advantages to be obtained, to check them when they are likely to be obtained, and to undo the mischief if it has been created by reason of the neglect of the law-maker. The State has a right to step in, and does step in, to protect all classes of the community who are supposed not to deal on equal terms with those with whom they are thrown in contact; clients as against lawyers, wards as against their trustees, infants as against persons of full age. Therefore some kind of protection was, in his judgment, due to industries which are likely to be subjected to an influence so baneful and sinister as the one which has been exercised by the Standard Oil Company.

It is needless to say that the general question of the relation of corporations to the community broadened very considerably in the fifteen years between 1883 and 1898. In an address delivered early in the latter year before the Academy of Political Science, Mr. Sterne deals with the economic aspects of corporate organisations and trade combinations in a more comprehensive way than the subject demanded at the date of the productions above summarised. He begins this address by assuming that the trade combinations upon which light was sought through the medium of the discussion to which his paper was a contribution, were the combinations familiarly known as trusts. He regarded the question as so intricate, and in many of its manifestations so novel, that all which could be put forth at the present day in regard to it are the mere acorns of thought from which trees of knowledge might grow, but no judgment which might be considered as conclusive could be ventured upon even by the most competent economists. It was his function to present the view of one who in the storm and stress of practical life had been compelled to modify a great many of the ideas which he had imbibed from the earlier economists, and who probably looked at the question from a different standpoint than the closet or academic economist. After quoting the language of one of the Justices of the Supreme Court in the prevailing opinion in the case of the *United States* against the *Trans-Missouri Freight Association*, in which occurs the following passage: —"It is wholly different, however, when such changes are effected by a combination of capital whose purpose in combining is to control the production or manufacture of any particular article in the market, and by such control dictate the price at which the article can be sold, the effect being to drive out of business all the small dealers in the commodity, and to render the public subject to the decision of the combination as to what price shall be paid for the article,"—Mr. Sterne went on to ask whether all which we call civilisation had not been effected by just this sort of combination by capital in its lesser forms, and accompanied by the sacrifice of independence on the part of individuals who make of themselves subordinates in the army of production, of government, or of distribution?

When the steam-power loom was established in

an industrial district, away went the independence of every home-industry weaver, and he had either to go to the workhouse or into the readjusted factory industrial conditions. All these sturdy independent weavers were, to use the language of the Justice of the Supreme Court, "independent business men, heads of their establishments small though they might be; and they were changed into mere servants or agents of a combination for selling the commodity which they once dealt in or manufactured, having no voice in shaping the business policy of the company, and bound to obey orders issued by others." Mr. Sterne argued that every human being who works labours for selfish ends, for the gratification of his individual desires; he produces, however, a general good. A trade combination which lessens the cost of production may wish to dictate prices, but inasmuch as it cannot, by any possibility, hide from the community the profits it makes, it tempts so much new capital in the line of production which it seeks to control, that it soon discovers it has lessened the cost of production for the benefit of others, and has failed to reap the profit which it expected to derive therefrom, and that thus but a small part of the saving which it has occasioned remains in its hands. But if trade combinations produce a sum of good overbalancing their evil, the question arises, Why has the law from time immemorial forbidden and punished with great severity, forestalling, engrossing, and combinations to control the markets for the prime necessaries of life? The answer is, That when the means of communication between the different parts of a country were so primitive that it was possible for famine to prevail in some districts, while in others there was great abundance, it became evident that if the individual capitalists, or a combination of capitalists, were permitted to purchase and withhold the necessaries of life in one part of the land, relief might not come from another part before people had reached the point of starvation. In these remote times of primitive development of the ways and means of intercommunication, the laws that were aimed against efforts to monopolise the necessities of life were just and wisely protective. Now, however, if a capitalist or combination of capitalists were to purchase every bushel of wheat and other cereals raised in a given district, that district would in a short time be glutted with food supplies from the outside until the price was restored to, if not reduced below, its natural point. Mr. Sterne held that every modern effort of a trade combination to control the price of a primary article of food had failed to produce a dearth of the article, and to illustrate his point, he recalled a conversation which he had with a famous speculator who, some time in the seventies, made an effort to corner the wheat market. In answer to a request for an opinion as to the probability of success, Mr. Sterne said that the attempt must inevitably fail: First, because he could not corner the wheat market of the world, and that, therefore, from every part of the globe wheat would be rushed in to supply the demand, and that he must either buy it or it would deluge the market, and thus depress the price below its natural limit; second, because any point beyond a normal price for wheat would bring into use substituted articles of food; that the withholding from the market of a food stuff did not operate in the same manner as the withholding from the market of an article of merchandise suitable for shelter or clothing. In the latter case the stock in use is exhausted, and must sooner or later be replenished. In the case of food the hunger that is unfed in one day does not increase the capacity for consumption on the following day, nor intensify the consumption at the end of the week or the end of the month. When there is an increase of supply, therefore, of cereals by importation, it adds to a stock which in a very short time will be larger than the demand can take up; hence there is a natural limitation which is generally lost sight of in all efforts for the cornering of a food supply.

It is argued that the trusts have a tendency to dismantle and put out of use industrial establishments and large quantities of machinery, and thereby lessen the opportunity for employment. To this Mr. Sterne replies that, when an amount of capital has by competition gone into a business in excess of that which could be profitably employed therein, there is continuing waste in its employment. When the New York Central Company acquired the West Shore Railroad, which was constructed merely for the purpose of dividing an existing business already adequately performed, had it felt satisfied that the whole of the business which was done by the West Shore could safely and satisfactorily have been done on the New York Central, what loss would there have been to the community if the rails had been taken up and sold for scrap iron, the ties removed, and the land returned to farming purposes? There would have been greater economy in the management, there would have been a great saving in repairs, and a still greater saving in the large *personnel* necessary for the carrying on the West Shore's business. If it be objected that the constant tendency of monopoly is to throw a large number of persons out of employment, the answer is that if any given result can be obtained by the employment of 200 persons instead of 400, assuming that the 200 can produce as much as the 400 had produced before, it is elementary political economy to find a positive gain to society in setting free the labour of 200 men who had been employed in excess of those who were essential for the accomplishment of a given purpose. Mr. Sterne admitted that it was a grave defect of our social organisation that no method had yet been devised by which, when such an improvement in machinery or economy in the methods of doing business takes place, those who have control of the machinery of these improvements can be required to make in some form direct compensation to those who are thrown out of employment, or are otherwise made to suffer for the general weal. It was Mr. Sterne's opinion that some general public insurance fund should be provided for those who must bear the hardship of the first shock of a change which inures, in the long run, for the general benefit.

The English law which forbade engrossing, and

trade combinations, was, at all events, consistent; because, in the first place, it fixed a price at which commodities were to be sold, and logically, made any contract to make a higher price unlawful; and, in the second place, it forbade all combinations of working-men to raise the price of their labour by any understanding or agreement among themselves. The modern law against trusts is accompanied by the securing of absolute freedom of combination among working-men to raise their wages, and entire exemption from the operation of the harsh statutes which formerly forbade such action. Mr. Sterne took the position, that so long as working-men are free to combine to raise the price of their labour, whether such increase is justified by the conditions of trade or not, trade combinations to raise, if possible, the price of commodities, or by any united action to resist the demands of the trade unions, should be permitted to the employer, and that, too, in the interest of the working-men themselves. He argued that all legislation which is aimed against the higher law of progress in a community must necessarily be abortive, and either become a dead letter or invite evasions of all conceivable kinds. We have for twenty years endeavoured to prevent trade combinations and trusts, but they still exist and flourish. It must, therefore, be evident that this kind of legislation lacks the essential element of being the crystallised form and embodiment of the most enlightened public opinion. If it be true that these failures to make the law workable are so uniform or so constant, it shows that the combinations are the fruits of civilisation and progress, and cannot be crushed, but can only be temporarily checked by these efforts to interpose legal clogs to their development.

Returning to this aspect of the subject, Mr. Sterne said that when a powerful tendency of centralisation of both capital and labour has, for a considerable period, set in, there is unquestionably underneath it a justification which cannot be affected by demagogical legislation nor have its currents diverted either by law or abuse. Within a period of time in the recollection of men of advanced middle life, the very simple art of obtaining place and power through party and political activity has developed into a scientific method which has given the control of government into the hands of a politician class which is equally potent in both the leading party organisations. The differentiation of employment has, in part, been responsible for the creation of this class. In part, the movement which created it has partaken of the general spirit of centralisation of power. The consequence has been that political guilds have been formed governed by an unwritten law which excludes from all participation in the work of Government such as are not included in their membership. The intrusion of a stranger is looked on with jealousy, and treated with a feeling of antagonism akin to that which would have been displayed in the Middle Ages if a shoemaker, a tailor, or a cooper had attempted to establish himself for the earning of an independent livelihood without passing through his trade-guild. These organisations have, in the course of a generation, perceptibly modified, and will, if unchecked, change in another fifty years the nature of our Government. Simultaneously with the formation of these politician guilds in their modern form, came a perception of the pecuniary value of legislation as a source of income to the politician. For, while the civil service in the executive department of the Government has been reformed, so as to loosen the hold of the politicians, they still have an undisputed control of the legislative departments of the Government, and their power to exploit in full the pecuniary advantages which these afford has been left untouched by the reformer. It seems probable that the politician class has found more than ample compensation for what it has lost to the people on the executive side of civil service reform, in what it has gained on the legislative side of its influence by the development and exploitation of this new form of industry. While at no period in the political history of the United States has there been such a general awakening as within the last twenty-five years on the intellectual side of politics, as exhibited by the activity on the part of the colleges in increasing their faculties capable of dealing with the political and economic questions which press for solution, and by the large number of students who avail themselves of the advantages of these studies, there had not been during the history of the United States so manifest and sinister a development of concentration of power in the hands of politicians, resulting in what is known as "boss rule."

Mr. Sterne was profoundly impressed with the idea that the creation of this new oligarchy operating through the forms of free institutions, constitutes a menace to capital of very threatening proportions, and, in somewhat lesser degree, to labour. Against this power there is for the present in sight but one peaceful and powerful counterforce, and that is, the concentration of capital in the form of trusts or other combinations, creating co-ordinate powers sufficient to hold such a government by bossism in check. Every effort to weaken this concentration of capital adds new strength to boss rule. It was, therefore, the conclusion reached by Mr. Sterne that in view of this new menace to thrift, it was dangerous to encourage the prevailing tendency toward anti-trust legislation and the enforcement of laws against all forms of combination of capital. Considering that the tendency toward concentration of political effort and the wielding of political power through persons having no official responsibility to the people is constantly becoming more accentuated, all weakening of capital under such circumstances tends to make it a prey to those who are living, under the guise of taking part in the government, upon the earnings of the producers of things useful to the community. Therefore, without concentration of capital so great as to make it capable of resisting with like force the tendency of the politician class, the only industry in which, in process of time, large fortunes could be made and accumulated would be the industry of the politician.

This later view of the question of corporate

responsibility may seem somewhat in conflict with that recorded fifteen years before, but the apparent contradiction is due rather to the way in which the subject is approached and the point from which it is regarded, than to any radical change of opinion on the subject. Mr. Sterne was too honest and courageous a seeker after truth to be specially careful about maintaining a reputation for uniform consistency of opinion. But on one point he is uncompromisingly consistent in his views of corporate responsibility, and that is the obligation of trusteeship devolving upon those who control a majority of the stock of any corporation. He achieved a somewhat remarkable professional triumph in the opinion of the Court of Appeals delivered in favour of his contention, and strictly in harmony with his views in the case of the New York and Northern Railway Company and certain appellants from judgments of the lower courts for whom he acted as counsel, and on whose behalf he found occasion to urge certain principles of corporate trusteeship which had been allowed to fall into neglect. The original action was brought to foreclose a second mortgage upon the property of the New York and Northern Railway Company made by it and given to the trustees—the Farmers' Loan and Trust Company—to secure the payment of second mortgage bonds issued by that Company to the amount of $3,200,000. The appellants being holders of a minority of the Company's stock protested against this foreclosure on the following among other grounds:—That the action was brought in pursuance of an unlawful plan and combination by and between the New York Central and Hudson River Railroad Company and others acting for it, to render the stock of the New York and Northern Railway Company valueless, and to secure its property; that in order to carry this plan into effect, the New York Central Company purchased a large number of the second mortgage bonds and a majority of the stock of the New York and Northern, thereby acquiring control of its management; that the affairs of the New York and Northern were so conducted by the directors and officers appointed in the interest of the New York Central that the obligations of the former Company could not be met, nor the default on the second mortgage bonds made good.

In the trial court the appellants offered evidence to show the character, extent, and purpose of the alleged mismanagement by the Central Company of the property of the New York and Northern, but the Court excluded all such evidence as immaterial and irrelevant. The General Term affirmed the position taken by the Special Term, which was, briefly, that all that was requisite for the plaintiff Trust Company to prove in suing for foreclosure was the making of the mortgage, its record, the issue of the bonds, the default, the acquisition of the property, the absence of other legal proceedings, and the amount due. In this, the Court of Appeals, in an opinion written by Justice Martin, held that the Courts below were in error. Before passing on the rulings made by the trial Court, the Appellate Court discussed the question whether a corporation, purchasing a majority of the stock of another corporation, may thus obtain control of its affairs, cause it to divert the income from its business, or to refuse business which would enable it to pay the interest for which it was in default, and then institute an action in equity to enforce its obligations for the purpose of obtaining control of its property at less than its value, to the manifest injury of the minority stockholders. Justice Martin and his associates held that with these facts established, a court of equity would not lend its aid to such a stockholder by enforcing the mortgage and decreeing a foreclosure and sale of the mortgaged property, at its request, in its behalf, and to accomplish such a purpose.

The salutary rule was laid down by the Court that where, as in this case, a majority of the stock is owned by a corporation or a combination of individuals, and it assumes the control of another company's business and affairs through its control of the officers and directors of the corporation, it becomes, for all practical purposes, the corporation of which it holds a majority of the stock, and assumes the same trust relation toward the minority stockholders that a corporation itself usually bears to its stockholders. It is a well-settled principle, however, much disregarded in practice, that the law requires of the majority of the stockholders the utmost good faith in their control and management of the corporation as regards the minority, and that in this respect the majority stands in much the same attitude toward the minority that the directors sustain toward all the stockholders. The

Court held that when the New York Central Company purchased the stock and bonds of the New York and Northern, thus obtaining a controlling interest in its affairs, "for the avowed purpose of destroying it, to serve a purpose entirely outside of that for which it was organised, and in hostility to it, it becomes clear that as such stockholder it owed a duty to the minority stockholders, that the law implied a quasi-trust upon its part, and that a Court of Equity will not aid it in the destruction of that corporation and a confiscation of its property, although it held a majority of its stock and the required amount of its bonds."

Thus, mainly through the efforts of Mr. Sterne, the law of this State in regard to the responsibility for corporate management, received, in several very important particulars, a new and authoritative interpretation. It has long been established in the private relations of life that one party cannot make impossible the performance of a contract and enforce a penalty for its non-performance by another. Through this decision of the Court of Appeals that became part of the law of corporations. One may be the creditor of a corporation while holding its stock, and may be able to enforce his right as creditor of the corporation against his fellow-stockholders ; but he cannot buy stocks and bonds with the avowed purpose, through the active power of the bond and the passivity of the stockholders, to work the destruction of the corporate entity and the absorption of its property. This the Court held to be taking an unfair advantage, to which it refused to lend its aid. The oppression of minority stockholders by the majority had so long been practised in the management of corporations that it had come to be regarded as a kind of vested right, the disturbance of which was inconsistent with the prosecution of accepted methods of speculation. Not the least important part of the decision in question, which has become a leading authority, was the finding of the Court that a trust relation arises the moment that a stockholder has in his own possession or under his control a majority of the stock. That possession confers the power of oppression, and from such a power the Court implied the existence of a trust which it was part of its function to see preserved against abuse.

The great weight which, in the judicial tribunals of the country, was attached to a decision of the New York Court of Appeals has rendered this one —delivered on October 20, 1896—of the greatest value as a weapon of defence for minority stockholders against majority oppression or spoliation. The exceptional value of the decision consists in the fact that it meets a clear issue without evasion or ambiguity, and furnishes a luminous exposition of what a Court of Equity can be trusted to do for the protection of a minority of the stockholders of a corporation exposed to a process not clearly distinguishable from highway robbery.

CHAPTER VIII

THE TWEED RING AND THE COMMITTEE OF SEVENTY

THE municipal corruption of New York in the later sixties has passed into history. But the full measure of its proportions was realised by very few even among those who took an intelligent interest in the public affairs of that time. That Mr. Sterne had pretty clearly apprehended the character and source of the evil, is apparent from several passages of his address on Representative Government, delivered at the Cooper Union on February 27, 1869. In one of these he says—

> The great cancer spot of our body politic—the corruption of our office-holders, consequent upon the low character in point of intellect and culture of the incumbents of our public offices—shows that in some one important particular our system must be vicious, and our policy wrong; that we either have delegated too much power, or distributed it badly, or both; and that our public life is not in accordance with the rules of political hygiene.

In another, in referring to the evidences of the insidious disease from which the body politic was suffering, he says—

You will find that our merchants are building palaces for the storing of merchandise. You will find in every department of the mechanical and fine arts a constant and steady progress. Dilettanteism is rapidly giving way to thoroughness. Even in our works of benevolence, we are more mindful of the duties which we owe to our fellowmen than we have been heretofore. We dive with a passionate charity into the darkest and remotest lurking-places of misery and of vice. If crime is on the increase it is because public justice is less repressive, not because private effort does not do its full duty in removing two of its mainstays—ignorance and drunkenness. And yet in the midst of all this progress there is one sore spot—inflamed, ulcerated, and mortified—our City's Government. This evil is not due to one political party more than to another. There is nothing in the tenets of either party which should make it a cover for spoliation and fraud. But it arises from the very existence of party and party necessities.

The vices of the City Government in New York are of somewhat ancient date. A Republican pamphleteer making, in 1786, a bitter attack on the rule of the Federalists found it to be "a matter of astonishment that a city so enlightened, and which has so eminently contributed to the restoration of public liberty, should have so long submitted to the abuses of its municipal administration." He was as much impressed as Mr. Sterne was, eighty years later, with the low character in point of intellect and culture of the incumbents of our public offices, for, in describing the character of the men who composed the majority of the Common Council, he said: "When we consider the slenderness of their influence as individuals; when we contemplate the paucity of their talents, we are impressed with mingled emotions of surprise and indignation that men so destitute of learning should have been permitted to become the despoilers of the rights of their fellow-citizens." Each succeeding generation seems to have echoed the same complaint which this critic had to make about the City Government of New York at a time when its population did not exceed 24,000. In 1820, with a population of about 120,000, and the suffrage restricted to property owners, New York was misgoverned; in 1850, with a population of 500,000 and manhood suffrage in untrammelled operation, the misgovernment of the city was still notorious. If the character of the City Council could be a subject of adverse criticism when the Republic was young, it had become a public scandal long before the Union was three-quarters of a century old. Thus it happened that when the Legislature of 1857 set about abridging the powers of the two boards of which that body was composed, there was no disposition to protest on the part of the business community or of the general body of taxpayers. In the estimation of most of these, New York was the worst governed city on the Continent. Some of them may have recognised the fact that it had come to be so largely by their own neglect, but they were so profoundly impressed by their inability to cope with the rowdies, jobbers, and wire-pullers who controlled elections, that they welcomed any legislation calculated to neutralise the power of the ignorant and purchasable vote, which did not demand of them any sustained exercise of vigilance or political activity.

Mr. Sterne perceived very clearly the uselessness of such a remedy, and, in the address already quoted from, he tried to impress his convictions on the minds of his fellow-citizens. His remedy was—

> Decentralise government to the utmost possible extent, give to each locality the absolute power of self-government, and under no pretext or seemingly valid excuse take such power from the locality. If New York City is given over to plunder by reason of the exercise, on its part, of such a power, let the bad grow worse until our merchants, our bankers, our lawyers, and our industrial classes find it to their interest to leave their counting-rooms and stock boards, their briefs and their workshops, to take an interest in our city's politics. And, as in no civilised community in this world having any social cohesiveness, the true and the trustworthy do not outnumber the designing and the criminal, the remedy will find itself. You therefore leave to the general government of the State such matters only which appertain to the general interest of all its inhabitants, and place nearer to the fountains of power, the people, all such matters in which they, as inhabitants of a locality, are especially interested. The more you centralise, the more you take from the people themselves the power to supervise the expenditure, the more you delegate, the greater your dependence upon the machinery of party. If the inhabitants of every street in the city of New York were compelled to make their own contracts, instead of the city making them for them, there would be less corruption, greater competition between individual contractors, and greater opportunity for the property owners to examine the relative proportion of services to expenditures.

The correctness of Mr. Sterne's diagnosis of the political evils with which the city of New York was afflicted at that time, was fully borne out two years later by an observer so expert and clear-sighted as Mr. Samuel J. Tilden. In tracing the development of the by-partisan system of spoliation, out of which grew the Tweed Ring, Mr. Tilden pointed out that the earlier Ring was one between the Republican majority in Albany and a few Democratic officials in New York. The Republican partners, however, had the superior power since they could create such institutions as the Board of Supervisors, and could abolish them at will. They could extinguish offices and substitute others; change the laws which fixed their duration, functions, and responsibilities, and nearly always could invoke the executive power of removal. The Democratic members of the combination were under the necessity of submitting to whatever terms the Albany legislators imposed, and having found out by experience that all real power was in Albany, they began to go there in person to share it. The lucrative city offices—subordinate appointments which each head of department could create at pleasure—with salaries at his discretion, distributed among the friends of the legislators; contracts; money contributed by city officials, assessed on their subordinates, raised by jobs under the departments, and sometimes taken from the City Treasury, were the pabulum of corrupt influence which shaped and controlled all legislation. Every year the system grew worse as a governmental institution, and became more powerful and corrupt. The executive departments gradually swallowed up all local powers, and themselves were mere deputies of legislators at Albany, on whom alone they were dependent. The Mayor and Common Council ceased to have any recognisable authority, and lost all practical influence. In the words of Mr. Tilden, "There was nobody to represent the people of the city; there was no discussion, there was no publicity. Cunning and deceptive provisions of law concocted in the secrecy of the departments, commissions and bureaus, agreed upon in the lobbies at Albany between the city officials and the legislators or their go-betweens, appeared upon the statute-books after every session. In this manner all institutions of Government, all taxation, all appropriations of money for our million of people were formed. For many years there was no time when a vote at a city election would, in any practical degree or manner, affect the City Government."

Thus the ground became fully prepared for the master combination of Tweed. The Tweed Ring was not a mere passing phenomenon in the politics and administration of New York City. It exercised, for a time, a controlling influence on the politics of the State; it had its plans laid for the capture of the Presidency of the United States and for the application of its characteristic methods to the conduct of the Federal Government. That the financial demoralisation of the war period—the unheard-of scale of national expenditures, the jobbery in contracts, the sudden growth of private fortunes, the development of the gambling spirit incidental to the varying fortunes of civil conflict, and the changes in value of an artificial currency—

had much to do with promoting official corruption in New York, there can be no question. But it is equally certain that the misgovernment of New York had its tap-root in the abuses to which the electoral system was systematically subjected. Under the Tammany system of which Tweed was a characteristic product, the cruder methods of repeating, ballot-box stuffing, the wholesale issue of fraudulent certificates of naturalisation, were much in vogue. But back of them all was the subtler and less easily eradicated vice, which Mr. Sterne never wearied in exposing—the failure to preserve a representative system of government. He insisted, in the heyday of Tammany corruption of the ballot-box, as strenuously as he insisted thirty years later, that official corruption in New York found its chief support in a system under which nearly one-half the community was virtually disfranchised.

It was but little over two years after Mr. Sterne's warning of February 1869, that the citizens of New York had a rude reminder of the utter failure of what is called partisan responsibility to keep the administration of city affairs out of the hands of a set of the most unscrupulous gang of thieves known to modern history. The corrupt combination which became notorious as the Tweed Ring, entered into complete control of the government of the city of New York on January 1, 1869, and held it until September 16, 1871. Within this period of two years eight and a half months the debt of the city and county, after making due allowance for unliquidated obligations, increased from $36,000,000 to $116,000,000. By far the larger part of the $80,000,000 thus added to the mortgage on the taxable property of the city was either squandered or stolen outright. Adding to this stupendous total of wasteful and corrupt expenditure which can be traced in the growth of the bonded debt, the large sums taken from the proceeds of taxation and from the amounts raised by assessments for local improvements, it has been held to be entirely within the mark to say that the brief term of power enjoyed by the Tweed Ring cost the taxpayers of New York not less than $100,000,000. When the *New York Times* published on July 29, 1871, the figures by which the people of New York were finally made aware of the enormous scale on which they were being robbed, they found the machinery of justice as completely under control of their plunderers as that of administration. But, when the crisis came, Mr. Sterne's confidence was fully justified in the readiness with which merchants, bankers, lawyers, and artisans left their counting-rooms and stock boards, their briefs and their workshops, to take an interest in city politics. It was out of this movement that there grew the Committee of Seventy—a body consisting of representative citizens of all shades of party opinion who had sunk their individual preferences in matters of national and State politics in a common effort to rescue New York from the slough of bankruptcy and disgrace into which it had fallen under the rule of the Ring.

The Committee had its origin in a public meeting attended by the foremost men of the city, held at Cooper Union on September 4, 1871. It is significant of the estimation in which Mr. Sterne was already held by some of the most eminent of his fellow-citizens, and of his associates at the Bar, that he was chosen to fill the office of Secretary of this body. The functions delegated to the Committee of Seventy had a gravity and importance probably beyond anything ever committed to such an organisation. They were, briefly, as follows :—

> To demand a full exhibition of all the accounts of the city and county, and an explicit statement of all the persons to whom, and the pretences on which, the large payments of the past two years and a half have been made; to enforce any remedies which now exist to obtain this information, if it is refused, and to recover whatever sums of money have been fraudulently or feloniously abstracted; and also to press upon the Legislature and Governor of the State such measures of legislation and action as may be necessary or proper to enforce the existing laws, and to supply their defects, and to remove the causes of the present abuses; and finally, to assist, sustain, and direct a united effort, by the citizens of New York, without reference to party, to obtain a good government and honest officers to administer it.

Mr. Sterne not only performed the arduous duties of general secretary to the Committee during the two years of its existence, but he was an active member of its most important committees, and bore the lion's share in the work of preparing reports, drafting resolutions, and keeping track of the details of the multifarious labours of this somewhat unwieldy organisation. He was a member of the Committee on Remedies, of the Committee on Elections, and of the Committee on Legislation. The high standard of ability represented in these bodies by which the real work of the Committee was done, may be inferred from the composition of the Committee on Legislation. Its chairman was Edward Salomon, and its members comprised the following well-known names:—Joseph B. Varnum, Henry N. Beers, John A. Dix, Edward Cooper, William C. Barrett, Benjamin B. Sherman, Edwards Pierrepont, Joseph H. Choate, Henry Nicoll, Samuel B. Ruggles, Theodore W. Dwight, and James M. Brown. Most of these men had a longer experience in public affairs than Mr. Sterne, and the lawyers among them were all his seniors at the Bar, but all of them were ready to defer to his clear judgment, and to place in his hands the formulation of the policy best fitted to the extraordinary crisis which they were called upon to meet.

Within a month after the formation of the Committee of Seventy, a partial investigation had been made of the fraudulent operations of the Ring with the following result:—(1) The debt of the city was found to be doubling every two years; (2) $3,200,000 had been paid for repairs on armouries and drill-rooms, the actual cost of which was less than $250,000; (3) over $11,000,000 had been charged for outlays on an unfinished court-house, for which building, completed, an honest estimate of real cost would be less than $3,000,000; (4) safes, carpets, furniture, cabinet-work, painting, plumbing, gas, and plastering had cost $7,289,466, which were valued by competent persons, after a careful examination, at $624,180; (5) $460,000 had been paid for $48,000 worth of lumber; (6) the printing, advertising, stationery, etc., of the city and county had cost in two years and eight months $7,168,212; (7) a large number of persons were found to be on the pay-rolls of the city whose services were neither rendered nor required; (8) figures upon warrants and vouchers had been fraudulently altered, and payments had been repeatedly made on forged indorsements. These were mere surface indications of the extent of the Ring frauds, but they afforded the standard by which to measure the scale on which the city was robbed.

The official title of the Committee of Seventy was "The Executive Committee of Citizens and Taxpayers for the Financial Reform of the City of New York," but its object being to secure for the city and county of New York good government and an honest administration of public trusts; the election of fitting depositaries of the public confidence was, obviously, a very important department of its work. As it happened, it was impossible to reach the chief malefactors through the ballot-box. Under the instrument known as the Tweed Charter, the term of the boards of aldermen and assistant aldermen holding office in 1870 had been extended to January 1, 1872, and discretion was given to the Mayor to extend their term of office until the following

June. The Mayor himself held office till January 1, 1873, and the only important officers to be elected were the representatives of the county in the State Senate and Assembly. The objective point of the Seventy's Committee on Election was therefore the defeat of the Ring candidates for these offices. The appeal issued to the voters of New York by the Committee smacks strongly of the style of Mr. Sterne. It was in part as follows :—

> Resolved—That the citizens of this city are earnestly entreated to make the reform of their own Government the one controlling issue at the next election, to support no man for office, and especially for the Legislature of the State, no matter what may be his party name, who is not known to be both honest and incorruptible, and determined and distinctly pledged, so far as he is able, whatever may be the consequences, to reform the city of New York; and that our fellow-citizens throughout the State are entreated to join in the effort to redress the evils which concern them hardly less than ourselves. We appeal to citizens of both parties to save us and the State from the possibility of such another degradation as has fallen on all of us. . . . No private business, no partisan end, can be so important to any right-minded citizen as the plain duties that are thrown on him by recent deplorable revelations.

It was inevitable that the Democratic organisation of the State should be held responsible for the iniquities of the Tweed Ring, and that popular indignation over the abuse of public trust in the city of New York should be visited on the party to which most of the members of the thieving combination owed allegiance. Accordingly, at the Fall election of 1871 there was a complete reversal of the results of the two preceding elections. In the State Senate, which had been chosen in 1869, there were 17 Democrats; in the one elected in 1871 there were but 7. The city and county of New York had sent 20 Tammany Democrats to the Assembly in 1870; in 1871 only 6 managed to pull through. Though the master-thief, William M. Tweed, had been returned to the State Senate by a constituency of more than ordinary moral obtuseness, his power was absolutely broken, and proceedings had already been begun to bring him to the Bar of Justice, On December 20, 1871, Tweed was arrested in his office under an order issued by Judge Learned of Albany, upon an affidavit of Samuel J. Tilden, in a civil action brought by the State for the recovery of $6,000,000 which Tweed was charged with having stolen from the city. This was the sum which had been disposed of by the so-called interim Board of Audit of notorious memory, which met but once and adopted a resolution setting forth that all claims against the county of New York incurred prior to 1870, and which were certified to by William M. Tweed, then President of the Board of Supervisors, and Joseph D. Young, clerk of the same, should be regarded as valid and should be paid. The county auditor, one James Watson, was a notorious rascal, and it was his duty to collect from the Committees of the Boards of Supervisors all the claims, chiefly relating to the county court-house, on which even that unscrupulous body had not found courage enough to act. In addition to these, claims were manufactured, for which there was not the slightest basis, and were duly certified by Mayor Hall, Controller Connolly, and "Boss" Tweed without examination. These certifications amounted to a sum slightly exceeding $6,312,000. The controller issued and sold bonds to that amount, and immediately after the pretended audit and allowance of each claim, a check or warrant in favour of the certified claimant was signed by the controller, the Mayor, and the clerk of the Board of Supervisors.

Mr. Charles O'Conor's succinct legal summary of this proceeding was as follows: "The accounts or claims so audited were all false, fictitious, and fraudulent; they were made up by fraud and collusion between James Watson and Andrew J. Garvey, James H. Ingersoll and Elbert A. Woodward (all agents and creatures of Tweed), and payments of such warrants were, pursuant to a corrupt, fraudulent, and unlawful combination and conspiracy to that end, agreed to be divided, and were divided accordingly between Ingersoll, Garvey, Tweed, and others unknown, their confederates." This was but a fraction of the plunder of the Ring, but it happened to be the most impudent of all their felonious transactions, and it furnished the chief basis for their subsequent prosecution. So far as any chance of bringing the Ring thieves to justice was concerned, the possession of the Controller's office was absolutely essential to the leaders of the forces of reform. Mr. Samuel J. Tilden and Mr. William F. Havemeyer thus performed an invaluable service to the cause of public justice, no less than to an honest and capable administration of the city finances, by inducing Connolly to appoint Mr. Andrew H. Green as his deputy. No man who has occupied, before or since, the position as head of the Finance Department of the city of New York has had so difficult a task as that which presented itself to Mr. Green. Under the rule of the Ring, the debt-contracting power had been exercised indiscriminately by all branches of the city and county government. Little or no regard was paid to positive prohibitory provisions against expenditures in excess of authorised appropriations, and the natural result was an annual spawning of a mass of illegal claims. Nearly every department had its own treasury, paid such bills as it chose, and acted without restraint, responsibility, or accountability. Annual expenses thus increased enormously, floated debt accumulated, and all kinds of obligations were created which came before those who had to administer on the estate of the Ring in the form of unadjusted claims.

Almost from the time of his entrance into the Controller's office, Mr. Green had recourse to the advice of Mr. Sterne in producing order out of the chaotic mass of obligations which had been bequeathed to him by the Ring officials. In another department of the work of reconstruction, Mr. Sterne was kept equally active. During the closing months of 1871 he had to devote all the time and energy at his disposal to the preparation of a new scheme of government for the city. This was nominally the work of the Seventy's Committee on Legislation of which he was a member, but abundant evidence is furnished by notes and corrections in his own hand that the Charter of the Committee of Seventy was very largely his own work. In the absence of these, the fact that its whole structure rests on the principle of minority representation would be conclusive as to its authorship, since none of Mr. Sterne's associates on the Committee was so profoundly impressed as he with the vital relation of that principle to local self-government, or was in any degree so conversant with the methods of its practical application to public affairs. In judging, therefore, of the value of the changes which the charter of the Committee proposed to introduce into the administrative system of New York, it must always be borne in mind that they were absolutely conditioned on the efficacy of the system of cumulative voting to elevate the whole tone and character of the city legislature, and to place in the hands of a minority of that body the same power to make their influence felt in the choice of members of the executive commissions which a minority of the voters had exercised in their own election. At the very foundation of the proposed charter was an effort to make the aldermen real, instead of sham, legislators for the city, and the more effectually to accomplish this, provision was made to give any compactly organised body of voters, in a given district, the opportunity to elect an alderman who should be independent of the dictation of the managers of either political party.

The precise language of the Charter on this subject was as follows :—

> At such election each qualified voter in each Senate district may give as many votes for one candidate as there are aldermen to be elected in said districts. The voter may give the whole of his votes for one and the same candidate, or may distribute them among nine different candidates, or a less number, in such proportion as he may see fit.

It was proposed to confer on the men thus elected a very important share of the power of appointment of the chief local officers. For example, the Department of Public Works, which was also to have supervision over the Docks, was to be placed under the charge of a Board of five commissioners, one of whom was to be appointed by the Mayor, and the remaining four were to be elected by the Board of Aldermen. The minority system was thus applied to the choice of these officers—

> At such election each alderman shall give not more than four open ballots, upon each of which shall be printed or written the name of one candidate for the office of commissioner, and each of which shall be signed by the member voting, and recorded by the Clerk of the Board. Each alderman may give the whole of his ballots for one and the same candidate, or may distribute them between four different candidates or a less number, in such a proportion as he may see fit. The four persons having the largest number of votes shall be deemed elected.

It was also proposed to entrust to the aldermen

the control over city expenditures in the following terms:—

> The Board shall have the exclusive power to appropriate money by proper ordinance for every branch and object of city expenditure; and no money shall be drawn from the city treasury, unless the same shall have been previously appropriated by the Board. They shall succeed to and be vested with all the powers now vested in any department of the city government, other than the Department of Public Instruction, to incur debt, and raise and expend public money.

The process of reasoning which led Mr. Sterne to the conclusion that a reform of the city government of New York might be found by investing the Board of Aldermen with the real power of local legislation appears to have been somewhat as follows:—The assumption by the State Legislature of the direct control of local affairs has necessarily involved a disregard of one of the fundamental principles of Republican government. The system of government by municipalities is inherent in our free institutions. In separate communities existing as integral parts of the commonwealth, but having local interests which immediately concern themselves rather than the State at large, the instinct of self-government has always asserted itself in some way as the basis of their organic life. From this germ has come the right which has been claimed and exercised of the administration of law and government by municipalities in respect of their local affairs, while retaining their allegiance as members of the whole nation. The lines which separate the functions of the central legislature from those which should be discharged by local Government boards is sufficiently distinct. Whatever concerns the right of all the citizens of the State, in respect either of persons or of property, belongs to the central authority, which is also charged with the duty of devising uniform plans by which the affairs of the various local divisions of the State may be administered by the people of those divisions. The representatives elected to the central Legislature are chosen expressly for the purpose of attending to these general duties. Among the reasons why they ought not to be charged with the direction of the local affairs of municipalities are these: They have neither the requisite time nor the knowledge of detail. Whether it is best in any particular city to open a particular street or avenue, or construct an aqueduct, or any other public work requiring the expenditure of money, cannot be determined without an accurate knowledge of the affairs of the locality which are usually possessed only by those residing in it. Consequently, when a local Bill is under consideration in the Legislature, its care and explanation are left exclusively to the representatives of the locality to which it is applicable, and sometimes by express, more often by a tacit understanding, local Bills are "log-rolled" through the Houses. Thus legislative duty is delegated to the local representatives, who, acting frequently in combination with some of the worst elements of their constituency, are able to shift the responsibility for wrong-doing from themselves to the Legislature. But what is even more important, there is lacking in the State Legislature that sense of personal interest and personal responsibility to their constituents, in dealing with the affairs of localities, which are indispensable to the intelligent administration of these affairs. And yet, the judgment of the local governing bodies and the wishes of their constituents, are liable to be overruled by the votes of legislators living at a distance of a hundred miles.

These considerations led to the conclusion that the original election or appointment of all local governing bodies, the duty of watching or checking them, and the duty of providing, or the discretion of withholding, the supplies necessary for their operations, should rest, not with the central Legislature, but with the people of the locality. The exercise by the State Legislature of inappropriate functions has had this among other mischievous consequences—the time which should be devoted to the thorough consideration of measures affecting the general laws and policy of the State is invaded and wasted, to the manifest injury of those general interests which it is the exclusive province of the Legislature to defend. The multiplicity of laws relating to the same subjects is itself an evil of great magnitude, and what the law is concerning some of the most important interests of our principal cities can be ascertained only by the exercise of the most patient research of professional lawyers. To the citizen it is a sealed book, and the officers who are called upon to administer it, are bewildered in the mazes of conflicting enactments. It may be true that the first attempts to secure legislative intervention in the local affairs of our principal cities were made by good citizens in the supposed interest of reform and good government, and for the purpose of counteracting the schemes of corrupt officials. But the notion that legislative control was the proper remedy was, nevertheless, a serious mistake. The corrupt cliques and rings which it was thus sought to circumvent, were quick to perceive that in the business of procuring special laws in regard to local affairs, they could easily outmatch the fitful and clumsy efforts of disinterested citizens. The transfer of the control of municipal resources from the localities to the State capital had no other effect than to cause a like transfer of the methods and arts of corruption, and to make the fortunes of our principal cities the traffic of the lobbyist.

Mr. Sterne found it idle to look forward to any remedy for the existing abuses of municipal government based on the limitation of the suffrage to property owners or rent-payers. As the French say of an individual that he has the defects of his virtues, so it may be said of our institutions that, taking into consideration the enormous benefits which arise from the exercise of the right of universal suffrage, we must be content to pay the price of the defects of such a system in its application to the concentrated expenditures and temptations incidental to municipal administration. In seeking remedies in other directions than in the restriction of the suffrage, Mr. Sterne recognised the low estate into which the Board of Aldermen had fallen. But he insisted that this was due to its election by a district system and by the majority plan, and that stripped of all truly governmental functions, such a Board could exercise no weight and perform no useful service. He regarded it, therefore, of the first importance, after securing a constitutional amendment which should compel the Legislature to keep its hands off all expenditures of strictly local concern, to obtain once more a municipal legislative body fitted to command the confidence and secure the services of the best men of the community. This he held could be done only by electing such a body on a plan of minority representation.

He argued that by adopting some method of minority or totality representation we should prevent the swamping of the more intelligent classes and of the property interests of the community. Totality representation is not in conflict with the rule of the majority ; but, on the contrary, it would ensure the rule of the true, instead of a fictitious majority. When the whole people are represented in the representative body, instead of only a part of them, the taking of a vote in that body would be somewhat analogous to taking the vote of the entire people represented, and then we should have at least an approach to an adequate representation of all our citizens, rich and poor alike. Were we to enact that the common council thus representing the whole of the people with its fair proportions of taxpayers, should have no power to incur expenses or create a permanent debt, unless sanctioned by the vote of three-fourths of the members elected, it would practically result in the giving of a veto to property interèsts against such expenditure for the reason that a combination of the taxpayers, under any proper scheme of minority representation, could secure at least a fourth of the members of the Board. Among the other benefits to be derived from minority representation, not the least in Mr. Sterne's estimation, would be the emancipation of independent voters from abject dependence on party candidates and the securing of permanence in office for men of proved capacity and honesty. In defending the reform against the accusation of complexity, Mr. Sterne was accustomed to say that were the political parties compelled to write out in a book the rules and regulations, their manner of holding primary elections and pre-primary ones, their system of making up slates and packing conventions, the machinery would appear too complex for practical action. The system of minority representation appears complex simply because it must be provided for by law and be written out in detail. Under the system provided for in the charter of the Committee of Seventy, by which each voter in the Senate district to which he belonged had nine votes which he could cumulate on one candidate or distribute as he saw fit, the power was given to a minority of one-tenth, plus one, of the voters of the district to elect one member of the Board of Aldermen. An objection to this plan on the score of the waste of votes which might result from it did not lie, Mr. Sterne argued, in the mouths of those who believed in the present system of representation by majorities only, because that results in the waste of a very much larger proportion of votes, namely, all the votes cast for unsuccessful candidates.

Substantially in the form in which it was drafted, the Legislature of 1872 adopted the charter of the Committee of Seventy. It was promptly vetoed by Governor Hoffman, mainly because he regarded its fundamental principle—that of minority representation—was of doubtful constitutionality. It is instructive to note the contrasted views on this question of a man like Mr. Sterne, devoted to the principles and practice of a broad and enlightened statesmanship, with those of a timid and truckling politician like John T. Hoffman. The Governor's method of stating his objections to the representation of minorities was as follows :—

A very serious question arises whether this method of voting is in conformity with the provisions of the Constitution. Many of the ablest lawyers of the State have not hesitated to express their convictions that it must be held to be unconstitutional. It is said, and with great force, that the election as regulated by this charter is not an election in the sense in which that word was understood at the time the Constitution was made, and in the sense that it has always been understood among us. An election is the choice of a public officer by his receiving a larger number of votes than any other candidate in the district entitled to fill the office, all the electors being entitled to vote once at such election for a candidate for the place to be filled. It is suggested also that the Constitution guarantees that all electors shall be entitled to vote for all officers who are to be elected by the people, and that if any elector exercises his right to vote once for each of the nine aldermen to be chosen for his district, his single vote as to any one of the candidates cannot be overriden by one of his neighbours voting nine times for some one man for the same place, without an infraction of his equal right of suffrage as an elector under the Constitution. There is, therefore, reason to fear that the election ordered under this charter might be declared invalid at a time when the Legislature is not in session, and that, meanwhile, great confusion may prevail in the affairs of the city. While in ordinary cases a threat of litigation is not, of itself, a sufficient reason why the Legislature should refrain from passing a law, or why I should refuse it my approval, yet, when the change to be made in the law is so revolutionary in character as it is in this case, when the doubts of its constitutionality are so grave and serious, and when complicated and injurious litigation is almost certain to follow, both the Legislature and myself are bound, by a prudent regard for the public interests, to abstain from making great innovations, not called for by any overruling necessity. The fundamental principle of our government, familiar to the people, is that elective officers shall be chosen by a majority of the votes of the people entitled to take part in the choice. In all questions submitted to the people the majority decides. When any other principle is sought to be introduced, a revolutionary change of great magnitude is proposed, which ought not to be tried under the sanction of an act of the Legislature only; if so great a change is to be made at all, it should be done only with the careful deliberation which pertains to revisions of the Constitution.

The independence of party organisation which the system of cumulative voting conferred, and which was regarded as one of its chief merits by Mr. Sterne, did not, naturally, commend itself to Governor Hoffman. He was too thoroughgoing a partisan to admit that the system of party responsibility for the government of New York had proved a costly failure, and he was at no loss to find specious arguments for the continuance of the system. As a fair sample of the kind of objections which the politicians have always interposed to the adoption of minority representation, the following additional extracts from his veto message may be worth quoting :—

> In all free governments the people divide themselves into two great parties. This tendency is so universal that it is not statesmanship to ignore it. Enactments will not overcome it. It is a natural, useful, and wholesome division ; it ensures a large body of men among the people interested in and intent upon fault-finding with the party in power, and struggling, by means of exposure of their errors, to bring over to the side of the minority enough of the electors to convert it into a majority, and so to take over the government. In politics, as in other things, it is agitation which purifies. Under this proposed new system of voting, the minority carry in their candidates without effort. The majority do the same. In a district where it is known that the political majority usually casts about two-thirds of the whole vote, there being nine aldermen to be elected, the caucus or nominating convention of the political majority will naturally concentrate all their votes upon six candidates ; the caucus of the minority will concentrate on three. There will be no actual contest before the people. The decrees of the party caucuses will be absolute. Neither side will be in fear, lest, by putting forward unfit candidates, it may lose the election.

For the two parties will be acting at the polls not against each other, but independent each of the other. This condition of things, where the decrees of the party caucuses on both sides are final, naturally gives rise to secret combinations between the leaders on both sides for an agreed upon division of power, against which combinations the mass of the voters might, under this system, struggle in vain. It is true there is an opportunity for a combination, in favour of one or two candidates, of independent voters, who may be regardless of party associations. But when the power of the regular party organisation is considered, will not this influence of combinations of independent voters make itself felt to a very limited extent, and very rarely? Will it be equal to the power which voters, disposed to disregard their party associations on any occasion, can now exert, by temporarily voting with the opposing party, by way of rebuke to their own?

Mr. Sterne was disappointed at this issue of the legislative effort of the Seventy on which he had built some very sanguine expectations of future reform, but he was not by any means discouraged. A Mayor was to be elected in the fall of 1872, and to the choice of a man who could be trusted to carry out his views of non-partisan reform, all the efforts of the working membership of the Committee were directed. On the platform drafted by the Committee, Mr. William F. Havemeyer was elected—a Democrat of the old school who had been already twice Mayor of New York in 1845-46 and 1848-49. Mr. Sterne was one of those to whom the mayor-elect turned for counsel and guidance, and there is ample evidence that Mr. Sterne was consulted in the preparation of the Mayor's inaugural message. In reviewing the laws relating to the government of the city, the message points out that, under the existing charter, the legislative power of the corporation is vested in the common council. But this was not the system which had governed the city since the law was enacted ; there had been form not substance—a legislature in name, but not in reality. Everything had been done as though there had been no legislative body ; as if no common council existed as part of the city government. While in theory the executive departments were subordinate to the Mayor, they had been by law made practically independent of him, and had absorbed to themselves all the legislative power, thus leaving the common council the direct representatives of the people, without influence and almost without functions. This, the Mayor held, should no longer continue. The legislative power should be restored to the common council. Elected by the people in a sense which could not be predicated of any election in the city during the past twenty years, the aldermen were reminded that they should act for the people, and for no particular party, political or otherwise. Their first duty should be to see that the legislative power of the government was in reality, and not merely in name, vested in themselves. Wherever they found this power to have been assumed by the departments without authority, the Mayor advised them that a change should be effected. He was persuaded that an examination would satisfy them that, even under existing laws, their powers were by no means so limited as the action of their predecessors would indicate.

Equally suggestive of the influence of Mr. Sterne was the passage in Mayor Havemeyer's inaugural counselling caution in the choice of the remedies by which the various defects in the city government might be cured. It was declared that the municipality of New York is intended to be and ought to be a government by and for the people of the city. The people of the city had shown their ability and determination to govern themselves, and they relied upon their elected representatives to maintain and defend their municipal right. From general and State politics, the government of the city should, as far as possible, be removed. Efficiency, honesty, and economy were the characteristics by which it should be distinguished. The legislation necessary to secure improvement in the government of the city should be promoted and approved by the corporate authorities, and by them officially presented to the Legislature. Legislation sought for by any single department for its own purposes, to extend its own power, must be prevented. The spectacle which had been witnessed during the preceding winter of the heads of some of the departments, with a lobby of retainers, besieging the Legislature during the whole session to keep themselves in office, and to retain their emoluments and patronage, should no longer be tolerated. All legislation for corporations, or individuals, designed to benefit particular interests at the public expense, should be determinedly opposed. Special legislation had been made an instrument of gigantic plunder of the city, and this channel for the advancement of private and individual interests, at the expense of the public, must be closed. If the Board of Apportionment was to continue in existence, its constitution should be changed so as to put an end to the anomaly of executive officers sitting thereon, and voting the amounts they are to have at their disposal to expend. No more executive officers should have such power; it should be placed exclusively in the hands of those city officers whose duty it is to watch and restrain.

Thus the reconstruction of the city government on a non-partisan basis began, but it had not proceeded far before complaints began to be heard that an attempt was being made to cheat the Republicans out of the fruits of a victory which was legitimately theirs. The spokesmen of the party, whose organisation had indorsed Mr. Havemeyer, said that if a party victory was to be claimed, they must claim it on behalf of the Republicans. By way of heading off any further attempt to get a non-partisan charter through the Legislature, the Republican Central Committee, early in November, appointed a sub-committee to prepare such drafts of laws relating to the city as might seem to be desirable. This committee began its work by the preparation of a number of amendments to the City Charter, which were practically equivalent to the entire recasting of that instrument. While they were left without any authoritative representation of the views of the Committee of Seventy, they claimed to have adopted in great measure the specific propositions which had been favoured by the Committee on Legislation of the Seventy. Indeed, the Republican sub-committee claimed that the only points of importance on which they differed on the sub-committee of the Committee of Seventy were that they did not introduce minority representation; that they gave the appointment of the heads of departments to the Mayor and aldermen, instead of to the Mayor alone; that they did not provide for a spring election; that they confined the preparation of the tax levy to municipal officers instead of conferring any authority over it upon State officers; and that they did not remove from office the four heads of departments who had been appointed after the fall of the Ring. The Committee frankly admitted that, acting as Republicans, they had not been indifferent to the wishes or interests of that party. They asked those who might be disposed to disapprove of their work to remember that any amendments to the Charter of the city were to come from a Legislature in which their party was in a large majority.

The Republican Charter was duly reported favourably by the Committee on the affairs of cities of the Assembly, and it evoked a letter of protest from Mayor Havemeyer, in the preparation of which the hand of Mr. Sterne is clearly traceable. The Mayor objected most strenuously to the provisions, that if the aldermen should object to any person nominated by the Mayor, he should promptly nominate another person in the place of the one so objected to, and continue so to nominate, until in case of a vacancy, twenty days should have elapsed since its occurrence, or until, in the case of the expiration of a term of office, not more than ten days of the term remained unexpired. If at such periods respectively, no nominations should have been made which shall have met the approval of the aldermen, it became the duty of the Mayor and aldermen to meet in joint convention within four days thereafter, and by the vote of the majority of those present to make such appointment. The Mayor insisted that this was a distinct and positive transfer of executive power to the Board of Aldermen, thinly covered by allowing the Mayor to go through the farce of making nominations for twenty days, which are to be rejected, and then, as a premium on such rejection, to make the Board of Aldermen supreme in the appointing power, by compelling the Mayor to act with them as one of their number only. He pointed out that to secure this end it would not be necessary for the Board of Aldermen even to act upon any nomination by rejection; if a sufficient number of the Board should remain away from the meetings to prevent a quorum during twenty days, the same end would be accomplished as though the Mayor had not the power to nominate conferred upon him. It was needless to urge that the Board of Aldermen would not seize and use such a power when the only price for its possession was absence from the meetings of the Board, whose members were thus to be relieved from even a slight responsibility of rejecting good nominations for public offices.

In addressing the Committee of Seventy on this subject, the Mayor endeavoured to impress upon them that this act had for its main object to give the city an entirely irresponsible form of government, and to prevent the people from changing it by an uprising similar to that of 1871, when such a Government should have produced its inevitable fruits of corruption, neglect of duty, and misappropriation of public funds. He recalled the fact that, in his inaugural message, he had urged the necessity of a reform giving back to the common council the legislative power which properly appertains to it, and stripping the departments of that independence which makes them separate and distinct governments. In place of this reform, however, it was not proposed to have one jot or tittle added to the proper function of the legislative branch of the Government. What was to be added was executive power, so that to the inharmonious government with which the city was already afflicted, and which presented the absurdity of frittering away the legislative power among the executive departments, there was to be superadded the monstrosity of a legislative body exercising the principal functions of the chief executive. The Mayor reiterated his opinion that the power of raising taxes and determining their amount should be left to the people of the city of New York, who were to be affected by its exercise. Answering the question of where this power should be lodged, he replied—

Clearly in the Board of Aldermen, under the check

of a two-thirds or three-fourths vote, frequent elections, direct and immediate responsibility to the people, with the additional safeguard of an executive veto by the Mayor of any of the provisions of the tax levy. Disclaiming all intention to reflect on the men composing the Board of Aldermen, or to claim new patronage for the office which he held, he insisted that when a new organic law, as the result of the reform movement of the past two years, was proposed, the true question is: "Is it an honest law? Does it furnish the reform for which our people have struggled and won victories, or is it an attempt of dishonest, contriving politicians to cheat the people of the fruit of their labours?"

In making his appointments for public office, Mayor Havemeyer had drawn largely on the membership of the Committee of Seventy, and the reputation of that body for disinterested public spirit became, thereby, somewhat impaired. Mr. Sterne himself would accept no office, although the Mayor had frequently solicited him to do so. The question was submitted to a sub-committee, of which Mr. Sterne was a member, whether the organisation, having done the work for which it was called into being, should be disbanded. The report rendered, in reply to this question, is among Mr. Sterne's papers, in his own handwriting, and may be presumed to be chiefly his work. The only signature appended to it is his own as secretary of the sub-committee. The report begins with the admission that its authors were alive to the formation of a popular prejudice against the Committee of Seventy by reason of the acceptance of offices of profit under the city government by some of its members. While it was but natural that the Mayor should look to those who had fought with him the battle of reform to share, to some degree, the responsibilities of office, and while it certainly would not be consistent to regard the acceptance of public trusts by worthy men as a ground of reproach, yet, as a fact, these appointments had caused the Committee no little embarrassment. It was clear to the minds of the authors of this report that the usefulness of the Committee of Seventy would be considerably impaired if the gentlemen who held public positions of emolument continued to be members thereof, and in recommending that the General Committee continue in existence, it was assumed that the resignation would be accepted of such of its members as were drawing pay as office-holders from the city or county treasury.

Reviewing the work done by the Committee of Seventy, the report goes on to say that while it might be true that the people of New York in calling the Committee into being did not mean to create a permanent political organisation, and that possibly it might be deemed a very liberal construction of the popular mandate to continue the organisation longer than was dictated by the absolute necessities of the hour, yet, when the very great service which the Committee had performed for the community was taken into account, it was felt that a capital of political power so useful in its character should not be lightly cast to the winds. There was no reason why, in the immediate future, as well as in the recent past, the activity of the Committee should fail to be productive of very great good through its positive influence in elections by the moral effect it could exercise in inducing a high average of nominations for public office, and by salutary efforts to promote wholesome and check pernicious legislation. In addition to the benefits to be derived by the citizens of New York from the existence of a body of gentlemen whose business it is to watch political parties in relation to city affairs, to exercise their influence in the election of fit men to office, and actively to exert themselves to secure the passage of necessary laws and defeat dangerous ones, there is the further advantage that whether at the moment, active or not, the Committee would furnish a rallying point for the better class of citizens in case of any public danger arising from future misgovernment, and would furnish a nucleus for organised resistance to any such combination as that from which the city had recently been delivered. It was pointed out that political power has the constant tendency in all countries to fall into the hands of the leisure class, but that in this busy country of ours the leisure class is not composed of men to whom the possession of wealth for generations has brought certain standards of education and conduct higher than the average, but is mainly made up of persons who have become unfitted by vice or ignorance for the active pursuits of life. Hence the moment that the pressure of immediate necessity is removed, busy men return once more to vocations which have a very remote connection with politics and political power, wrested for a time from the grasp of those who possess it, reverts once more to the men whose only business is politics. The only means of counteracting such a tendency is to keep alive by means of some organisation like the Committee of Seventy the watchfulness of our much occupied citizens, and to scrutinise closely acts done or intended to be done, affecting the city government, so that it may not fall back into the condition from which it had but recently emerged. Many evils continue to exist which required a remedy, and the City Charter which had passed the Republican Legislature was very far from being such an instrument as would best subserve the ends of good government. It was, therefore, held to be scarcely proper for the Committee to surrender the mandate received at the hands of the people while there was so much left to be accomplished in the way of reform. The report concluded by the statement that while these and kindred considerations had caused its authors to recommend that the Committee of Seventy should remain together as an organised force against fraud and corruption in local politics, the recommendation was based on the hope that the report would be adopted by the great majority of the members. Should a respectable and influential minority differ from the views which the report had expressed, and hold that it were better to dissolve the Committee, Mr. Sterne and his associates said that in such a contingency they would recommend a surrender of the functions of the Committee rather than continue it as a divided and crippled organisation, shorn of all that could make it formidable, and hence respectable, as a political power.

This was, in fact, the contingency which had to be faced, and the Committee of Seventy was accordingly dissolved. It will live in the history of the city as part of a *régime* of reform to which, whatever its defects, must be accorded the distinction of having brought administrative order out of chaos, of having found the credit of the city absolutely wrecked, and having left it fully restored. The eyes of the people had been opened to the monstrous character of the pretension that the city of New York could be treated by contending sets of partisans like a conquered province. Though the victory of the advocates of non-partisanship in the city government had been far from complete, and was not destined to be lasting, the fight had been fairly begun which, continued intermittently to the present time, and more seriously prosecuted now than it has been in all the thirty years since the first Committee of Seventy was organised, bids fair to assure the permanence of business methods in the city government of New York.

In 1871, the leading merchants of New York closed their places of business on Election Day, that nothing might be left undone to bring out a full vote against the nominees of the Tweed Ring. It was Mr. Sterne's suggestion that this precedent should be established by law, and the designation of Election Day as a legal holiday will be remembered among his services to the cause of good government.

CHAPTER IX

THE SISYPHEAN LABOUR OF MUNICIPAL REFORM

THE immediate issue of the municipal reform movement to which the Committee of Seventy had given shape and direction was sufficiently discouraging. With the election of mayor in the fall of 1874, the city administration of New York began to settle into the old partisan rut again. The cause of non-partisanship in city government found its sole advocacy in the platform of a body of "Independent Democrats," whose candidate for mayor was Mr. Oswald Ottendorfer. This organisation declared that while in its general political action effect was given to its partisan views by supporting candidates of like sentiments, its members deemed it to be their duty to support local candidates, without distinction of party, whose election would aid in relieving the city from the rule of political bosses, and all good citizens, irrespective of party, were invited to unite with them in the accomplishment of that object. Tammany placed in the field as its candidate for mayor, Mr. William H. Wickham, a business man of respectable repute, and the Republicans nominated a straight party candidate in the person of Mr. Salem H. Wales. How quickly the lesson of the Tweed Ring had been forgotten by New York voters is demonstrated by the fact that the combined vote of Ottendorfer and Wales was less than that received by the Tammany candidate. The fact that the mayor-elect was a man of reputable character and antecedents did not change the character of the organisation, whose candidate he was, and whose interest he must needs serve. The feeling with which reformers viewed this collapse of the movement which was started with so much promise in 1871 may be inferred from the comment made by the *New York Times* on the result of the municipal election of November 1874: "If anybody had said in the fall of 1871, when the public indignation against the Tammany Ring was at its height, that in three years the same political organisation, with but a slight change of leaders, would be able to control the affairs of this city, that person would have been laughed to scorn. Yet, with but one important exception (the register), every Tammany Hall nominee for local office was elected yesterday."

The breakdown of the cause of reform in the city had, however, been accompanied by a triumph of the reform movement in the State, in the election as Governor of Mr. Samuel J. Tilden. Mr. Tilden had borne a conspicuous part in the impeachment of the Ring judges and the prosecution of the Ring thieves. The analysis of the Broadway Bank accounts showing the percentages on which the Ring plunder had been divided was done under his direction, and was virtually his work. Mr. Tilden's nomination for Governor was scornfully regarded by the practical politicians of his party, and nobody could have been more surprised than they at its brilliantly successful issue. On the question of municipal reform Mr. Tilden entertained sentiments in substantial accord with those held by Mr. Sterne. One of the first deliverances of the new Governor was the preparation of a formal message on this subject in which he laid down as among the essentials of local self-government the following:—"(1) That there be an organism under which the elective power of the people can act conveniently and effectively, and exercise an actual control at one election over those who represent it in the local administration; (2) that in voting upon the administration of local affairs, the popular attention and the popular will be freed, as far as possible, from disturbing elements, especially from complications with State and national politics." Governor Tilden had previously pointed out in his inaugural message to the Legislature that it was often asked to pass laws from New York City under the pressure of a public opinion created by abuses and wrongs of local administration that found no other method of redress. When the injured taxpayer could discover no mode of removing a delinquent official, and no way of holding him to account in the courts, he assented to an appeal to the legislative power at Albany; and an Act was passed whereby one functionary was expelled, and by some device the substitute selected was put in office. Differing in politics as the city and State did, and with all the temptations to individual selfishness and ambition to grasp patronage and power, the great municipal trusts soon came to be the traffic of the lobbies. It was long since the people of the city of New York had elected any mayor who had the appointment after his election of the important municipal officers. There had not been an election in many years in which the elective power of the people was effective to produce any practical results in respect to the heads of departments in which the active governing power really resided. A new disposition of the great municipal trusts had been generally worked out by new legislation. The arrangements were made in secret; public opinion had no opportunity to act in discussion or power to influence results. Inferior offices, contracts, and sometimes money were means of competition, from which those who could not use similar weapons were excluded.

It was to endeavour to find a remedy for this state of things that a Commission was appointed, on the recommendation of the Governor, to report to the Legislature such laws or constitutional amendments as might be required for the better government of cities. Of this Commission Mr. Sterne was a member, and he had as his associates Messrs. William M. Evarts, Oswald Ottendorfer, E. L. Godkin, Samuel Hand, Joshua M. Van Cott, James C. Carter, William Allen Butler, Judge John A. Lott, Edward Cooper, and Henry F. Dimock. It is needless to say that the report submitted by this body was a very able one ; but as one of the amendments which it recommended to the City

Charter contemplated the election of a Board of Finance by a restricted vote, the whole scheme fell under the popular disapproval which this part of it had excited. Speaking of the subject ten years later, Mr. Sterne said that the amendments to the Constitution proposed by the Commission were never submitted to the vote of the people, partly because they were misunderstood, and partly because of the absence of courage among the political leaders of the State. His own position in regard to this matter had been so constantly represented and misunderstood, that he felt impelled to make public the following explanation:—

I was, from the outset, in favour of the adoption of a plan of minority representation, being firmly convinced that the citizens of New York would not favourably entertain anything that savoured of any limitation of the suffrage. When I found, however, that that was hopeless of accomplishment through that Commission, I felt that the only alternative was to create an entirely new organisation to exercise a veto power over expenditures, leaving to universal suffrage the election of mayor, aldermen, and all other officers now elective, and strengthening instead of diminishing their functions, as the Commission recommended, stripping from the Legislature the power of interference which it now has, and lodging all political power in relation to the city in the hands of properly elected city officers. I felt, in common with my associates, that somewhere within the limits of that city some Conservative power should be found to exercise a mere veto upon extravagance and corrupt expenditures, and this was the only power which was attempted to be lodged in the hands of the so-called Board of Finance. But it is useless now to discuss this plan, because, without any direct vote of the people ever being had upon it, there seems to be a general impression that political power, once granted, cannot be modified, even if not withdrawn, although such modification is for the good of those to be affected thereby.

This statement was made before a meeting of the German-American Citizens' Association in 1887 on the proposed constitutional convention and the work before it. Mr. Sterne was steadfastly of the opinion that not the least important part of this work related to the transfer to the people of the cities of the State an effective control over the management of their own affairs. He recalled the fact that in the fifteen years preceding 1887, New York City had had a succession of so-called business men as mayors. Messrs. Havemeyer, Ely, Wickham, Grace, Cooper, Edson, and Hewitt were all business men who had achieved distinction in their respective walks in life, and yet the burden of taxation had not been lifted. The city had grown enormously, and the taxable value of its property was constantly increasing. The improvements alone which had been made within the past decade, and had, therefore, added to the taxable area, should have considerably lightened the percentage of taxation ; but notwithstanding all this, together with the marked reduction in the interest charge, there was a constantly growing accumulation of debt, and a slow but steady rise in the scale of taxation from year to year. The Mayor, however good his intentions, could effect but little practical reform so long as the Legislature was able to impose on the city, against its will and against its protest, vast expenditures for so-called public improvements. Since 1857 no session of the Legislature had passed by without creating a vast number of changes in the laws relating to the government of the larger cities of the State. In 1857, in 1869, in 1870, and in 1871, and again in 1873, and so on downward, the Charter of the city of New York had been changed, had been tinkered with, and had been modified and controlled as party dictates demanded. Power had been taken from one department and transferred to another ; vast amounts of expenditure had been imposed upon the city of New York by mere legislative will and direction, which never would have been sanctioned even by a corrupt city aldermanic Board, and not only the government of the city of New York, but that of every other large city of the State, had been a prey to the legislative will, swayed by party motives and by sinister and pecuniary interests.

Hence the desire of residents and citizens of incorporated cities had been well-nigh universal for true instead of assimilated Home Rule, and that in some way or another a form of charter for the various cities of the State should be incorporated into the fundamental law of the State, so that for weal or for woe, the cities should have in their own hands the control of their own destinies. Thus, Mr. Sterne held, that the primary amendment to be demanded from the Constitutional Convention was, that even if New Yorkers could not otherwise improve their city administration, they should be permitted, at least, to enjoy their misgovernment close at home, and to exercise whatever influence they might be able to use quite under their own eyes at the City Hall, and not be remitted to the tender mercies of the members from Sullivan, St. Lawrence, and Hamilton counties, in the determination of how much they should be taxed, and for what purposes and objects. But the securing of Home Rule was but one step in the right direction; and Mr. Sterne argued that, if possible, such a home government should be secured that the people might live under it with pride and decency. To do this, he held it to be necessary so to reorganise the city government as to create two elements which were sorely wanted—one, efficiency on the part of the executive department; and the other, true deliberation and advice on the part of the Legislative department. His plan was to give to the Executive the power of removal, as well as the power of appointment of the heads of departments, and to make departments single-headed except, possibly, the department of police, or in lieu thereof, a larger department of public safety, which should include the departments of police, public health, and fire—correlative jurisdictions requiring co-operative aid,—and wherein alone it might be judicious to have a commission of five persons to wield collectively these important functions. He advised that it should be made incumbent on these departments to send to the Legislative chamber of the city one of its members or its chief to answer questions and take part in the deliberations without voting, so that the department should be constantly under public scrutiny and subject to a public examination.

All this presupposed not only an increase of the dignity of the Legislative department, but its election in a different way and by a different constituency from that established by law. It was the Charter amendments which the Tweed Ring bought from the Legislature in 1870 and 1871 which stripped the Board of Aldermen of all substantial legislative functions, and thereby of all character, and left the Board the mere power of granting away franchises without any power to exercise control for good. As a consequence, only such men sought the office as discovered in the only function left to the aldermen—that of granting franchises in relation to the use of the streets of the city of New York—an opportunity for profit. That the Board of Aldermen had grown from bad to worse since 1871, Mr. Sterne held to be a direct consequence of the law which stripped its members of truly legislative power. He therefore insisted that it must either be restored to its proper legislative function or abolished altogether, since an absolutely despotic Government was better than a sham democracy. The Board must be enabled to hold the executive officers of the city to a well-defined responsibility, and there should be conferred on it part of the function exercised by the Legislature, properly to supervise and determine the objects and purposes of city expenditure. In short, his position was that if the dignity of the position of the aldermen could be raised, and the character of their election and their constituency could be changed, legislative power might be safely lodged in their hands.

It was not till 1896 that Mr. Sterne had the satisfaction of seeing incorporated in the organic law of the State radical changes in the relation between the State and incorporated cities. These fell far short of the changes which he had advocated, but they marked at least a considerable step in the right direction. Under the Constitution, as then amended, the cities of the State are classified according to the latest State enumeration into three classes, of which the first includes all cities having a population of 250,000. Laws relating to the property, affairs, or government of cities, and the several departments thereof, are divided into general and special city laws—general laws being those which relate to all the cities of one or more classes, and special laws those which relate to a single city, or to less than all the cities of a class. As a partial check upon legislative interference with the affairs of cities, it is provided that after any Bill for a special city law has been passed by the Legislature, the House in which it originated shall immediately transmit a certified copy thereof to the Mayor of such city. The Mayor is required to return the Bill within fifteen days to the House from which it was sent, or if the legislative session is ended, to the Governor, bearing the Mayor's certificate as to whether the city has or has not accepted the Bill. In every city of the first class the Mayor acts for the city in regard to such a Bill. If the Bill relates to more than one city, it must be transmitted to the Mayor of each city to which it relates, and is not to be deemed accepted unless it bears the formal acceptance of every such city. If a Bill be returned without the acceptance of the city or cities to which it relates, it may, nevertheless, again be passed by both branches of the Legislature, being then subject, like other Bills, to the action of the Governor. We have expounded to very little purpose the views of Mr. Sterne in regard to the relations between the Legislature and the cities of the State, if this summary of the municipal amendments does not carry on its face convincing demonstration that to the teaching and influence of Simon Sterne the people are largely indebted for such benefits as they have brought in their train.

Like most believers in the possibility of municipal reform on a non-partisan basis, Mr. Sterne had steadfastly insisted on a separation of City from State elections, and it was held to be a most important gain for the cause of better government when there was inserted in the amended Constitution a provision that all elections for city officers should be held in an odd numbered year, leaving the even numbered years for national and State elections. That is to say, the voters of a city were thus enabled to make a clear distinction between the issues to be decided at elections of national and State officers, and those involved in the choice of the holders of the chief positions of municipal responsibility. It became possible under this provision to make the separation complete between municipal questions and those which form the dividing line between the great political parties. A principle earnestly contended for by all who have tried in the last thirty years to secure better government for the city of New York was thus finally incorporated in the fundamental law of the State.

With the consolidation of the various municipal and other divisions which went to the formation of the Greater New York, it became necessary to prepare a charter suited to the necessities of the new metropolitan constituency. This work had been entrusted to a commission which finished its labours early in 1897, and which gave public hearings early in that year to citizens or public bodies desiring to be heard. As intimated in a previous chapter, Mr. Sterne made a plea before this body for the introduction of the principle of minority representation in the new charter, but without effect. At the same time, the Bar Association appointed a committee to examine the proposed charter, of which Mr. Wheeler H. Peckham was the chairman, and Mr. Sterne was one of the members. In setting forth what they conceived to be the essential requisites which any scheme for the local government of such vast territory and population should possess, the Committee gave due weight to certain principles for which Mr. Sterne had always contended. These were : First, A large measure of local governmental power should be bestowed so as to give as little occasion as possible for the intervention of the legislative authority of the State ; in other words, wide, though not unlimited, scope should be given to the policy which goes under the name of Home Rule. Second, This power should be wisely and skilfully distributed among the different branches or departments of the local Government so as to prevent the abuse to which it is always liable. Third, The scheme should be so shaped as to make it easy to trace the credit for good, and the responsibility for bad government to the particular department or officer to which it really belonged, and the people should be able to exercise a real corrective power through popular elections. Fourth, The scheme should be carefully adapted to the habits and needs of the people which it is intended to serve, such adaptation to be shaped, not so much by a regard to theoretical principles, as to the teachings of actual experience as found in the history of the former local government of the same population. The Committee found that the Charter failed to conform to most of these requisites, and viewed with particular disfavour the constitution of the proposed Municipal Assembly. In this body was vested what was described in the language of the Bill as the legislative power of the city of New York, but the actual legislative power accorded to it was really very meagre. The direct grants of power were substantially those held by the existing Board of Aldermen, and while other and far larger grants were apparently conferred upon the Municipal Assembly, it was only to be curtailed and restricted or altogether destroyed by other provisions of the law. By far the larger portion of all local legislation as to matters of importance was to be transacted or controlled not by the Assembly, but by the heads of some twenty departments, appointees of the Mayor. The Committee found, however, that the obstructive power of the Assembly would be very considerable. They did not find that its opportunities for useful service were so much greater than those afforded by membership in the existing Board of Aldermen as to encourage them to expect a substantial improvement in the quality either of the candidates for election or of those elected to seats in the Municipal Assembly. They, therefore, regarded the establishment of a local legislature such as the Bill contemplated as a measure of most doubtful utility, and they anticipated what was shortly to be demonstrated in practice, that the division of the Municipal Assembly into two Houses would be a serious obstacle to its efficiency, would tend to divide and obscure responsibility, and would enhance the danger of unwise and corrupt obstruction. It was apparent to the Committee that in adopting the numerous checks and balances on the action of the Assembly, the Charter Commission had recognised the fact that the establishment of a Municipal Assembly, under the conditions accepted, was a hazardous experiment. Further demonstration of this was supplied in the recommendation by the Commission of a constitutional amendment authorising minority or proportional representation in municipal elections.

Mr. Sterne set forth, clearly and succinctly, his personal objections to the Greater New York Charter in the following communication to Governor Black :—

New York, *April* 17, 1897.

To Hon. Frank S. Black,
Governor of the State of New York.

Sir—Imperative professional engagements, which do not admit of adjournment, alone prevent me from joining in person the representatives of all the organised professional and business interests of New York City to ask you to veto the Bill recently passed (notwithstanding the disapproval of Mayor Strong) by the Legislature, and known as the Greater New York Charter.

It is true that a majority of the citizens of New York voted in favour of consolidation, but it is reasonable to suppose that this vote was given on the assumption that the Greater New York Charter would be a monumental work founded upon experience, would have enlisted in its practical accomplishment the ablest men in New York, that abundance of time would be afforded to them to produce a legislative measure harmonising the incongruous laws which now govern the municipalities which are to be united, and that a great opportunity would be afforded to guard the public treasury against extravagance and incompetency, and that no too great sacrifice would be imposed upon any portion of the city to be consolidated by the terms of settlement between the associated bodies politic.

It was also hoped that in the organisation of the municipal legislative body, a recognition of the principles of minority representation would give to each section of our community an opportunity to elect representatives of their own choosing, so as to emancipate the voters of New York from the thraldom of party machinery, and allow greater freedom for the issues of a municipal campaign to be fought out on lines affecting the municipal welfare only, and not disturbed by questions of national politics.

It was also hoped that substantially and freely a larger measure of Home Rule would be afforded to the citizens of New York, when their city will comprise almost half the voters of the State.

In all these expectations, the citizens of New York have been sorely disappointed, and, therefore, asked for time for the reconsideration of the terms of the instrument of consolidation, and for the prior enactment of the constitutional amendments which will secure to the municipality the benefits of a united Government unhampered by the continuance of county government, and to give to its citizens minority or proportional representation to prevent the absolute domination of some one political organisation in its government, and thereby enslave the greatest city of the Union for its personal and partisan ends.

The citizens of New York also ask for due time for the amendment of the sections of the Bill, so that its many defects, iniquities, and provisions of questionable constitutionality (which will be more particularly pointed out to you by my associates) may be eliminated, and the great fear of confiscation through excessive taxes, by well-guarded provisions, be lifted from the owners of real estate in the part of the consolidated city which has heretofore been known as New York.

Perhaps never before in the history of the municipality of New York has there been such unanimity of apprehension of evil from State legislation as is felt and expressed as to the measure which we ask you to disapprove.

It is safe to say that this feeling has already adversely affected real estate values, in the city of New York an appreciable percentage, and the consummation of the mischief by your approval will still more largely and injuriously affect such values. But were it known that by a large view of your duty, this ill-digested and dangerous Bill would be vetoed, and that time would be afforded for the elaboration of a scheme of consolidation, founded in fair dealing and wisdom, a corresponding rise and activity would ensue in real estate values, instead of doubt, depression, and loss. No better test of real benefits for injuries could be had than this gauge of value. If consolidation under any condition would give to New York City the impetus and advantages which the enthusiastic supporters of the measure before you claim for it, the first reflex of its passage would have been in an advancing market for real estate. The contrary result is its effect, and this effect has continued long enough to give pause to the most blinded advocate of the Bill before you.

I therefore ask you to heed the protests of the Chamber of Commerce, of the Bar Association of the city of New York, of the Board of Trade, of the Real Estate Exchange of the city, of the Reform and Union League Clubs, and of the many citizens who, independently of organised action, unite in asking at your hands a veto of this measure. This veto will not be a reversal of the popular vote in favour of consolidation, but will grant such delay as will enable a union of municipal interests to be formed which will be fruitful of benefits in place of evils and regrets.

These observations are not intended as a reflection upon the gentlemen who framed the Charter. Many of them are men of eminent ability and probity. Several of them I count among my own friends, who, doubtless, with reluctance, signed a charter which contained the defects of a many-headed police department and a dual chamber which tends to destroy responsibility, but all of them would candidly admit that the time allotted by the last Legislature for the completion of the stupendous work which they were called upon to perform was much too short to enable them to create such a measure as they must have desired to produce, and since its submission to the Legislature, no such thought, deliberation, or time has been by the law-making body given to it to have remedied in any particular the defects from which the draft of the Bill suffered.—I am, respectfully yours,

SIMON STERNE.

In the fall of 1897 the cause of municipal reform suffered a serious reverse in the election of the Tammany candidate for mayor. This was the more deeply deplored by the friends of good government, because the combined vote for the Citizens' Union and Republican candidate would have sufficed for the defeat of the Tammany candidate. What Mr. Sterne called the reconquest of New York by Tammany furnished him with a text for a very instructive review of the causes which had contributed to so deplorable a result. In an article in the *Forum* of January 1898, he pointed out that when, three years previously, the citizens of New York wrested from Tammany Hall the control over the city government and elected as mayor a gentleman of good repute as merchant and bank president, there was inaugurated what was supposed to be a new era in municipal administration of efficient, honest, and faithful public service. He admitted that the return of Tammany to power without the element of patronage to assist it seemed to confirm the views of those who look with distrust upon Democratic institutions, particularly in their application to urban population, and apparently supported the disparaging opinions as to the intellectual and moral qualities of the New York electorate, which had been expressed by eminent foreign critics. But he held that the causes of the reconquest of the city of New York by Tammany in 1897 must be sought for in the history of the economic and political conditions of the city during the three years of Mayor Strong's administration, in the State legislative proceedings during these three years, and in the use which was made by the citizens of New York and the city administration of the opportunities for better government afforded by the election of 1894.

Referring to the twenty years prior to 1895,

during the greater period of which New York had been under Tammany rule, Mr. Sterne thought it fair to assume that a large proportion of the annual budgets and a considerable proportion of the indebtedness of the city incurred during that time represented waste and extravagance, unnecessary expenditure, and crystallised fraud. During the last year of Tammany administration the tax-rate had been $1.79 per hundred. This was a large enough exaction from the thrifty and industrious part of the people whose money is invested in real property, and who had the well-grounded expectation that the saving which would be effected by the bank president's administration of the affairs of the city would result either in a considerably lower expenditure of money, and thereby in a reduction of the tax-rate, or in an enormous increase in the efficiency of all the departments by the expenditure of a like sum of money. In this expectation the citizens of New York were lamentably disappointed. During the first year of Mayor Strong's administration the tax-rate went up to $1.91, though the assessed valuation of property had increased $13,615,625, while the city debt increased $6,672,165. There was a further increase of debt in 1896 to the amount of $8,260,505, and in 1897 to the amount of $8,310,832. The increase of the ordinary expenses, which kept pace with the increase of the debt, was a sore and serious disappointment to the taxpayer, because he argued, in the rough-and-ready fashion of popular logic, that either it was true that the preceding Tammany government was an extravagant and dishonest one, and that, therefore, the amount of expenditure in these departments was ridiculously in excess of actual needs; or it was not true, and the money expended under Tammany was a necessary expenditure; or, as a third alternative, that the new administration, from which so much good was hoped, was, for some cause too occult for him to understand, incapable of affording relief. The second year after the reform administration came into power the tax-rate rose to $2.14, the assessed valuation of real and personal property having been increased $89,537,243 over that of the previous year, and $103,152,868 over 1894. During the third and last year of the reform administration the tax-rate was $2.10, though the assessment had been increased $62,150,951 over that of 1896, and $165,303,819 over that of 1894. During those three years the actual values of property had, through the erection of huge office-buildings, been more largely increased than during any previous period in the history of the city, and the tax-rate should have decreased accordingly.

For years the Legislature and the City Government had vied with each other in multiplying offices so as to strengthen the political organisation in power, or, when the party in control of the State differed from that in the city, in adding to such offices so as to divide between the party in control of the State and the political organisation in power in the city the incumbents of the new offices thus created. Mr. Sterne pointed out that it was the duty of the reform administration to get rid of all these useless and expensive additions of increased office-holders and clerical force, to make an official day of labour in the public offices six or seven hours instead of three or four, and in every way to diminish the expenses of the various departments of the city of New York to reasonable business limits. What was done was to put in every office originally created for mere purposes of expenditure a follower of one of the factions or organisations which made up the army of the reform movement of 1894, to increase instead of diminish many salaries in every department, and to make a more lavish distribution of public money for new construction of highways and buildings than had theretofore been done. It is true that in one department of the city administration—that of street-cleaning—a degree of efficiency was attained hitherto unknown in the city of New York, and also that the judicial administration of the police justices' courts was raised in dignity by the selection of a higher order of incumbents. Had the superior efficiency in the work of street-cleaning been attained without the expenditure of a dollar more than the amount which the commissioner had at his disposal when the department was under Tammany rule, it would have furnished a complete demonstration of the corruption and inefficiency of Tammany as compared with the work of the reform administration. It did, however, involve an expenditure of an average of about $500,000 a year above previous appropriations to accomplish the result.

So with the Department of Education, it would have been a fine object-lesson for the citizens of New York if they could have had the administration of the public schools removed from improper influences and conducted upon a high plane of efficiency at an expense no greater than that which had been incurred under the waste and knavery of Tammany rule. But the superior efficiency of the schools was attained at a cost in 1895 of $266,770 in excess of that of 1894, in 1896 of $1,028,867, and in 1897 of $1,437,501 in excess of that of the last year of Tammany administration, and this without counting additions to expenditures provided for by the issue of bonds. Still, in Mr. Sterne's judgment, the people would have found no fault with these expenditures if in other departments compensating savings had been made, because they argued that if 20 per cent of the $34,000,000 theretofore annually expended by the city of New York, exclusive of the interest charge on the public debt and the city's proportion of State taxation, was wasted under Tammany control, there should have been a saving of almost $7,000,000 a year, out of which these beneficial additional expenses for education and street-cleaning could have been made, and still leave $4,000,000 to go to the credit of the tax-payers and the reduction of their burdens. But the expenditures of public money during the three years of the term of Mayor Strong, who stood before the community for decency as compared with the professional politicians banded together under the name of Tammany, were, with some few exceptions, as large as in the years which had preceded his incumbency.

Mr. Sterne desired it to be understood that no one more than he deplored the unfortunate mixing up and confounding of the work of the outgoing city administration with the general desire for the reform of our American municipal governments. He said that he had been striving since he arrived at manhood to remove from that government the reproaches which might justly be laid at its door, but he could not shut his eyes to the fact that the administration of Mayor Strong had, from the economic side, been a lamentable failure, and that any movement which was allied with it, or stood for the same class of thought, could not for the second time "enthuse" the people of the city of New York. On the financial side there was the record of the total expenditures, which, starting with $38,395,094 in 1894, went on increasing every year until they reached $48,229,558 in 1897. Deducting from this an increase of $2,500,000 in the State taxes, and about $400,000 for increase of interest on the public debt, there still remained an increase of about $7,000,000 in the general expenditures. The debt of the city, which at the close of 1894 was $105,777,855, had reached by 1897 the sum of $129,021,357, showing a total increase of $23,243,502 during the three years of Mayor Strong's administration. Before that administration came into existence, the heads of the city government had been accustomed to answer the charge of extravagance by the excuse that the expenditures were imposed by the action of the Legislature. To some of the expenditures of the three years in question the same excuse will apply, but simultaneously with the beginning of Mayor Strong's administration there came into force a constitutional amendment which subjected any Bill involving expenditures by the city government to the Mayor's veto, reserving to the Legislature, however, the right to pass the Bill over such veto. The expenditures involved in such legislation which met with the approval of the Mayor are, therefore, fairly chargeable to his administration.

But if the administration which made way for Tammany in 1897 was a failure from the economic side, it was equally a failure, in the judgment of Mr. Sterne, from the political side. Early in the year 1895, the Legislature passed a bi-partisan police Bill which was of such a character as to challenge the adverse criticism of almost all the conservative elements which aided in the election of Mr. Strong. It continued to enforce that feature of police management which had divided responsibility and aided corruption. It was, in the opinion of competent judges, worse than the law which preceded it and for which it was substituted ; yet it was approved by the Mayor. The commission to draft the Greater New York Charter seemed to recognise the fact that, without minority representation in the municipal legislative Boards, the experiment which that Charter initiated might prove a dangerous one. They expressed a doubt, however, about the constitutionality of such a provision, and yet, despite its importance in the scheme of government, no serious effort was made, either on their recommendations or by the city authorities, to postpone the adoption of the Greater New York Charter until minority representation could be constitutionally secured in the Municipal Assembly, so that should the city be recaptured by Tammany, a substantial proportion of political power could still be retained by the better class of the citizens of New York. The matter was disposed of by the Commission, of which the Mayor was a member, recommending that the Legislature pass a constitutional amendment providing for minority representation in municipal bodies. This recommendation was wholly disregarded by the Legislature. The Charter was thereupon promptly passed, and through its instrumentality the hold of the powers that work for evil upon the city treasury and upon the appropriation of other people's money was strengthened instead of loosened. The term of office of the Mayor was lengthened to four years, and his powers greatly enlarged; the incumbents of office were made more dependent upon the Mayor; the length of the terms of office of heads of departments was increased, and no safeguard was placed anywhere to guard against the event which happened, of a sinister and dangerous organisation once again taking possession of the city of New York.

The liquor law passed during Tammany's control of the city was enacted with the view of not being strictly enforced in a cosmopolitan community like that of New York, and probably also with the view of a corrupt acquiescence in its breach. During Mayor Strong's administration, and in the hottest summer months, Mr. Roosevelt, the President of the Police Board, ordered this law to be strictly and rigidly enforced, and in this he had the full support of the Chief Executive of the city. This action alienated from the reform movement thousands upon thousands of its supporters, who regarded such strict enforcement as an impairment of their personal liberty, and a senseless and needless aggravation of their discomfort during a protracted period of an extreme heat in 1895. Finally, the Republican party insisted upon placing upon the statute book an excise law whose enforcement went far beyond Mr. Roosevelt's position during the summer of 1895, and interfered with the habits of the German population of the city to a greater extent than had been attempted before. They met the taunt that they should not allow Sunday beer to be of more importance to them than good government by the answer that they should not be asked to sacrifice an innocent indulgence to Puritanical legislation; that the question of their personal liberty was quite as important, as a matter of principle, as good government in this city. Mr. Sterne did not attempt to decide whether they were right or wrong in this contention, but contented himself by showing that there was thus produced in a large class of the voting population a feeling of positive hatred against everything labelled Republican, which told with great force against the candidacy of Mr. Low.

Thus, when the question was agitated in the

summer of 1897, of nominating a Citizens' Union candidate for the Mayoralty of the city of New York, account had to be taken of a widespread feeling of resentment and disappointment with the existing administration, and it required the utmost delicacy and tact to overcome the mass of opposition which had been accumulating because of these successive blunders, and to weld it into a united movement against Tammany. Under the existing system of representative government, which recognises majorities or pluralities only, a community has no means of making its protest against misrule effective except by voting for those in opposition. Such a vote, Mr. Sterne insisted, could in no way be held to imply sympathy with, or confidence in, the organisation helped by the protest of 1897. It was his opinion, that of the 234,000 votes recorded in favour of the Tammany candidate for Mayor, not one-half were in sympathy with Tammany. A very large proportion of this vote represented the voters' disappointment at the measures which, and resentment against the men who had, during the last three years, oppressed and disappointed them. Unfortunately, Mr. Low's candidacy was publicly supported by many of the men in close affiliation with Mayor Strong's administration and by the Mayor himself. The result, therefore, in 1897—the reconquest of New York by Tammany—Mr. Sterne held to be no indication of the breakdown of American institutions or of free government. It was the better element of New York which made the mistakes that resulted in the weakening of the garrison and the opening of the gates for the entrance of the enemy who had been ejected three years before. Nor was it true that New York had deliberately chosen a corrupt government, and that it might be legitimately inferred that New York was itself corrupt. New York was resentful at the miscarriage of its efforts three years before. No people living under democratic institutions as now organised, and without true minority representation in full operation, has an opportunity to exhibit such resentment except by inflicting upon itself another wound, and that was the unfortunate situation in the city of New York in the autumn of 1897. Mr. Sterne concludes his judicial review of the causes of Tammany's reconquest of New York by the following personal statement :—

The writer of this article hesitated for some time as to the wisdom of setting forth before the community the facts herein stated, he having participated in every reform movement undertaken in the city of New York from Tweed's day down to and including the advocacy of the candidacy of Seth Low for the Mayoralty at the election of 1897, and sharing with his fellow-committeemen of seventy of 1894 the responsibility of the election of Mayor Strong. Yet the battle of municipal reform must be fought again and again until success perches upon its banner, and when won it should be made a permanent victory over the enemies of good government, and that can be done only by fighting on better lines than the platforms of 1894 and 1897. And to do this effectually, there must also be a clear understanding and no illusions about the causes of the failure of the friends of good government in the campaign of 1897, and any contributions to public discussion having that end in view must ultimately have beneficial results.

Into the municipal contest of 1899 which turned upon the question of an independent and unassessed judiciary, Mr. Sterne threw himself with unabated ardour. In a speech delivered at the Citizens' Union meeting in Cooper Union on October 28, Mr. Sterne pointed out that the issue once more presented to the citizens of New York, was whether they should rule themselves or permit Tammany Hall to designate the occupants of the seat of justice. He remarked that New Yorkers could not complain in that year, that they had but a Hobson's choice of taking the adherents of one or the other political party, both equally objectionable, for non-partisan offices. A club of citizens of every shade of political opinion, bound together by but one tie, and that of a public-spirited interest in the welfare of the city of New York, had invited all the interests not under the dominion of Tammany Hall to unite in the formation of a ticket which was to be expressive of the best sentiments of citizenship, and represent in its make-up the assurances of high service by special fitness to fill the various offices for which they were selected. The City Club, the Citizens' Union, and the Republican Organisation, which had at this time truly subordinated partisan advantage to the higher call of patriotism, asked the citizens of New York to avail themselves of the opportunity to give Tammany Hall an unmistakable intimation that New York was weary of its domination.

As viewed by the great body of voters, the question really narrowed itself down to the re-election of Judge Joseph F. Daly, since the other reform nominee for Justice of the Supreme Court —George C. Barrett—was also on the Tammany ticket, and the other judicial nominations were not of sufficient prominence greatly to excite public interest. In the words of Mr. Sterne, Judge Daly had been denied a renomination by the Boss of Tammany Hall, on the avowed ground that he had not given proper consideration to that potentate, meaning thereby, to his financial interest and political favourites. In the language of the organisation, Judge Daly had been "turned down" by the Boss because he refused to be faithless to his trust. Mr. Sterne, therefore, appealed to the citizens of New York, if they respected their rights, if they had any decent regard for the value of an independent judiciary, if they knew how dangerous it was not to resent this displacing by a political boss of a faithful judicial officer, to put Judge Daly back, by their votes on November 7, where he ought to have been a year ago. Judge Daly's candidature represented a principle; it represented the eternal ideas of justice, and the more one respected his fellow-citizens the more confidently would he expect such a principle to triumph.

But the time was not ripe for the popular uprising that swept Tammany out of power in 1901, and Mr. Sterne and his associates in the Citizens' Union movement of 1899 pleaded in vain. Nevertheless, up to the date when the illness which was destined to prove fatal overtook him, Mr. Sterne did not cease to raise his voice and bend all his energies to the promotion of the cause of good government in the city of New

York. One of his last public deliverances on this subject was a speech he made at the City Club on January 19, 1900, on the revision of the Charter of the Greater New York. He began by the reminder that this charter had been opposed by every conservative interest in the city. It was urged that it would increase municipal expenditure and make the task of the independent voter who desired to emancipate municipal government from partisan control more and more difficult. These prognostications came to pass. The expenses of the city increased, and the political organisation which had formerly controlled the Government was aided in its recapture shortly after the passage of the Charter. The question of its revision was before the community once more. Mr. Sterne, therefore, embraced the opportunity to plead with all the force at his command for the one safeguard which he felt would most effectually guarantee to the minority of the citizens of New York some proper representation in the Municipal Assembly, and under which it would be expedient to give that Assembly substantial power over the executive department of the city. He remained thoroughly convinced that if minority representation were intelligently introduced in the election and organisation of a municipal body, the cleavage would no longer be between the Democrats of the organisation stripe and Republicans of the organisation stripe, but political parties would become disintegrated on the subject of municipal administration, and the citizens would divide upon municipal questions into smaller congeries, leaving to each quota of voters capable of electing one member to such municipal body a special organisation and domain.

Mr. Sterne had impressed these views on the Charter Commission, but the only result obtained was the recommendation of the passage of a constitutional amendment applying minority representation to municipal bodies after the passage of the Charter. He argued that we have tried every conceivable palliative against political corruption, and they had all failed, except the one remedy which promises success, which is drastic in its effect, which trusts the people finally, enlarges their scope of choice, and gives true effect to their voting power, and which makes of a legislative assembly a reduced photograph of the whole community. For the last twenty-five years efforts had been made by civil service reform, by the substitution of the Australian ballot, and by putting nominations under the ægis of the law and protecting the citizen's right to the exercise of his nominating power, to stay corruption, and to undermine the rule of the boss; and yet the rule of the boss was stronger than ever before. Why not, asked Mr. Sterne, try what some of the most eminent political thinkers believed and now believe to be the true safeguard for Democratic institutions and the only preventive of the degeneracy of the whole political machinery and its falling into the hands of the political organiser? It is the law of differentiation in employments, and the intensity of the competition of modern life which create and make as a condition of success the exclusiveness of thought and occupation on the one side of the mass of our citizens to their respective industrial and professional vocations; and on the other, produce a class of politicians who are politicians all the year round, and who are infinitely the superiors in management to the volunteer and occasional politician. A contest between the two represents the trained intellect against the amateur, and it produces the same result in politics that it does in every other occupation in life. That we must, therefore, make it easy for the citizen to produce a result commensurate with his efforts, and to secure a representative in the municipal body selected to act for him by a comparatively slight effort. Impose on the citizen the condition that he must belong to a majority before he can be represented at all, either in the city or in the district, and you place him at so hopeless a disadvantage as against the trained politician, that he prefers to go a-fishing rather than attempt the impossible.

Had an intelligent appreciation of the effect of minority representation existed in the minds of the authors of the new charter and the Legislature which passed it, and had provisions securing its benefits been incorporated therein, in both municipal chambers a clear majority would have been elected against Tammany in 1897 instead of an overwhelming majority in its favour. In a representative body elected on the system of minority or proportional representation every influential class of our citizens would find itself represented by its ablest spokesmen. The taxpayers, as such, would then be represented; the merchants would be represented; every form of communal interest in the city of New York which could attach to its banner a one-hundredth part of its voting population would be represented, and the Municipal Assembly would, indeed, be a reduced photograph of all the financial, industrial, educational, and other interests in the city. We have, said Mr. Sterne, tried two municipal bodies, and they were as corrupt as one. We have tried short terms for mayors, and their incumbents were as incapable as those holding longer terms. We have tried everything but the true remedy. So Mr. Sterne was moved to make this last appeal for a reform in whose adoption he profoundly believed lay the solution of most of the problems with which the people of New York had been vainly trying for generations to deal:—

> Is it not about time for a community which has intelligence enough to vie with every other part of the world in commercial and manufacturing activity, to see the hopelessness of every attempt heretofore made to remedy the political evils which afflicted, and accept the just and larger remedial measure of a fuller effectiveness of the vote, and of a larger and freer expression of public opinion which is alone afforded by minority representation?

CHAPTER X

PROFESSIONAL ACTIVITY

MR. STERNE had the common experience of members of the Bar who begin their career without influential connections, of finding it difficult to obtain a firm foothold in his profession. But his indomitable will and tireless energy, coupled with a training more than usually thorough, an engaging manner and unswerving uprightness of conduct, combined to gain for him clients whose lasting respect he seldom failed to win, no less than that of the men with whom he was brought into contact on the Bench or at the Bar. Mr. Sterne entered into co-partnership in 1867 with Mr. Max Goepp, under the firm of Goepp and Sterne. His partner dying in 1872, he continued in practice alone until 1878. During the seven succeeding years, Mr. Sterne formed partnerships with Mr. James A. Hudson, Mr. Oscar S. Straus, and Mr. Daniel G. Thompson, resuming practice alone in 1885, and continuing it, under his own name, until his death in 1901.

It is obviously impossible to make more than a passing reference to the professional work performed by a man like Mr. Sterne during a long and active practice at the Bar. Among the clients whom he represented early in his career were certain security-holders interested in the management of the Chesapeake and Ohio Railroad Company; The Central Crosstown Railway Company, for which he acted as counsel from 1874 to 1880, when it was one of the prominent street railroads of New York; Mark Twain, the well-known humorist, in a suit to prevent infringement of copyright; Joaquin Miller, the poet of the Sierras, in a like suit; and Sir Morrell Mackenzie, the well-known English physician. Mr. Sterne early showed his ability to handle satisfactorily matters involving large financial transactions, and in this class of cases he was very frequently consulted. He was a good equity lawyer, and was noted for his familiarity with and sound knowledge of corporation and railroad law. He was frequently called upon for an opinion relating to questions involving the construction of the Constitution of the United States, the Constitution of the State of New York, and the Interstate Commerce Act. The prominent position which Mr. Sterne secured at the Bar, and the reputation which he gained for learning in the higher branches of the law, are indicated by his appearance in certain extradition proceedings brought in the name of the Austrian Government; in cases before the United States Supreme Court on questions affecting the validity of the issues of bonds of the States of Louisiana and North Carolina, payment of which had been repudiated; in a suit involving the question of the right of the city of New York to apply the bonds in its sinking fund toward the extinction of its debt; in a proceeding in relation of the right of the city of New York to expend money for the opening of Van Courtlandt and Crotona Parks after the debt limit had apparently been reached; in a matter before the Executive Department of the United States involving the retention, against the interests of American citizens, of a certain diplomatic representative in one of the States of Africa; in proceedings before the Department of the Interior in relation to public lands, and others in relation to certain old Spanish grants affecting title to a large tract of land in the territory of New Mexico; in a hearing before the Secretary of State, as representing the President, in regard to signing a bill which indirectly brought about a change in the position of the United States Government toward the Nicaragua Canal question; in the submission of an argument to the President of the United States in regard to his signature of a bill prohibiting the acquisition by alien corporations of more than a specified amount of land in the territories of the United States; in proceedings before the Court of Claims of the State of New York with reference to the construction of an addition to the new Capitol building at Albany; in *quo warranto* proceedings as to the right of certain railroads in Brooklyn to use steam on the streets of that city; in patent infringement suits affecting, among others, an important chemical preparation largely employed in the industrial arts, a well-known air brake used on railways, and the question of the priority of invention of a weapon used in modern warfare; in a suit determining almost for the first time that a seat on the New York Cotton Exchange was property subject to sale under a judgment against a member, and in another suit, also pioneer in its nature, decided in his favour by the New York Court of Appeals, determining that the interest of a stockholder in a foreign corporation is not subject to attachment in any State other than that in which the corporation was organised.

Mr. Sterne's familiarity with Wall Street affairs, and the convictions he had formed as to the evils of speculation, led him, as one of several contributors to a series of newspaper articles by prominent lawyers on the subject of success at the Bar, which appeared in New York in 1883, to point out that one of the causes of failure among lawyers was the temptation, too often indulged, to take a speculative interest in the enterprises of their clients. By endeavouring to seize the opportunity of acquiring wealth without much effort, Mr. Sterne held that the attention of the lawyer became diverted from his more immediate responsibilities; his money being invested in an uncertain risk, his time was often wasted and the gains of many years swept away, with the sure result of professional demoralisation and loss of clients.

Mr. Sterne's appearance, in 1879 and 1880, as counsel for the New York Chamber of Commerce and New York Board of Trade and Transportation before the Committee of the State Assembly, known as the Hepburn Railroad Investigation Committee, and his arduous and successful services in that investigation, have already been referred to in an earlier chapter. He spent nearly eight months in this work, and employed all the resources of his professional knowledge and ability, no less than his insight into human nature, in dealing with unwilling witnesses. The efforts of opposing counsel to introduce unseemly wrangling and to belittle his labours on behalf of the mercantile community, were met with the greatest urbanity and firmness. His manner of examining the leading railroad officers who appeared before the Committee was such as to command respect and admiration. He declared that he was not attacking the men but the system they represented. This formed the key-note of his conduct of the investigation, and by closely adhering to it he succeeded in exposing the evils then connected with the administration of New York's great systems of transportation, despite the denials of the railroad Presidents that any such evils existed. The testimony taken is contained in five bulky volumes of printed matter which stand, to this day, as a monument to the industry and acumen of the man who elicited it, and as a contribution whose value has never been excelled, to this branch of railroad literature.

In his closing argument before the Committee, Mr. Sterne took occasion to reply to a remark of one of the opposing counsel who had referred slightingly to his work. He pointed out that the legal representatives of the railroad companies in their summing up, which occupied several days, had ignored all the evidence presented and had treated the controversy as though no proof had been adduced to support the allegations of the complaining merchants, in spite of the fact that the truth of these charges had been overwhelmingly established. To an allusion which one of them, Mr. Depew, had made to him as a Don Quixote, he replied in the following terms :—

> I have been called by my friend, Mr. Depew, in several parts of his address a "Don Quixote." I did not know to what degree or extent that remark was apposite or pertinent until towards the end of this third day of discussion. I am now disposed to confess that there is something Don Quixotic about this controversy as it now shapes itself. If I am a Don Quixote, this Committee had the exhibition that instead of Don Quixote fighting the windmill, two windmills have, during the last three days, been fighting Don Quixote!

Reference has already been made, in a previous chapter, to Mr. Sterne's legal services on behalf of the city, in 1874, in connection with the sinking of the tracks of the New York and Harlem Railroad on Fourth Avenue, above Forty-Second Street, in New York City. He was unable to obtain a final determination of this case on appeal, on account of the death of Mayor Havemeyer, for whom he was acting as private counsel, and the decision of the then Corporation Counsel to discontinue further proceedings after the decision of the lower Court. In Mr. Sterne's opinion there was no valid, legal, or other reason for such a discontinuance, but as he was acting merely as the representative of the official attorney of the city, he was helpless in the matter.

He always felt confident that if he had been allowed to argue this case on appeal, he would have carried his point, and saved a large sum of money for the city.

As counsel for the city of New York in several suits brought against certain local banks to recover interest on money deposited during the Tweed *régime*, and which the banks claimed had been deposited without any agreement for the payment of interest, Mr. Sterne achieved at least the partial success of recovering for the city the sum of over $200,000.

Suits against the New York Elevated Railroad for damages to property by reason of the obstruction which they made to the passage of light and air have long ceased to excite attention in New York, or to be regarded as anything remarkable in legal practice. But in the earlier history of the elevated roads, the questions involved were regarded as of the highest importance, and the absence of any controlling precedents gave a profound legal significance to their determination. In the earliest period of these suits, Mr. Sterne was retained on behalf of a certain corporation to recover damages claimed by reason of the operation of one of the west side elevated railroads in front of its building which was situated opposite one of the stations of the road. Mr. Sterne's client occupied the entire building, and derived no rental from it. But it was deemed necessary to prove loss of rental as one of the elements of damage. The loss of light due to the darkening of the building by the station in front of it had been somewhat lessened by the construction of a large skylight, and it seemed as if the amount recoverable on that ground would be trifling. It was also necessary to prove depreciation of the property. This would not have been difficult but for the fact that during most of the period for which damages were claimed, there had been a steady rise in real estate values in many parts of the city, including the district in which the plaintiff's property was situated. Mr. Sterne claimed that this was due to a reaction from the pre-existing depression, and not, as was claimed by the defendant, to any benefit gained by the existence of the elevated railroad. This situation, however, added greatly to the difficulty of Mr. Sterne's position, and it was regarded as a decided legal triumph when, through the testimony of expert real estate agents, and by a process of exhaustive reasoning on the facts presented, he overcame all the objections urged against the recovery of damages, and succeeded in obtaining a judgment for the full amount claimed. This decision was sustained on appeal, and the Company decided to pay the judgment before the time set for argument in the Court of last resort, fearing the effect of an adverse decision there upon the suits of other claimants.

Another case of considerable public interest occurred in the course of Mr. Sterne's practice in the early eighties. He was called upon by the Board of Trade and Transportation to appear on its behalf against certain railroads which were refusing to accept freight for shipment on account of what was then known as the "Freight-handlers' Strike" for higher wages. The case was argued by Mr. Sterne at the Special and General term of the Supreme Court, and resulted in a decision by the latter tribunal in favour of Mr. Sterne's position, which was, that railroads, though in private hands, are affected by a public interest; that the business done upon them is likewise affected by a public interest, and that it is the public duty of the railway corporation to handle and forward freight offered to it, the disaffection of its working-men furnishing no excuse for the non-performance of that duty. This decision (in *People* v. *New York Central and Hudson River R. R. Company*, 28 Hun.) has been frequently referred to in similar strikes in other states, and was among the first of its kind rendered in the state of New York. It has commanded acceptance by the Courts of other states wherever a similar question has been raised.

But, as Mr. Sterne himself argued, in discussing the question of "The Duties of Railroads and their Employés" with Prof. Hadley before the Commonwealth Club in March, 1888:—It is equally true that not only the railway performs a public function, which it may not neglect or discontinue, but that as a necessary legal and logical corollary, its officers, employés, and working-men are likewise engaged in the performance of a public function which they cannot be permitted to discontinue at will. More specifically, these employés cannot be permitted to combine to discontinue this public service, however humble may be their part of the functions performed, inasmuch as the occupation partakes of a public character, and the employé should be held in the same measure of responsibility to the public as his employer. Mr. Sterne went on to argue that if the law as it stands does not sufficiently recognise this duty on the part of employés, there should be no hesitation about adopting amendments to the law by which the acceptance of employment for the performance of a function which is so essential to the public weal as the regular transportation of passengers, freight, and mails, should be regarded as an enlistment for a term of years in the public service. Manifestly, under any such rule, a railway engineer would no more be permitted, at the instigation of the chief of his trade-union, to take his engine to the round-house, than a soldier would be to lay down his arms without a command from his superior officer. Mr. Sterne scouted the idea that such legislation would lead to paternal government, though he admitted that so long as private interests could be relied upon to perform this transportation function duly and thoroughly, it was as well to leave things as they stood. But when the community is in danger of the stoppage of a service upon which its welfare depends, the community has the right to step in and to attach such conditions to the service as will insure its performance and its continuance, precisely for the same reason that it insures the regularity and continuance of the service of its armies and of its navies, by terms of service made independent of caprice and conspiracy.

There have been many acute reminders since these words were uttered of the necessity of incorporating in the law of the land the principles here contended for, but they have so far passed unheeded.

That Mr. Sterne's fairness to his opponents was fully appreciated in his profession, is shown by an incident which occurred a few years before his death. On behalf of certain foreign bond-holders largely interested in the Chicago and Northern Pacific Railroad Company, he had become a member of the committee, of which he was also one of the counsel, engaged in the effort to bring about a reorganisation of the affairs of that company, then in the hands of a receiver. Many claims, conflicting as against each other, of different classes of lienors, general creditors, and stockholders had to be dealt with, and each counsel or representative of the various claimants was engaged in the endeavour to obtain as large a concession as possible for his client. The complicated relations of the Corporation with the Northern Pacific Railroad Company, then also in the hands of receivers, were matters of frequent discussion and serious consideration on the part of the committee and their counsel, and Mr. Francis L. Stetson, counsel for Messrs. J. P. Morgan and Company, who were largely interested in the Northern Pacific Company, and who were, like the other claimants, endeavouring to secure the best results for themselves. Toward the later stages of the reorganisation proceeding, a dispute arose as to the claims of one of the parties interested, the decision of which was of vital importance to all concerned. After much talk, there seemed to be no prospect of coming to an agreement. Mr. Stetson, though opposed to Mr. Sterne and other members of the committee on the question involved, finally suggested that in view of the judicial spirit which Mr. Sterne had shown in dealing with the problems considered by the committee, he felt sure, if the matter in controversy were submitted to Mr. Sterne, it would be decided on its merits, and full justice done to all. He added that, so far as his own clients were concerned, he was willing, on their behalf, to make the submission. In this suggestion Mr. Stetson was warmly seconded by others interested in the controversy. Though at first reluctant to consent, Mr. Sterne was finally induced to serve as arbitrator, and when his decision was rendered, it was accepted as eminently satisfactory.

Nothing is more gratifying to a lawyer than to have his judgment of the law vindicated by a decision of the Court, when associate counsel have disagreed with him and taken the view of his opponents. Mr. Sterne had this satisfaction in a series of litigations in which half a dozen prominent attorneys were associated with him, and the other side was represented by counsel of equal eminence. The question arose under the terms of a railroad mortgage which was being foreclosed, whether the complainants were entitled to the payment of interest upon the defaulted coupons. The mortgage itself was silent on this point. All the attorneys, except Mr. Sterne, insisted that each coupon constituted a separate contract, and that, as there had been a default on each coupon, interest thereon ran from the time that each became due. Without having the opportunity of examining the authorities, Mr. Sterne insisted that, from the nature of the mortgage contract and the provisions of the law of New York, where the mortgage had been executed and the bonds and coupons were payable, interest as claimed was not recoverable. His position was that the mortgage was similar in its nature to a real estate mortgage, upon which, on default of the payment of the bond, simple interest only could be recovered, unless, of course, as was not here the case, the mortgage provided otherwise. He argued the question before one of the judges of the United States Circuit Court, in one of the Western Districts, who, after an examination of the authorities, submitted by Mr. Sterne in an elaborate brief, agreed with his conclusions, and by so doing enabled Mr. Sterne to save for his clients nearly $150,000. The attorneys on the other side became so fully convinced of the justice of Mr. Sterne's argument, that they decided not to appeal from the Judge's order.

Mr. Sterne was full of resource in his mastery of the practical details of his profession, and was equally conscientious and industrious in the effort to accomplish, by every honourable means, the object of his retainer. He uniformly gave the impression of thorough earnestness and unwavering belief in the justice of his client's cause. He was gifted with an extraordinary memory, which enabled him to recall, without apparent effort, and with great accuracy, all the facts bearing on a given matter, and the arguments on both sides of a question which had at any time been presented to him. He was accustomed to say, when wonder was expressed at his ability to recall, after a long lapse of time, and in the midst of the pressure of other matters, some incident, fact, or argument, in connection with the subject under discussion, that he saw things with an almost microscopic eye, and retained them unconsciously in his memory as clearly as he had at first received them.

The cases in which Mr. Sterne's professional activity dealt with questions of public interest would make a long list, and some of them have already been referred to, at length, in the earlier chapters of this volume. One of the latest of these related to what is known as the "Amsterdam Avenue grab." One of the street railroad companies of New York had attempted to occupy that section of Amsterdam Avenue between Fifty-Ninth and One Hundred and Twenty-Fifth Street, for the purpose of laying tracks for cars to be run by electricity, although another company was already in possession, and the available width of the avenue precluded the possibility of safe operation over two sets of double tracks. The intervening space which it was proposed to allow between the two sets of tracks of the two companies was so small as to involve a certainty that any one caught between the cars while in operation would be injured or killed. The danger of accident was so apparent, and the fear of injury to women and children using the street was so great, that there was a general public protest against the proposed further occupation of the Avenue. Mr. Sterne was retained as counsel to protect the rights of the people, and succeeded in obtaining an injunction from the Courts restraining the invading company from carrying out its plans. To this he added his services in drafting a Bill which was enacted into a law, by which similar attempts by railroad companies likely to endanger the lives of the public were prohibited.

For many years Mr. Sterne had appeared, without fee or reward, before the Legislature at Albany, in support of a Bill which he had drafted to regulate telephone charges. In common with many others, he thought these charges extortionate, but, owing to the influence and power of the telephone monopoly, he had been unable to make much progress in his efforts to have them reduced. When, therefore, a few years before his death, the Telephone Company increased its rate for unlimited service, Mr. Sterne's objections took the determined form of obtaining a preliminary injunction to prevent the removal of his telephone, because of his refusal to accede to the demands of the Company. He insisted that the additional charge was unreasonable, and that the books of the corporation would sustain his contention. The Company fought the suit in every way, and, on a technicality, evaded an examination before trial. The Court, however, continued the injunction, holding, practically for the first time as a matter of law, that the service rendered by the Telephone Company was analogous to that rendered by a common carrier; that the public was entitled to it on the payment of a reasonable price, and that what was a reasonable price should be determined by a trial upon the merits. This trial, however, in which the examination desired would have been made, had not taken place at the time of Mr. Sterne's death, and there appeared to be no necessity for a determination of the question by his heirs. The suit was productive of benefit to the public, inasmuch as the decision on the motion for an injunction served to call attention to the rights of telephone users, and is said to have induced the Telephone Company to arrange for a system of reduced charges based upon the number of telephone calls issued.

Mr. Sterne was, from its foundation, a member of the Association of the Bar of the City of New York, the leading organisation of lawyers in the United States. When the power of the Tweed Ring began to exert its influence on the Bench and Bar of the city, he was among the first to suggest the organisation of a body of lawyers, for the purpose of maintaining the honour and dignity of the profession, and raising the standard of its culture and ability. His name does not appear among the founders of the Bar Association, because, when it was organised, he was, under the advice of his physician, travelling in South America. On his return to New York, he immediately became a member, and continued to be one until his death. He took an active part in the affairs of the Association, serving at frequent intervals on its more prominent committees, and being consulted on all important occasions by his fellow-members.

The contrast between the compensation paid by the English Government to its judges, and that paid by the Government of the United States, was a subject to which Mr. Sterne frequently referred, both by tongue and pen. He made a notable contribution to this discussion in an article contributed to the January, 1892, number of *The Counsellor*, a magazine devoted to the interests of the New York Law School. The article was entitled "The Salaries of the United States Supreme Court Judges," and in it Mr. Sterne brought out a number of considerations which seem at length about to bear fruit in long-deferred Congressional action on this subject. In illustration of his theme, he referred in the following language to the impression produced on him when as a boy he had gone with his law preceptor, Mr. John H. Markland, to call upon Chief Justice Taney in Washington:—

> We found that legal luminary living with his family over a candy shop on Pennsylvania Avenue, between Fourth and Fifth Streets. The chamber in which the Chief Justice wrote his opinions was partitioned off by a calico curtain from another apartment in which apparently was done the family cooking. Of course there was an impressiveness and an air of refinement which emanated from the dignity of his person and which no mean surroundings could overcome, and there was also the stamp of superiority given by the law books which filled the pine-wood shelves. But more forcibly there was indelibly engraved upon the mind of the young lad the conviction of the penuriousness of the country which demanded of the leading law-officer of the State a life-long devotion,

and exacted from him an unsullied and unblemished integrity, together with entire abstention from any speculations to advance his worldly concerns (for such speculations would in themselves involve a suspicion of bias as to the vast and varied interests coming before the Court), while it at the same time lodged that self-same officer in what was little better than a garret, and left him cause for anxiety even for the mere subsistence of his family after his death.

Mr. Sterne instanced the cases of the late United States Supreme Court Chief Justice Waite and Associate Justice Samuel F. Miller, on behalf of whose family contributions were solicited, after their death, from members of the Bar. After dwelling upon various unsatisfactory conditions existing with reference to the Court, he added :—

> That in active competition for talent of a high order the United States is constantly outbid in the markets, and cannot, therefore, in the long run pay to have in its judicial service the measure of ability that is generously contended for by railway corporations, banking establishments, and private institutions of every character, would seem from what I have said too obvious for comment, were it not for the fact that, notwithstanding the shabbiness of the Governmental bid, ability of a very high order has from patriotic motives been forthcoming, and its services offered to the people of the United States. If this system continues successfully in operation, it is a mere exploiting speculation by a vast nation to deplete and cheat a few people of their brain products for its own benefit and without a single justifiable excuse, either of expediency or honesty.

At the time of his death, Mr. Sterne was the General Counsel of the Missouri, Kansas, and Texas Railway Company. He had been retained in 1888 by certain foreign clients to protect their large stock-holding interests in that corporation as against the machinations of those controlling it. The road was operated under a lease by the Missouri Pacific Railway Company, and its revenues had been so depleted through bad management and diversion of traffic, that a default occurred on the payment of interest on its bonds. Foreclosure proceedings were instituted by the trustees of various mortgages on the road, and receivers appointed, and those previously in control or interested with them expected, as was believed, to be able to buy in the property at a nominal figure. This expectation was disappointed. Mr. Sterne interposed a vigorous and effective opposition to proceedings not in the interests of the stock- and bond-holders. By his sagacious counsel in the various litigations, in which the road became involved after the default, and with reference to the steps to be taken for the protection of the general interests of those concerned, together with his skill in negotiation with opposing interests, he produced such a spirit of confidence in the ultimate prosperity of the road, as, coupled with the promise of adequate financial aid toward its rehabilitation, brought about an amicable arrangement with the foreclosing trustees, whereby the railroad was turned over to the new management without a sale at auction. The old bondholders were paid under the plan of reorganisation either in new bonds or in cash, and the stockholders received new stock and certain securities on paying a prescribed assessment.

The expectation of the Company's ultimate prosperity was subsequently realised, and Mr. Sterne's share in promoting it was fully recognised by its officers. In the negotiations leading to the final reorganisation he took a prominent part, and was instrumental in receiving the largest concessions obtainable from those inimical to the Company. His laborious duties were performed so faithfully and well, and resulted so much to the benefit of the Company, that when the new management took the property out of the hands of the receivers in 1891, and began to operate it on its own account, he was unanimously elected the Company's General Counsel, and so continued to act until his death. In that capacity he was able to render many and varied services in important and serious litigations, and to conduct negotiations in many threatening legal complications endangering the corporate life of the Company. In all of these more than ordinary legal abilities and great foresight were required. When it is remembered that the Missouri, Kansas, and Texas Railway is to-day one of the great railroad systems of the country, operating over two thousand miles of road, and running through three states and one territory, the importance of the duties which devolved on Mr. Sterne, and the nature of the transformation which he was largely instrumental in effecting, may be partly appreciated.

The high appreciation in which Mr. Sterne was held by his associates in the management of the road is shown by the following extract from a resolution adopted by the directors and stockholders after his death :—

> Mr. Sterne was identified with the Missouri, Kansas, and Texas Railway Company for many years, and both in his capacity as legal adviser and as a director he served its interests zealously and loyally. His wise counsel and untiring energy have been of valuable assistance to the executive officers in the Company's business, and in times of stress and emergency he was always found fully equipped to protect the rights and property of the stockholders and unswerving in his fidelity to their interests. The history of the Company's success during Mr. Sterne's connection with it is full of evidence of his high professional acquirements. In counsel he was wise and conservative; in conflict he was aggressive and fearless. As a man he commanded the respect and warm regard of all those with whom he came in contact, and his unfailing courtesy and the brightness of his disposition endeared him to those with whom he was closely associated.

It will be admitted by those who knew Mr. Sterne that the tribute of the stockholders and directors of this great corporation is not an overstatement, and that it is justly applicable to his representation of other interests and clients.

INDEX

THE END

Printed by R. & R. Clark, Limited, *Edinburgh*.

www.ingramcontent.com/pod-product-compliance
Lightning Source LLC
LaVergne TN
LVHW011200110826
845150LV00006B/1274

* 9 7 8 1 4 2 5 5 7 3 0 9 6 *